SEX,
RELIGION, AND
THE MAKING OF
MODERN MADNESS

SEX, RELIGION, AND THE MAKING OF MODERN MADNESS

The Eberbach Asylum and German Society, 1815–1849

ANN GOLDBERG

New York   Oxford

Oxford University Press

1999

Oxford University Press

Oxford   New York

Athens   Auckland   Bangkok   Bogotá   Buenos Aires   Calcutta
Cape Town   Chennai   Dar es Salaam,   Delhi   Florence   Hong Kong   Istanbul
Karachi   Kuala Lumpur   Madrid   Melbourne   Mexico City   Mumbai
Nairobi   Paris   São Paulo   Singapore   Taipei   Tokyo   Toronto   Warsaw

and associated companies in
Berlin   Ibadan

Published by Oxford University Press, Inc.
198 Madison Avenue, New York, New York 10016

Oxford is a registered trademark of Oxford University Press

Library of Congress Cataloging-in-Publication Data
Goldberg, Ann.
Sex, religion, and the making of modern madness : the Eberbach
Asylum and German society, 1815–1849 / Ann Goldberg
p.   cm.
Includes bibliographical references and index.
ISBN 0-19-512581-9
1. Psychiatry—Germany—History—19th century.
2. Mental illness—Germany—History—19th century.
3. Eberbach (Asylum)—History—19th century.
4. Psychiatric hospitals—Germany—Sociological aspects.
5. Psychotherapist and patient—Germany—History—19th century.
I. Title.
RC450.G4G64   1998
616.89'00943'09034—dc21   98-13682

1 3 5 7 9 8 6 4 2

Printed in the United States of America
on acid-free paper

FOR MY PARENTS

Acknowledgments

Funding for the research and writing of this book was generously provided by the Fulbright-Hays Commission; the Center for German and European Studies at the University of California, Berkeley; and the Max-Planck-Institut für Geschichte, Göttingen. I also thank the Hauptstaatsarchiv, Wiesbaden. The staff graciously offered their services and were indispensable in helping to decipher the sometimes impossible handwriting of nineteenth-century physicians' reports. At the Center for German and European Studies, I owe special thanks to Gerald Feldman.

A number of people in Göttingen made my stay there an extraordinarily stimulating intellectual experience: Peter Becker, Reinhard Blänkner, Hans Bödeker, Bill Clark, Isabel Hull, Bernhard Jussen, Carola Lipp, Hans Medick, Jürgen Schlumbohm, and Rudolf Vierhaus. I am also grateful to Jürgen and Ute Schlumbohm for their warm hospitality. Michael Kutzer, at the Medizinhistorisches Institut, Mainz, offered hours of his time and his expertise in the history of medicine. My stay in Wiesbaden would not have been the same without the hospitality of the Roder family and the wonderful times spent with my friends Birgit and Alex Coridass. Steve Wight was a great source of support, thought-provoking conversation, and good cooking in Frankfurt.

My greatest intellectual debt goes to David Sabean. His graduate seminars—critically engaged, interdisciplinary, unorthodox, and good humored—were inspirations that shaped my view of history and the historian's craft. He originally alerted me to the existence of the Eberbach sources; since then he has generously and tirelessly supported me in innumerable ways, including reading in their entirety and commenting upon several drafts of the manuscript. I am also grateful to Peter Reill, another teacher from whom I have learned so much, and who, as director of the Clark Library and the Center for Seventeenth and Eighteenth Century Studies, UCLA, arranged for my presentation of several conference papers based on chapters of this book. Kathleen Canning read an earlier version of the manuscript and offered incisive, very helpful suggestions and criticisms. I have also benefited from the comments of several annonymous readers.

My warm thanks go to the members of the history department of the University of Mississippi. They welcomed me with open arms and made my stay in Oxford both a pleasure and an intellectually valuable experience. For this book, conversations with Kees Gispen, Jeff Watt, and Doug Sullivan-Gonzalez were particularly helpful. At the University of California, Riverside, I would like to thank Sharon Salinger and Kenneth Barkin, who read and commented on parts of the manuscript, and Randy Head for numerous thought-inspiring conversations and bibliographical references. Two research assistants, Peter McCord and Laura York, helped in gathering source material. Over the years, I have benefited from the suggestions and/or support of a number of people. My thanks to Ed Berenson, Dirk Blasius, Sharon Gillerman, Carol Groneman, Mitch Hart, Karin Hausen, Doris Kaufmann, Jonathan Knudsen, Michael Kushner, Peter and Isabel Paret, Joan Scott, and Jonathan Sperber. Finally, I am grateful to my editor, Thomas LeBien, and the editorial staff at Oxford University Press, for the prompt, professional, and friendly way that they shepherded this project to its completion.

Riverside, California   A. G.
Summer 1998

Contents

Part II: SEXUALITY AND GENDER

SEX,
RELIGION, AND
THE MAKING OF
MODERN MADNESS

Introduction

In 1838, an indigent tailor arrived at the Eberbach asylum terrified, dazed, and repeatedly crossing himself. At home before his committal, Martin M. had become violent and been bound and beaten. He had experienced, as he later explained, "an irresistable urge to spit in people's faces and hit them." Now, during his eleven-month incarceration, he incessantly begged for "mercy" from the asylum physicians.[1] Rituals of authority and submission were built-in features of doctor-patient relations in an institution where doctors wielded almost absolute power and where acts of submission were a necessity for any patient who wanted to leave the place. Curiously, Martin M. understood this fact in a language foreign to the medical designs of the asylum—a language ("mercy") of the prisoner or penitent, of criminal justice or the church, not that of the patient. Martin M., it seems, felt he needed either divine salvation or judicial clemency, not medical treatment.

The treatment of Martin M. in an insane asylum was an innovation of the nineteenth century. Just twenty-five years earlier, such a man would have been left at home to face the punishments of family and community or placed in one of the multifunctional work-, poor-, and madhouses that housed the castoffs of society—beggars, petty criminals, prostitutes, orphans, the insane, and the infirm. In contrast to these detention institutions, the new asylums of the nineteenth century contained only the mentally ill, with the aim of medically treating and rehabilitating them through methods that affected the mind. The birth of a new medical specialty and a new set of experts—the alienists, later known as psychiatrists—thus accompanied the founding of modern insane

3

asylums in a movement that spread throughout Europe and North America beginning in the late eighteenth and early nineteenth centuries.

As a result of these changes, masses of deviant and mentally ill people in the nineteenth century came to be incarcerated and subjected to new kinds of medical and psychological treatment (although their numbers remained limited in the first part of the century). We know that most of these people came from the lower classes; certainly such people made up the overwhelming majority of patients in public asylums. Further, while empirical studies are mostly lacking, it can be safely assumed for preindustrial or developing areas that the social profile of asylum patients was, in addition, primarily rural and small town.[2]

The historical implications of these social facts have yet to be explored. A literature on the social disciplining of patients, based on the analysis of prescriptive sources (such as asylum ordinances and medical tracts), has illuminated the bourgeois social agenda of asylum policies.[3] But patients were not, as the literature suggests, passive, blank slates on which psychiatry imposed itself. What is most interesting about this history are the gaps between physicians and patients, disparities that were cultural and based not only on class, but, in female and Jewish patients, also on gender and ethnicity. The personal psychodynamics behind Martin M.'s behavior are irretrievable. But this much can be said for sure: his misreading of both his own condition and the purpose of the asylum—his transposition of them into a language of criminal justice and/or religion—was not unique to him; it derived at least in part from a mentality, rooted in the rural world of *Vormärz* (1815–1848) Germany, removed from the thinking of his educated, middle-class physicians.

This book is about what happened when educated physicians and officials encountered the rural, lower classes for purposes of psychiatric evaluation, incarceration, and treatment. A rich set of asylum sources, the patient files of the Eberbach asylum (1815–1849), in the western German territory of Nassau, form the basis of this analysis. The files of 463 of Eberbach's 758 patients have survived.[4] These records are valuable not only for their length (some are hundreds of pages long), but also for the variety of documents they contain. A standard patient file included at the minimum a medical case history, written by a Nassau medical officer, documenting the patient's background, familial circumstances, history of illness and its prior treatment, and justification for incarceration; a report by the local official (*Schultheiß*) on the individual's familial and financial circumstances; a certification of commitment by the *Landesregierung*; the asylum's admission case history; an asylum log (a staff record of treatment and twice-weekly examinations), and either an autopsy or release report. Numerous files went far beyond these documents to include sources ranging from patient writings (letters, stories, sermons, and even, in one case, literary criticism) to reports by clergymen and former employers, letters from family members and friends, testimonies of community members in local investigative reports, prison reports, correspondence regarding the escape of an inmate, medical case histories by different physicians who treated the patient over time outside the asylum, and so forth. In other words, these files allow access not simply to the thinking and practices of the asylum, but to the wider world that produced mental patients and to a multitude of perspectives on madness and the lives of the patients.

While lacking a brilliant and high-profile reputation, Eberbach was in most ways entirely typical of those asylums at the forefront of innovation in the early years of their founding. This study, however, does not offer an institutional history. Nor is it an intellectual history concerned with the origins and development of psychiatric ideas. The book is rather a social history of insanity that explores how a society (doctors, officials, families, and communities) responded to insanity, and how, in turn, madness and personal distress were shaped by social experience.[5] The institutional history of Eberbach, though a part of this story, is too narrow a focus to encompass the many extramedical (social, cultural, and political) forces and groups that shaped this history. On the other hand, a broadly focused, comparative survey of a number of German asylums, though sorely needed, would not have allowed for the kind of close, textual reading of sources, the exploration of the subjective meaning of beliefs and behavior, and their contextualization within very specific settings (asylum, village, family) that is methodologically at the heart of this work. What this study searches for, in other words, is not generalizable laws, but contextualized meanings of madness.[6]

The book's approach is thus by necessity local and "micro," an *Alltagsgeschichte* that examines the everyday experiences of "ordinary people" and takes as its starting point the life stories and individual cases of mad people.[7] Very little is known of asylum patients, and there is mounting agreement about the need to incorporate them more fully into histories of psychiatry. Recent attempts to do so with the anecdotal usage of patient case histories have not solved the problem of how to tease out the historical meaning from such sources.[8] These sources present a number of problems, not the least of which is the variety and seeming uniqueness of individual patient life stories and experiences, which seem to defy historical generalization. The search for patterns in medical diagnosis (among other possible variables) has the virtue of allowing the historian to move beyond anecdote. However, the primary diagnostic categories used in psychiatric nosologies (mania, melancholia, and dementia) were too vague and all-encompassing—one or more were used to describe all patients—to enable a meaningful classification of the patients for the purposes of social history. These diagnoses present solely the voice of physicians, and a very abstract one at that. They tell us something (but not much) about medical practices of the time, but next to nothing about the patients.

Buried within case histories, however, I found another set of medical categories, which, by contrast, were applied to specific groups of patients who shared certain common social characteristics—those of gender, class, and ethnicity—and, in all but one case (masturbatory insanity), distinctive experiences of madness and personal distress. These medical categories were religious madness, nymphomania, and masturbatory insanity. Usually subsumed under the broader rubrics of melancholia, mania, and dementia, these terms could refer to either illness entities or symptoms of another underlying pathology. To these, I have added an examination of "Jewishness," which, though not a diagnostic category, shared many of the social and discursive functions of diagnosis.

Although the patients' experiences of madness often overlapped with medical diagnosis, the former were, as I argue, quite distinct from the "illnesses" they became in medical discourse and practice. Physicians and alienists, in classifying, explaining, and treating these people's problems, transformed them into illness entities ("nymphomania," "masturbatory insanity," and "religious madness"). The interpretation of madness by doctors thus reveals as much (or more) about the doctors themselves—their medical categories, social prejudices and concerns, and cultural background—as it does of their patients. The illnesses of this study were thus areas where two fairly distinct worlds collided, where the experiences of personal and social crisis of the rural lower classes confronted the knowledge, expertise, and authority of the educated bourgeoisie (physicians, alienists, and officials) of Vormärz Germany.[9] Within the context of these illnesses, I show the everyday struggles that took place between doctors and patients over a range of issues far beyond the purely medical—over definitions of identity, truth, self, God, the supernatural, and sexuality—that accompanied the project of early psychiatry as it developed into a profession and shaped the experience of "modern madness."

My approach to the history of madness draws largely from a body of scholarship outside of the field. The idea that the history of the public asylum should be viewed as an aspect of the broader historical encounter of "elite" and "popular" cultures; that there were different cultures and experiences of madness shaped by class, gender, and ethnicity; and that psychiatry, as a social activity of asymmetrical power relations between physician and patient, was the site of struggle over competing values and definitions of the self—all of this should come as no great surprise to readers familiar with microhistory, recent approaches to women's and social history, and cultural studies. Within a very disparate literature, historians have been questioning the earlier dominant "grand narratives" (generally Marxist and Weberian) that assumed a universal, inevitable model of historical development and looked to large-scale structures and social forces. Instead, attention has shifted to the "experiences of human actors," as mediated by culture, class, and gender; to the ways that ordinary people appropriated, transformed, and resisted dominant institutions and scientific discourses; and to the negotiated and contingent nature and experience of the self in history. Even the work of Michel Foucault, instrumental as it has been in stimulating much of this trend, has come under attack for substituting a new kind of grand narrative in the form of the history of hegemonic, scientific discourses of power.[10]

These new approaches have made almost no inroads into the historiography of psychiatry.[11] The questions and research strategies of historians of psychiatry have instead largely been determined and limited by a long-standing debate between essentialists and social constructionists. In the first case, madness is understood to be a real disease entity. Different historical periods and places have named and treated it differently, but the illness itself is universal and transhistorical. Therefore it is entirely valid (if not always possible) for the historian to apply present-day psychiatric categories to understand the psychodynamics and psychological traumas of people from the past.[12] Historians of this persuasion have therefore treated the development of the modern asylum as a history of humanitarian progress, since this institution provided for the first time (however inadequately) medical approaches to the treatment of insanity. Taking their cue from Foucault and the anti-psychiatrists of the 1960s, social constructionists, by contrast, approach madness as a social artifact—a label or "discursive formation"—that has been used by societies, especially modern society, to mark off (and control) the abnormal and deviant from the rest of society. Madness, therefore, is by definition a question of power, and understanding madness in history requires analysis not of the individual mad person, but of the social, political, institutional, and professional forces and structures that determine how and why a society treats that person as mad. Such accounts thus cast the history of the asylum as one of intensifying institutional control of social deviants.[13]

This polarization, once productive, has outworn its usefulness and now only limits the sorts of questions posed and research areas pursued in the field. In this study, I am not interested in fighting old battles about whether the asylum and the psychiatric profession were instruments of social control or humanitarianism; or whether madness was socially constructed or real. I take as a given many of the positions of social constructionists, such as the historicity of medical diagnosis and the asylum as an institution of social control. But I do so with the anthropologically informed methodology of *Alltagsgeschichte* and the insights of feminist scholarship, and thus in ways that also challenge and diverge from the work of Foucault and other poststructuralist histories. For the discourse of medical practitioners represented only one, albeit dominant, voice in the history of the asylum—a voice that can not be sufficiently comprehended without analysis of the many other, often contending, voices and

interests—of patients, families, communities, and officials. It is only by first separating out these different perspectives and grasping the divergent meanings
ascribed to matters of mental trauma by the actors, that I have been able to
come back to the question of the medical construction of mental illness to explore its historical significance and impact in the practice of early psychiatry.
This study thus treats the patients and their communities as historical agents in
their own right, not merely as the objects of hegemonic discourses. In this
sense, it seeks to contribute in the area of the history of madness to an emerging body of scholarship engaged in rethinking poststructuralism through attempts to incorporate the experience and agency of historical actors.

   Madness in this study is understood as a social construct and something
more. I analyze official "illnesses" in terms of the various social and medical
components in the thinking of the medical authorities, the professional interests of psychiatry, and the power dynamics of the doctor-patient relationship.
But there is also another dimension to madness, which, though not separate
from medical discourse (and practice), is not reducible to that discourse—
namely, the experience of the patients. I have tried to understand this experience in a way that captures the personal dimension of mental crisis, but does
not, in essentialist fashion, dehistoricize it. For many patients, mental crisis,
while formulated in terms often distinct from their physicians and asylum keepers, was real, terrifying, and destructive to their lives. Before incarceration,
many had been marginalized, teased, and brutalized as abnormal and crazy in
their communities.

   How does one approach this material? From a clinical perspective, there
were patients who displayed symptoms that match any number of present-day
psychiatric illnesses: depression, schizophrenia, paranoia, general paresis. This
said, there are nevertheless serious problems with using such categories to understand Eberbach's nineteenth-century patients. In a different context, the
historian Caroline Bynum has cogently summed up the problems in her explanation of why the fasting behavior of medieval female mystics can not be
equated with modern anorexia/bulimia. Quite simply, the psychodynamic approach is "reductionist and individualistic": it reduces the social and cultural
phenomenon of female religious fasting to "dynamics in the psyche or the
psyche's personal history." In so doing, it misses the social meaning of this behavior: the theological interpretations of behavior by both the mystics themselves and their society. The views of these female mystics were not mere
"epiphenomena" of a more "real" underlying (medical) causation, but the very
stuff of what fasting behavior was about. Finally, a psychodynamic approach
ultimately "can . . . explain only individual cases," not the "widespread pattern" of female fasting and other forms of piety Bynum studied.[14] Thus, while
she recognizes the dimension of deep, personal conflict, and even biology, that
could propel the mystics into their self-punishing behavior, it is in the arena of

medieval culture—to the "images and symbols" of the female mystics and their meaning within the broader culture—that she seeks to understand and embed this behavior.

Indeed, as the anthropologist Gananath Obeyesekere has argued in his study of twentieth-century Sri Lankan female ecstatic priestesses, the distinction between public and shared social meaning, on the one hand, and that of the private and unconscious, on the other, is in many cases not an accurate or useful one. For example, the symbol of the snake-like, matted hair worn by some ecstatics functioned simultaneously at several levels of meaning: as expression of both unconscious, psychic conflict and as public communication understood by the culture (the communication of "fear and revulsion" associated with the ecstatic's connection to the supernatural).[15]

While recognizing the personal and psychodynamic content of patients' experience, this study likewise looks to the cultural and social meaning and context of that experience. One may object that the marginalized, stigmatized, and incarcerated patients at Eberbach cannot be compared to socially integrated priestesses and female mystics, whose behavior, while pathological in a modern, Western context, was "socially acceptable and intelligible" to their societies. Indeed, Obeyesekere makes just such a point when he distinguishes "personal symbols," such as the ecstatic's matted hair, which operate at the levels of both unconscious and social communication (and thus serve to integrate otherwise disturbed individuals into society), from the "psychogenetic symbols" of Western psychotics. These latter symbols, so he argues, derive solely from the unconscious and thus lack public meaning. This distinction, however true sociologically, is based on an ahistorical and curiously decontextualized and essentialist notion of Western psychosis.

What, more than anything, made Eberbach's patients unintelligible and ultimately banished them to outsider status was not an innate psychosis but particular sets of social relationships (between doctors, patients, communities, and officials) and the historical development of psychiatry and the insane asylum. Even further, to the extent that patients were considered insane by their families and communities, this was not necessarily because the former were communicating in a wholly private and unintelligible language of the unconscious. To the contrary, what was often so frightening and disconcerting about these people was the way they both used and abused a common public language and set of cultural symbols. The fact that in deep personal crisis, anxiety, and confusion this language was distorted and appeared delusional in the hands of mad people should come as no surprise. But in articulating individual problems, the patients spoke and experienced in the idiom of a wider public culture. As such, the stories of these people form a meeting place between private trauma and history.

The madness I am thus interested in was a kind of cultural idiom of its own, shaped by gender, class, and ethnicity, and understandable within the social and institutional dynamics of its society. Thus, the questions I posed to the sources were not what patients "really" suffered from or whether they were "really" insane, but what they were trying to communicate about themselves in a given set of historical circumstances and within a given set of cultural idioms available to them; and how, in turn, they got their messages "wrong."[16] I have thus sought out where possible the social patterns and cultural logic of what, at first glance and filtered through the viewpoints of the many doctors and officials who wrote much of my source material, appeared as merely idiosyncratic, private, and "crazy."

In treating the behavior and statements of patients as strategic and communicative acts situated within the social and institutional framework in which they took place, I do not, however, assume that those acts were necessarily the result of consciously willed intentions (although sometimes this was the case). Neither, on the other hand, are the actions I am interested in reducible to either unconscious mechanisms or to "internalized norms."[17] Perhaps what comes closest to the approach I have taken here is the sociologist Anthony Giddens' concept of "practical consciousness," which he defines as "tacit knowledge that is skillfully applied in the enactment of courses of conduct, but which the actor is not able to formulate discursively."[18] And yet this rationalist formulation of action is hopelessly inadequate for capturing the often seemingly irrational and self-destructive behavior of traumatized people, who could be profoundly *unskillful* in applying their "knowledge" (of institutions, social mores, and power relations). This is one of the reasons why I have found it so important to find the common patterns of action and thought in patients, and why I believe it is so crucial to maintain the tension between the shared, socially sanctioned cultural idioms from which patients drew, on the one hand, and the ways in which, traumatized, patients misconstrued and misused them, on the other. One of the benefits of this approach is that by making madness historically intelligible, it also, I hope, helps to shed new light on a number of issues in the broader history of German society in the Vormärz—issues ranging from class relations and state-building to religious politics, anti-Semitism, gender, sexuality, and the history of the self.

How the book addresses these issues, its organization and arguments, is the subject of this final section. The history of the nineteenth-century public asylum was, this book argues, above all, a history of class relations. In Vormärz Germany, those relations were closely tied to and impacted by state-building and the formation of a bourgeois public sphere,[19] on the one hand, and the social-economic crisis of the countryside, on the other. As I explain in chapter 1, the founding of the Eberbach asylum in 1815 was only one aspect of a broader rationalization and centralization of state power that was taking place in Nassau and elsewhere in Germany at this time. As state administrators extended and restructured the role of the state in matters concerning the deviant poor, they brought to their tasks a range of concerns, assumptions, and values that were stamped by a developing bourgeois culture and, in many cases, by the influence of political liberalism.

The bourgeoisie, bearers of new values and practices identified with Western, modern society (capitalism, liberalism, Victorian morality) that in the course of the nineteenth century became generalized and institutionalized in economy, politics, and culture, have long been key to scholarly understandings of the history of modern German and European society.[20] Most recently, Doris Kaufmann has shown how a bourgeois discussion with itself (in popular journals, scholarly treatises, letters, diaries) about probing and mastering the irrational, uncontrollable, and potentially mad aspects of the self was central to the lunacy reforms of early nineteenth-century Germany, spurring and shaping the outrage over the condition of the mad and the movement to decriminalize, medicalize, and humanize their treatment in the spate of asylum foundings of the period.[21]

It was thus middle-class groups who initially developed the new vision of insanity, largely in reference to their own health and identity, and many early psychiatric concepts bear witness to this fact. The literature on nymphomania, for example, was, in bourgeois fashion, preoccupied with a critique of the excesses of aristocracy and luxury.[22] But the institutionalization of this new vision of insanity occurred in quite different settings, where alienists confronted a very different set of social problems in the form of the lower-class patients who filled the new asylums. These were people whose anxieties, despair, and mental confusions were rooted (in part) in the economic crisis and social dislocations that characterized the lives of the lower classes in these years of mass pauperization, and in the mental world of rural culture.

It is the intersection of these three elements—state, bourgeoisie, and rural lower classes—that forms the broader context in which I investigate the rise of the asylum and the professionalization of psychiatry. Recent pathbreaking studies have examined the professional interests at work behind the discovery of certain mental illnesses and the medicalization of deviancy in the nineteenth century.[23] We now understand, for example, how intimately intertwined the "illness" of monomania was with attempts by early French alienists to forge the new medical speciality of mental medicine, which used monomania to make claims for a monopoly over matters dealing with mental maladies.[24] My work builds upon such studies by showing how the process played itself out in the everyday practices of doctors and patients and within the wider social arenas of families and communities.

Religious madness is a particularly interesting and important diagnosis in this context. The medical discourse of religious madness drew much of its force and meaning from both the religious politics of the Vormärz and the development of bourgeois culture and self-identity. And the heyday of religious madness (the late eighteenth and early nineteenth centuries) coincided with the first foundings of asylums. That is, it was a diagnosis prevalent among the first generation(s) of asylum patients. I show how this fact was related to both the professional interests of early psychiatry and the social composition of asylum patients. Chapter 2 begins the analysis of religious madness by situating it within the broader contexts of culture, politics, and medicine of early nineteenth-century Germany. In the latter case, I argue, the medicalization of certain religious experiences served not only in attempts by medical practitioners to wrest institutional (and intellectual) control away from churches and other religious healers, who had long been involved in the care of the mad. "Religious madness" was also closely bound up with training superstitious rural people in the modern, secular experience of illness, that is, the willingness and ability to understand one's problems in medical, rather than supernatural, terms. This endeavor, as I explore in chapter 3, involved physicians in a larger cultural project of refashioning some of the fundamental belief systems and even subjective experiences of the self of rural society. Martin M. would have to be taught to be both "ill" and patient; and the lessons to be learned were as much cultural as medical, as much about changing his beliefs as curing his illness.

Part II focuses on sexuality and gender. Sex-based insanity was, according to the staff, rampant in Eberbach. It took particular and gender-specific forms in the diagnoses of nymphomania (female) and masturbatory insanity (male). Neither the word nor the concept of nymphomania was new to the nineteenth century. The image of dangerously oversexed females stretched back centuries, as did such female "illnesses" as hysteria, uterine fury, lovesickness (not exclusively female), and, since the seventeenth century, nymphomania, which were associated with pathologically out-of-control sexuality.[25] New to the nineteenth century, however, was the institutionalization of nymphomaniacs in insane asylums. Before the advent of the modern mental hospital, women with social profiles and behavioral characteristics very similiar to Eberbach's nymphomanics had been treated as delinquents and disciplinary problems, not medical cases—either incarcerated as "lecherous women" in prisons and workhouses, or fined and left in the custody of their families.[26] The same could be said for the male patients suffering from masturbatory insanity, many of whose symptoms would earlier have either gone unnoticed or been treated as disciplinary problems.

The treatment of "nymphomaniacs" and "masturbators" as ill thus reflected a movement underway since the eighteenth century to decriminalize acts of sexual deviancy. The view of this process from the Eberbach sources is one of both change and continuity. At the local level, the new pedagogical and medical approaches to sexual deviancy, while reconceptualizing this area, did not necessarily mark a sharp break with past practices. Particularly in the cases of nymphomaniacs, as we will see, communities, the state, and the medical profession worked jointly to regulate sexuality along traditional lines consistent with village norms.

Nymphomania and masturbatory insanity were ideological constructs with the power to suppress and transform into "illness" the complex events of patients' lives and the social referents and contexts of their behavior. This analysis draws from and contributes to a body of recent feminist scholarship that is exploring how a modern ideology of fixed, "natural," gender differences has been historically constructed on the basis of "the refusal and repression of alternative possibilites" and identities.[27] Medical understandings of nymphomania and masturbatory insanity, as argued in chapter 4, contributed to the development of a polarized definition of gender norms, which was under way in bourgeois culture. The subsequent chapters on nymphomania explore the process of being and becoming a nymphomaniac within the two settings that produced it: the asylum and the community.

Chapter 5 examines the everyday practices of nymphomania and sexuality within the power dynamics of the asylum and the doctor-patient relationship. It reveals two contrasting understandings of female sexuality: the medical one of pathological genitals and a set of patient gestures and words linked to social and interpersonal matters. The nymphomania diagnosis worked to erase this female narrative of sex and to replace it with a reified body of urges, desires, and malfunctions. Something similiar occurred in the setting of the community, a context where many of the women had already been marked as either "man-crazy" (the popular term) or clinically nymphomaniacal. Here, in chapter 6, I examine the social profiles of nymphomaniacs, the sources of their problems, and the way these women drew upon (but also often distorted) to express themselves a female language of rights, duties, and sexual honor rooted in peasant culture. I show, finally, the differing but overlapping views and interests of medicine, state, family, and community in having these women locked up as lunatics.

Part III explores within the themes of masturbatory insanity and Jewishness the fluid and murky boundaries in this period between insanity, on the one hand, and criminality and delinquency, on the other. While medical writers struggled in print to elucidate the meaning of, and fine distinctions between, mental maladies, the situation on the ground for practicing physicians and alienists could be utter confusion: how, in particular, to distinguish between real lunatics and any number of other social types, such as the delinquent or the dissimulator, whose behavior either overlapped with or mimicked that of the mentally ill? Chapter 7 shows how useful the concept of masturbatory insanity could be in this situation, allowing physicians (and other self-appointed masturbation "experts") to read as mental illness a broad, vague, and now disputed area of indiscipline and deviancy in males, thereby serving to medicalize acts and attitudes that had long been treated as disciplinary matters (or simply neglected). Chapter 8 explores instances where the opposite outcome occurred, where epistemological confusion resulted not in the medicalization of deviants, but in the inability and unwillingness to see the person as ill. Anti-Semitism and the association of Jews with criminality were the key factors here, structuring (when it was triggered in certain Jewish cases) both the everyday practice of psychiatry and the madness of Jewish patients.

I

The Duchy of Nassau and
the Eberbach Asylum

State-Building and the Origins of the Asylum

Eberbach's founding in 1815 coincided with the lunacy reform movement that swept Europe and North America in the first half of the century. That movement in Germany took peculiar shape in the central role played from the start by the state. Unlike England and France, the primary initiative for the lunacy reforms in Germany came from above, by enlightened state bureaucrats under the tutelage of the German neoabsolutist states.[1] If the (apocryphal) founding image of French psychiatry is the alienist Phillip Pinel famously striking the chains off the inmates of the Bicêtre during the French Revolution, its (real) German counterpart is that of the Prussian Minister Karl August von Hardenburg charging J. G. Langermann (medical officer, later privy councillor and head of Prussian medical affairs) in 1803 with the responsibility of turning the Bayreuth madhouse into Germany's first mental hospital.[2] Other states and areas of Germany followed suit in the decades after the Napoleonic wars.

Eberbach was no exception to the German pattern, where new, enlightened ideas about insanity, concerns of state security with respect to the deviant poor, and the desire to keep abreast of the most progressive trends united to lead even the small and impoverished state of Nassau to embark on costly lunacy reforms. Further, in Nassau both the founding and functioning of the asylum were closely tied to state-building, that is, to the consolidation of state power, the political integration of the population, and the extensive administrative reforms that this entailed—in the penal system, medicine, local government, education, religion, and so forth. State reforms in the area of culture (religion and education) will be discussed in chapter 3. The following section focuses on the penal, medical, and (local) governmental reforms, which formed the broader institutional context of the asylum.

The duchy of Nassau, which achieved its final form in 1816 (bounded by the Rhine, Main, Sieg, and Lahn rivers), was one of the new *Mittelstaaten* (medium-sized states) to emerge out of the Napoleonic wars and the Congress of Vienna. An artificial creation of historical circumstance, this territory united within its borders one of the most heterogenous populations to be found in the German Confederation: two dozen former secular and ecclesiastical states of differing religious confessions, traditions, and political systems. Confessionally, it was made up of both Lutheran and Reformed Protestants, who, together, slightly outnumbered Catholics; further, the three Christian faiths overlapped in a number of administrative districts.[3] There were, in addition, minority communities of Jews and Mennonites.[4]

The enormous task of political integration and rationalization of the state apparatus proceeded simultaneously on several fronts in the years during and after the Napoleonic wars.[5] A number of these reforms are important to the history of madness and the asylum in Nassau. First, the founding of the asylum was only one part of a broad reorganization of the penal and poor law system beginning in 1803, which dissolved Nassau's three multifunctional prison-workhouses that had been hitherto used to house an enormously heterogenous inmate population of convicted criminals, delinquents (e.g., "lecherous women," alcoholics, vagabonds), orphans, the indigent, and the insane. The combined prison and workhouse had, by the late eighteenth century, come under sustained attack by an enlightened public shocked by its abuses and resolved to humanize and reform the care of orphans and the mentally ill through separating and freeing them from their criminal status.[6] These humanitarian impulses, together with practical administrative and economic motives, were behind the governmental decrees that in Nassau led to the reforms. These designated the *Zuchthaus* at Diez as the territorial prison solely for convicted felons (1803), while delinquents and the insane after 1812 were transferred to the newly opened correctional house and, after 1815, to the asylum at Eberbach.

Penal reform had suddenly become possible in 1803 with the secularization of church properties. Former monasteries, such as the Cistercian monastary of Eberbach, could now be put to use for secular purposes. In an 1805 report, the state Health Commission, charged with the planning of the asylum, expressed its intended medical and humanitarian goals:

> We must provide an abode for those unfortunate classes of people who are so robbed of their minds that they can no longer remain in human society. [However, it should not be] considered a mere place of detention for these

poor people, but rather a place whose purpose is to bring to bear every possible means in order to free those wretched people from one of the saddest of all plagues.[7]

However, as a result of the Napoleonic wars and disagreements among state and medical officials about the nature and site of the asylum, the decision to locate the institution at Eberbach was not made until 1812, and it would not be until 1815 that the asylum was ready to admit its first patients. In this year, the asylum opened with a mere four patients (one woman and three men) who had previously been housed provisionally in the correctional house. By the following year, the number had jumped to twenty-five.[8] By the 1840s, the admissions rate averaged about 33.6 patients per year. Given that many of these patients were "incurable" and could thus languish in the asylum for years, there was a steady increase over the years in the total number of patients at the institution, from fifty-six in 1822 (already more than the fifty patients for which the asylum was originally designed) to 100 by 1830 to 161 in 1844.[9]

Despite the early optimism and high humanitarian goals, the limited funds of the state treasury as well as new information about the kinds of mad people to be incarcerated in the asylum meant that, initially at least, Eberbach was to open its doors as a purely custodial institution—a place of confinement to rid society of public disturbances—and connected spatially and administratively to the correctional house that existed since 1812 on the grounds. In the intervening years since 1805, concern had grown over the high costs required of a medical institution. Two other arguments were raised in favor of a detention institution: there were not enough "curable" insane in Nassau to justify a hospital, and the asylum must first gain the "trust" of the population before it could be transformed into a hospital. These arguments appear to have directly proceeded from the class background of Nassau's mad, which an 1811 census had made plain. The census had established that of the 180 mentally ill in Nassau (fifty-four "qualified" for admission to the asylum), most were from the rural poor, and their illnesses had been left entirely untreated. Medical theories that mental illness was only curable soon after its outbreak and only in types of insanity associated with "civilization" (that is, the urban educated classes), clinched the case for the incurable nature of Nassau's mad and thus for the erection of a purely detention asylum. The "trust" the asylum needed from its population (in order to become a hospital dispensing psychic medicine) was, presumably, that of the "educated classes."[10]

Hence, from its inception, Eberbach's functions were tied to state security policy, particularly as it related to the rural poor. At the same time, there had been strong opinion in favor of the medical and humanitarian functions of the asylum, and thus a compromise had been worked out: the medical functions were to be only provisionally abandoned until that "trust" could be gained among Nassau's inhabitants and all "incurable" lunatics had first been taken care of through detention. At least the second prerequisite was considered to be fulfilled by 1816.[11] In the next few years, Eberbach embarked on its original medical mission, becoming a joint institution that housed not only the chronic and incurable insane for purposes of security, but also a modern mental hospital applying the most up-to-date theories of asylum administration and medical treatment of the "curable" insane. By the 1820s its German- and European-wide reputation as a modern mental hospital was such that Eberbach was even able to draw numerous applications from other German territories by wealthy and influential families.[12] The majority of its patients continued to come, however, from Nassau's rural poor.

The asylum represented a new experiment in the centralized and state-controlled management of madness. It was not merely a question of a qualitative shift in treatment (the transfer of the insane from prison-workhouses to asylums), but, in the long run, of an enormous increase in the numbers of those people diagnosed as insane and incarcerated as a result, an increase that closely accompanied the asylum wherever it appeared in Europe and North America in the nineteenth century.[13] In Nassau, the institutionalization of madness was greatly facilitated and impacted by the simultaneous restructuring of the medical system and local administration, both of which in turn became the central points of contact between the asylum, on the one hand, and state and society, on the other.

The commitment of an individual to the asylum required legal certification of insanity by a qualified physician. Before the nineteenth century, the availability of such physicians and their access to remote and poorer rural communities had been all but nonexistent.[14] This situation changed dramatically with Nassau's 1818 medical reform edict, which established a (for the period) uniquely comprehensive system of state medical care that extended to all Nassau inhabitants. Each of Nassau's twenty-eight districts (*Ämter*) were equipped with three civil-servant medical personnel: an accredited doctor or medical officer (*Medizinalrat*), an assistant doctor, and a pharmacist. Through this unified medical civil service, health care by qualified physicians was extended for the first time to the poor. Fees for these people were minimal and offset by public funds from the state treasury and local communities (*Gemeinde*), which amounted to two-thirds of the medical officers' salaries.[15]

In the broadest sense, then, the medicalization of madness in Nassau occurred within and as part of the broader medicalization of society that state policy had created, a process that brought even the poorest rural folk into closer contact with educated physicians and their conceptions of illness. A record of that contact and the complex ways in which local and familial conflicts were translated by medical officers into problems of mental illness has been left in the form of the state-mandated medical case histories these physicians wrote for purposes of committals to the asylum. An essential set of sources for this study, these reports, which ranged from one to dozens of pages,[16] detailed everything from the familial and work background of prospective inmates to their circumstances of insanity, diagnosis, prior treatment, and justification for incarceration.

Special training in medical psychology was very limited at German universities of the time. It was not a prerequisite for the position of medical officer in Nassau, and it appears that many of these officials, particularly at the beginning of the period, had little or no familiarity with either insanity or the field of psychic medicine.[17] Whatever training in the field they did have appears to have been arbitrary, dependent on where they had studied or on personal interest in the topic.[18] Thus, the medical models and levels of sophistication vis-à-vis insanity varied tremendously, from those doctors who seem to have been extremely uncomfortable with treating and diagnosing insanity and even explicitly made reference to their inexperience in such matters, to those who wrote extensive reports demonstrating familiarity with the very latest psychiatric theories. The different explanatory models used by these doctors were also the product of both the eclecticism of contemporary theories of madness and the lack of consensus even among trained alienists regarding its nature and cure. In contemporary psychiatry, the etiology of madness could be ascribed to any number of social ("moral"), psychic, environmental, hereditary, and organic causes. Humoral medicine continued to be employed, together with the newer neurophysiological theories, particularly those of the Scottish physician John Brown (1735–1788). The medical reports reflected both this eclectism, often providing a dizzying range of possible causes of the patient's illness (and using both humoral and neurophysiolgical models) as well as the split in Germany between the "somaticist" and "psychicist" schools of psychiatry (explained below).

The 1816 administrative reform of local government created the basis for the second arm of the committal process. The reform worked to consolidate state control at the local (*Gemeinde*) level with the transfer of most local authority to state-appointed officials—*Schultheißen*. In the 1848 Revolution, it was these official representatives of the state, with their lifetime, nonelected appointments, who became the chief targets of angry, rural communities.[19] These *Schultheißen* also played a crucial role in the committal process to the asylum. This was because the second legal prerequisite for committals was an official report of the *Schultheiß* on the familial and financial circumstances of the patient, which often included in addition the *Schultheiß'* own views of the person's mental condition and whether that person required incarceration. But as the highest local authority, the *Schultheiß'* role in community responses to insanity was even broader than his legal mandate. The *Schultheiß* functioned as a mediator between various interests: between villagers and family members in conflicts that erupted, and between the village or family, on the one hand, and the central government and asylum, on the other hand. As the case histories and *Schultheiß* reports reveal, it was, for example, often this official (as opposed to a doctor) who was first called to deal with a disruptive and disturbed family member. It was also the *Schultheiß* who, in turn, contacted the government to initiate commitment proceedings, and with whom the asylum negotiated when the latter sought a suitable living arrangement within the community for the patient as a prerequisite for release. The *Schultheiß*, as spokesman for the community, could block such releases by claiming that no villager was willing to take in the patient.

Asylum Administration

In his historical typology of asylums, Dieter Jetter classifies Eberbach as an old-style, multifunctional absolutist institution, which had typically combined prison, workhouse, and, sometimes, madhouse in one facility (the *Zucht-Arbeits-und Tollhäuser*).[20] By contrast, the ideal-typical modern asylum of the nineteenth century ensured the strict institutional separation of the mentally ill from all other types of inmates.[21] Many influential alienists, most notably Maximilian Jacobi (1775–1858), director of the model Vormärz asylum Siegburg (in the Prussian Rhine province), further advocated (and realized) even the institutional separation of the mad themselves into the "curable" and the "incurable," the former to be treated in the new mental hospitals, and the latter to be housed in separate nursing (detention) homes. Only after 1849, when Eberbach was moved down the road and renamed Eichberg, did the asylum, according to Jetter, come into its own as a modern mental hospital in line with the ideal of the time.[22]

There is something to be said for Jetter's classification of Eberbach. The continued physical proximity of asylum and correctional house at Eberbach did indeed differentiate it from the most progressive asylums of the period. Spatially conjoined, the asylum and correctional house also shared the same administrative, medical, and clerical personnel. Further, while the correctional and asylum inmates were housed separately from one another—and lived under different house rules and with different legal statuses—there was some interaction between the two groups: the inmates of both institutions participated together in religious services (though they were seated separately); and some recuperating patients with applicable craft skills worked in the correctional house workshops. In addition, legal links between the prison (the *Zuchthaus* in Diez) and the asylum were fostered through the process by which the asylum's criminally insane inmates were subject to retransfer to prison if and when they were cured or deemed falsely diagnosed as insane. In at least one case, the asylum acted as a quasi-judicial/police body, transferring a patient who had committed murder to the judicial authorities after taking his confession.[23]

Finally, Eberbach's administrative chain of command failed to conform to cutting-edge medical opinion, which called for asylum directorships to be filled by physicians. That position at Eberbach was instead held jointly by a jurist, Philipp Heinrich Lindpaintner (1794–1848), and the house physician, Ferdinand Wilhelm Windt (1780–1848).[24] "Director" Lindpaintner and Dr. Windt, both of whose tenure spanned almost the entire period of the asylum's operation, were responsible, respectively, for the administrative and medical affairs of the asylum and correctional house. Paid civil servants, their decisions in almost all matters—including admissions, releases, building improvements, and even the use of corporal punishment—however, required the approval of the *Landesregierung*, to whom they directly answered.

Responsibility for the restructuring of Eberbach into a medical institution after 1817 lay with both these men, and Lindpaintner, in all of his written statements, took great pains to stress the shared nature of the directorship and the important role played by Windt—statements that reflect, at the least, the close and harmonious working partnership the two men seem to have established early on. The historical evidence, however, suggests that it was the jurist Lindpaintner who was the leading personality in asylum matters and its relations with the political authorities and medical community at large. It was Lindpaintner, not Windt, who reported directly to the government in his quarterly administrative reports. Published works on Eberbach and other asylum matters, which furthered the reputation of both the author and his institution, were written by Lindpaintner and the assistant physician, Andreas Basting.[25] Lindpaintner, but not Windt, is listed in the recent multivolume historical lexicon of German psychiatrists.[26] In contrast to Lindpainter's reputation, particularly for his founding in 1829 of an innovative organization for the placement and support of released Eberbach inmates, Windt was, and remains, a completely obscure figure in the history of psychiatry.[27]

Lindpaintner's training was not in medicine, but in law. Born in Koblenz in 1794, the son of a landowner and *Privat-Sekretair*, Lindpaintner studied at the Lyceum in Mainz (during the French occupation), where he learned "the practical benefits of order in public and domestic life" through an education that combined academic subjects with training in "strict military discipline, obedience, order, and industriousness. . . ."[28] At university (Aschaffenburg, Augsburg, and Heidelberg) in the years of French hegemony in Central Europe, Lindpaintner not only received the education that would prepare him for civil service, but was exposed thereby to a strong dose of liberal and natural law traditions in courses that ranged from the natural sciences (natural philosophy, botany, agriculture) to taxation, law (constitutional law, legislation, institutions of Roman law, French statutory law, and Confederation of the Rhine constitutional law), police science, and political economy. Later, as Eberbach's director, he would bring the two poles of his educational experience—military discipline and order, on the one hand; natural law, on the other—to his civil-service career, implementing both in the asylum setting. In 1814, after passing the civil-service exam, he began his career as *Receptur* in the town of Eltville, followed in 1817 by his appointment as Eberbach's director (at the young age of 23), a position he would hold until his death in 1848, and which would bring him respect, reputation, and multiple promotions (he achieved the title of *Geheimer-Hofrath* in 1842).

The medical staff at Eberbach consisted of a house physician and an assistant physician, who, until 1838, doubled as administrator. Windt, who in 1818 achieved the positions of both medical officer for Amt Eltville and house physician to Eberbach's asylum and correctional house, had begun his career in 1800 as a lowly *Amtschirurg* (state-employed surgeon). The son of a privy councillor and physician (*Bade-Medicus*) in the Nassau town of Diez, Windt went on to be promoted to *Landphysicus* in 1803, a position he held until the assumption of his positions in Eltville and Eberbach, which, like Lindpaintner, he would retain until his death in 1848 (with promotion to the grade of *Obermedicinalrath* in 1821).[29] Unlike the rest of the personnel at Eberbach, Windt did not live at the asylum; his examination of patients occurred in twice-weekly visits. The bulk of his duties and salary rested on his second position as medical officer for the town and district of Eltville, where he resided.

On a day-to-day basis, therefore, most of the therapeutic measures and medical contact that patients had were with the assistant doctor. Following two unsuccessful attempts at filling the position after the death of Dr. Ramspott in 1824, the asylum hired Andreas Basting (1819–1888) in 1826, who remained at Eberbach and its successor, Eichberg, until his retirement in 1866. The son of a landowner (*Oeconom*) from the Rheingau, who had studied medicine at the University of Gîttingen before assuming his position at Eberbach, Basting was considered to have particular talent for the job and to be sympathetic and sensitive to the patients.[30] Under Basting were the asylum attendants who, literally, lived with the patients, sharing both sleeping and eating quarters. Like the majority of the patients, these attendants came from the lower classes. Only same-sex attendants were used in the separate male and female sections of the asylum.

There was thus a transitional quality to Eberbach, both in its administration and in the contradictory and complex ways in which the legal, criminal, and medical coexisted and interacted in the institution. The 1849 geographical separation of asylum and correctional house in the transfer of Eberbach's patients to the newly opened Eichberg asylum (several kilometers away) was a self-conscious attempt to fully modernize the asylum at long last (as well as to deal with the long-standing problem of overcrowding). Eberbach's institutional confusion, it should be noted, only exacerbated the mental confusion of the populace at large about the nature of the asylum. It was a very narrow stratum of enlightened bureaucrats and educated public who were the purveyors and supporters of the new medical strategy, which employed a disease model of insanity and sought to separate or "free" the insane from their criminal status in the new asylums. This view had not yet prevailed at the local level, where an older, absolutist, and disciplinary model of insanity still existed. Families, communities, and local officials, as I will demonstrate, often thought about and used the asylum as the equivalent of a prison or workhouse, to rid themselves of social disturbances and to punish and reform the socially deviant.[31] Indeed, there were even medical officials who had trouble distinguishing between penal institutions and insane asylums. There was, for example, the medical official who, after establishing the existence of a form of "mental bondage" in one patient, recommended that the latter be committed to the "correctional [house] *or* the insane asylum" (my emphasis).[32]

However, despite its backward aspects, Eberbach should be seen not as an anomaly, but as a prototypical asylum of the early nineteenth century. First, even the most modern German asylums of the era were themselves something of hybrid institutions, combining as they did medical treatment with the pedagogical and disciplinary practices of the asylum's forerunners, the absolutist workhouse and prison.[33] Second, the reforms of Lindpaintner and Windt successfully (though gradually) introduced the most up-to-date asylum management and medical treatment, known as "moral treatment" (discussed below). From the outside, Eberbach looked like an old-fashioned, multifunctional institution; on the inside, however, the story was quite different. Eberbach's backward elements were seemingly linked to Nassau's financial poverty and its small population (which did not allow for the support of a separate mental hospital, not to mention two asylums, for the curable and incurable, respectively). It certainly did not reflect any lack of will or "backward" thinking on the part of its staff, who were steeped in the newest medical paradigms of insanity and its institutional care, as well as in the enlightened cultural context from which the lunacy reforms had arisen.[34] Lindpaintner was clear about his and the asylum's mission, and it was one that placed the institution fully in the mainstream of enlightened reforms and progressive medicine:

> [In the] darkness of the Middle Ages, out of ignorance or a bias for the miraculous, one imagined the unfortunate condition of the insane to be partly divine inspiration, partly hellish sorcery. The [flames of the] stake blazed for our mentally ill, pitiable brothers. Later we committed them to eternal confinement in prisons and workhouses; and it is not long since we finally felt and understood how disgracefully we violated the holy human rights [of the insane] by such treatment. [Then, recently], the demands of humanity found enlightened, courageous defenders. They triumphed. Everywhere we are beginning to found [specialized], appropriate asylums for our mentally ill, because we again value them as people. . . .[35]

Such sentiment and the practical reforms that derived from it had, by the 1820s, brought Eberbach an established, if not brilliant, reputation as a modern medical institution. This fact was recognized by Lindpaintner's contemporaries and by the staff's own self-perception.[36]

Anthropological Psychiatry and Moral Treatment

The psychiatric paradigm that held sway among German writers and practitioners of psychic medicine in the first half of the century is known as anthropological psychiatry. In stark contrast to the later (post-1850) mechanistic theories of a natural-scientific psychiatry, which reduced mental illness to "brain disease," anthropological psychiatry took as its object the whole person and, embedded as this psychiatry was in the broader mental universe of German Romanticism and Idealism, posited the fundamental "unity of body and soul . . . the idea of man as a psychophysical unity."[37] Within this "anthropological" (psychosomatic) conception of the person, debate raged over "two different interpretations of the soul-body relationship"—a debate that was, consistent with its German context, peculiarily philosophical and speculative in nature, and which split the field of psychic medicine into two hostile camps (from about 1820 through the 1840s) of psychicists and somaticists.[38] Psychicists claimed that mental derangement, while it might be indirectly affected by somatic factors, is at base a disease of the soul. In the sin-theory of the leading psychicist, J. C. A. Heinroth (1773–1843), reason, defined in religious terms as the "receptivity" to God (the highest form of consciousness), becomes enslaved and the soul thereby diseased through a life of sin (especially sins pertaining to physical passion and material pleasure).[39] Somaticists, whose bulwark lay in asylum alienists, countered that the soul, being incorporal, "cannot therefore become diseased"; only the body is subject to illness, and thus "underlying all psychic diseases there is a somatic dysfunction."[40] In a seeming paradox befitting its times, Maximilian Jacobi and his somaticist colleagues positioned themselves to root out the reprehensible mixing by psychicists of metaphysics and religion with the legitimate concerns of medicine, in order (among other goals) to preserve the integrity of the incarnate soul.[41]

The theoretical position taken by the Eberbach staff in this debate was a pragmatic middle ground. On the one hand, while eschewing any dogmatic position, Lindpaintner clearly leaned towards the somatic camp:

> Embracing no hypothesis exclusively, but united over the fact that the psychic can only be understood through the agency [*Vermittlung*] of the somatic, thus with respect to the impenetrable mystery which prevails regarding the connection between the body and the soul, [it is clear to us] that only the physical organ—but not as it can be thought of in abstract terms—is subject to illness.

[Thus] with lunatics whose affliction is not stamped with recognizable signs of curability or incurability, we first seek in the physical being the condition which seems to be connected with the abnormal mental functioning.[42]

On the other hand, Lindpaintner could be scathing in his criticism of any "one-sided" position, either of the somaticists or the psychicists. In a comment on one case history written by a medical officer in 1818, he quoted the renowned German alienist Johann Christian Reil on the "revolting spectacle" of the "purely physical doctor" who "like a mole burrows into the intestines, searching for the soul in the region where nature has placed the equipment for carrying out the lowest bodily operations."[43]

Treatment at Eberbach was in turn pragmatic and eclectic, reflecting both the belief in the manifold (psychic and somatic) causes of mental illness, as well as the various and intertwined functions of its treatment, namely, discipline, education, and medical cure. Therapy was divided into two categories: the "direct" and the "indirect psychic method,"[44] which broadly corresponded, respectively, to "moral" (psychological) and somatic treatments. Given contemporary medical theories of the interconnectedness of body and mind, such a distinction can, however, be misleading, for the aims and effects of both types of therapy could be conceived in somatic and psychic terms.

The "direct psychic method" supposedly worked directly on the patient's mind. Usually referred to by contemporaries as "moral treatment," it was the therapeutic method at the heart of progressive asylum management everywhere and in the minds of proud alienists that, more than anything, distinguished the new institutions from their purely repressive forerunners. In other words, through this method, the asylum sought not merely to control and manage the mad, but to make an impression on the mind and thus begin to effect changes in the internal state of the patient. No detail was too trivial in the creation of total environments for this purpose—from the architecture, the masked window bars, and the gardens, to the patient's daily routine, to, most importantly, the moral authority and influence of the alienist. The supposedly soothing, pleasant, and healthful environment of Eberbach's bucolic and wooded setting was, for example, itself considered therapeutic according to experts of the time. Patients were also strictly separated according to gender, class, and level or type of illness (curable vs. incurable and/or raving). In the latter case, this was to prevent the raving and "dirty" patients from upsetting (or reinfecting) the quieter and convalescing patients.

Then there were the measures designed to induce the patient to internalize the norms and values of the asylum's order, what Klaus Dörner has called the "internalization of coercion."[45] The irrationalities of the mind were to be eradicated by the external, rational influence of the asylum's rigidly ordered existence, by the moral authority of the alienist, and by indoctrination in the values of industriousness, cleanliness, and discipline. To this end, the patient had first to learn the lesson of complete dependency and unconditional submission to the will of Eberbach's authorities:

> [Even] those [newly arrived patients] whose capacity for reflection is severely exhausted must necessarily perceive how he [sic], helpless to resist, has been entirely given over to unfamiliar powers. In such a situation, a serious, but kind and humane, type of treatment according to the level of the [patient's] receptivity, must make a deep impression on him, and substitute external constraint for the lack of internal strength [in the lunatic] . . . We bind the newly arrived to the rules of the asylum. At the same time, we often gain his trust . . . With a healthy, strong will we are easily able to master the timid resolve and the sick mind of the lunatic.[46]

Lindpaintner was especially adamant about the need to accustom patients to a "regulated mode of life," through a rigidly set daily routine regulated by the "stroke of the clock" and constant occupation with hard physical labor or, in the case of "educated" patients, with such intellectual activities as reading and writing. Work served a number of purposes, from the "dietetic" benefits to the body, to disciplining and diverting the mind from its irrational thoughts, and re-placing the disorders of illness with an external social order. It also had distinct (and openly acknowledged) financial advantages for the institution itself. Eber-bach was a state-run asylum, but it largely depended upon the patients them-selves (or, more precisely, their families) to cover expenses for their daily up-keep—for food, clothing, fuel, cleaning, washing, and so on. This came in the form of direct payments by the families of patients with means and by a combi-nation of patient labor and local poor funds for indigent patients.[47]

Originally, the patients were divided into two classes based on their ability to pay the asylum costs. In 1827, a four-class system was introduced, again based on the amount and type of payment, which determined the level and type of housing, food, and daily activities of the patients. The well-off patients received better and more food, were housed in their own rooms or ones shared with only several other patients of their class, were occupied with light work or intellec-tual occupations during the day, and were taken on special day-excursions.[48] Occupation for the poorer patients (the majority), by contrast, meant for men gathering and chopping wood, gardening, construction and repairs of the asy-lum grounds and buildings, and, in winter, spinning. Those who had a specific trade and were deemed mentally competent worked in the correctional house workshops. Lower-class female patients worked at equally arduous, but "femi-nine" work: washing, cleaning, ironing, sewing, knitting, and spinning for the correctional house factory, and in later years, some light garden work.[49] But even these lower-class patients were periodically given special treats and recre-ation: coffee, tobacco, games, and excursions into the countryside on Sundays and special holidays.

The "indirect" method of treatment acted on the mind indirectly through the body. It included blood purgings, and the administration of emetics, purgatives, and blistering agents, the effects of which were conceived largely in terms of Brunonian medicine as means to either increase or decrease an imbalanced level of brain activity or nervous energy by ridding the body of excess fluids (particularly blood from the head) and/or redirecting them to other areas of the body.[50] Baths and showers of all types, including the extremely painful *"Sturzbad,"*[51] were used as either calming or shocking and stimulating agents. Water was also used in something called "unfurling" (*Aufrollen*), described by Lindpaintner as follows:

> To moderate the flight of thoughts of those suffering from lunacy [*Narrheit*], to awaken their prudence and attention to their own person, we used an eighty foot high church vault to unfurl [*Aufrollen*] them from a swing. This process and the unexpected plunge into a water container is in part [responsible] for the cure [of patients].[52]

The arsenal of "indirect methods" also included a number of ingenious (and ghastly) mechanical instruments, such as the hollow wheel and the rotary chair. The hollow wheel, devised by the alienist C. A. F. Hayner, was "a huge padded wheel, designed the same way as a treadmill, in which the patient was imprisoned. Unless he remained completely motionless, the patient had to run either forward or backward, and the decision to rest or to move about was his alone."[53] The rotary chair, in which the patient was strapped, would be turned on its axis at a very high velocity, thereby creating a centrifugal force that caused extreme discomfort and fright from intense pressure to the brain, nausea, and the sensation of suffocation.[54] For raving and "disobedient" patients there were also such punishments and restraining mechanisms as the straitjacket, forced standing, enclosure in a closet, and solitary confinement in a *"Blockzimmer,"* whose painful effect could be immeasurably increased when the patient was confined naked in the dead of winter.[55]

Dörner argues that, consistent with their neoabsolutist origins, German asylums exhibited a degree of authoritarianism and brutality without parallel in the West, as witnessed by their regimented daily routines, military drills, "sadistic punishment" devices, and "physically punitive coercion."[56] In short, Prussian asylum therapy can be characterized as a "pedagogic-military, authoritarian imposition of reason and moral duty."[57] Britain's "Non-Restraint" movement (the abolition of mechanical restraints), which began in the 1830s, had no German counterpart until as late as the 1860s.[58]

Treatment at Eberbach only partly supports Dörner's *Sonderweg* interpretation of German psychiatry.[59] On the one hand (as indicated above), it did indeed display the very elements of authoritarianism, brutality, and military regimentation, which drew their sources from the absolutist workhouses and prisons and from the bureaucratic state. One would be hard-pressed to distinguish, for example, Basting's formula of "work, order, and cleanliness" for one "hot-tempered" and "immoral" patient from the typical regimen of prisons and workhouses.[60] The asylum even experimented (unsuccessfully) with drilling the male patients in military exercises.[61] Discipline at Eberbach, whether arrived at through effects on the psyche (the "direct" treatment) or through acting on the body (the "indirect" method), formed one of the cornerstones of treatment. Indeed, in this institution, there existed both in practice and in the thinking of its staff no distinct demarcation between discipline and punishment, on the one hand, and therapy, on the other. Physical methods, such as the hollow wheel, were used interchangeably (or simultaneously) as both therapy and punishment.[62]

On the other hand, the discipline and authoritarianism in no way excluded more progressive, psychological methods of treatment that drew upon Enlightenment pedagogy and psychology, the moral treatment of the West, and political liberalism. Discipline itself took on new meaning within this context, employed as it was not merely for purposes of restraint and punishment, but for affecting the mind and, as I explore in chapter 3, for reshaping the experience of selfhood. The "Casino" evenings at Eberbach provide the most striking (and outlandish) illustration of the incorporation of a modern, liberal sensibility into asylum life. Three times a week in winter, the "distinguished" (middle- and upper-class) male patients gathered with the higher-level staff in the asylum library (*Casinosaale*) for evenings of cultivated leisure and sociability that included billiards, chess, newspaper-reading, and conversation over tea and tobacco.[63] The patient August G., who thought he was the French *dauphin*, graced the company each opening season with his inaugural addresses on noted asylum events.[64] Later, a separate woman's version of the Casino evening was set up. The curative value of these evenings was seen in terms of the discipline of bourgeois morality and self-fashioning. As Lindpaintner explained, the Casino served to "accustom [patient-participants] to the sense of order" and to reawaken the "sense of propriety . . . decorum [and] honor."[65]

Salons, reading clubs, and other voluntary associations, which the "Casino" mimicked, were vital institutions of an emerging bourgeois public sphere and the movement for liberal reform in Germany.[66] The notion of an asylum salon therefore seems like an ironic and bizarre contradiction in terms: the salon's rituals of individuality and free sociability became in the "Casino" staged reenactments. These used all the signs of the salons and clubs—not only the cultivated, leisure activities, but also the antihierarchical mixing of patients and staff within a still-exclusive circle based on class and education—but put them to use in the wholly artificial and unfree environment of a "total institution."[67] And yet, as Isabel Hull explains, the array of associations that made up civil society in Germany were themselves exercises in self-disciplining, requiring their members to "submit to rules of demeanor and judgment that ordered social intercourse in a new way"—towards the "goal of social self-creation through morality."[68] The asylum Casino did not contradict this project; to the contrary, it provided an ironically faithful reflection of the latter.

Military exercises and Casino sociability symbolize the two poles of absolutist and liberal models of treatment. The fact of their coexistence in the asylum best describes the nature of this institution and is emblematic of its tensions and contradictions. Lindpaintner prided himself on Eberbach's banishment of chains and beatings, but substituted for these an array of virtual torture machines and medical treatments, all in the name of humanitarianism and enlightenment. The rhetoric of liberalism—of individual freedom, education, and the restoration of reason—joined hands here with force and repression. Eberbach's model of governance and order was in fact a type of enlightened despotism.

Economic Crisis and the Social World of the Patients

The transitional character of the Eberbach asylum matched the transitional nature of the society in which it was embedded. Old and new coexisted in a still-preindustrial society undergoing not only administrative modernization, but the spread of market capitalism. This development, together with a rise in population, were in turn responsible for the economic and social crisis of mass pauperization that stamped the history of the Vormärz in Nassau and elsewhere in central Europe.

Nassau's population was overwhelmingly rural and poor, and it was steadily growing. In 1819, only 7 percent of the population lived in towns of over 2,000 inhabitants. Nassau's largest city and capital, Wiesbaden, contained only slightly over 5,000 residents.[69] As late as 1847, 83 percent of the population still lived in rural communities.[70] With the notable exceptions of the areas of wine-growing and small-scale industry in (respectively) the Rheingau and the flatlands near Frankfurt am Main, Nassau's terrain was mountainous (the Westerwald and the Taunus), and its agricultural conditions poor. Particularly in its poorest region, the Westerwald, an economy of cattle-raising and oat cultivation was by the early nineteenth century increasingly dependent on potatoes, with catastrophic results in the years of crop failures in 1816/17, 1829, and 1846/47.[71] Nassau's demographic growth exacerbated these conditions, leading in this area of partible inheritance to the splintering of agricultural holdings into tiny plots of land, which were, as a result, in many cases no longer able to support their owners.[72] Out of a total of 26,864 peasant households in 1818, only 365 were taxed at the rates for middle to upper-class holdings.[73] This partitioning of land contributed to the creation of a landless, "proletarized" rural underclass, who eked out livings as servants and day laborers.

For men, this often involved seasonal migration to work as paid laborers in the industrially advanced areas in and around Frankfurt, or in the mines of the Westerwald. Many poor peasant women were likewise drawn to towns and larger cities to work as servants for the wealthy. But even peasants who owned land were usually forced to supplement their living as day laborers or in home industry (making faience and stoneware, basket-weaving, spoon carving, sewing, and weaving).[74] Their products were in turn either sold to entrepreneurs or peddled by the peasants themselves in towns. The existence of a secondary trade or supplemental area of work was one of the distinguishing features of the Nassau economy and a "sign of the difficult economic situation of broad sections of the population."[75] Poverty also drove large numbers of Nassauer to emigrate to North America.

State reforms aimed at creating a free-market economy played a major role in the increasingly desperate plight of Nassau's urban and rural lower classes. An 1808 law abolishing the remnants of serfdom set peasants free from what had remained of feudal tax and labor burdens, but at the same time meant the loss of the protection and welfare duties of their former lords. Furthermore, more than half of the agricultural holdings in Nassau continued to be burdened by the *Zehnte,* a "tax" of 10 percent of the yearly harvest of demesne, church, and other lands held by corporations and private owners.[76] Reforms aimed at ridding Nassau of the three-field system in order to increase agricultural productivity threatened peasant grazing and other rights to common lands.[77] The abolition of guild monopolies in 1819 had a devastating effect on artisans who found themselves unable to compete both with the influx of craftsmen into the trades and increasing competition from peddlers and entrepreneurs. By the 1830s and 1840s these dislocations had taken on the dimensions of mass pauperism and provided direct fuel to the revolutionary uprisings of 1848. In this year, Nassau was the first German state swept by revolution, which became a "mass movement . . . that encompassed practically the entire population."[78]

The Eberbach asylum housed some of the victims of these developments, and, consistent with Nassau's demographics, the majority of its patients came from the rural lower classes. Males, however, consistently outnumbered females by a ratio of about two to one.[79] Patients in the two lowest payment categories made up about 70 percent of the asylum population, and those patients whose upkeep was paid out of poor funds formed the largest (43 percent) of any single patient group at Eberbach. The previous occupations of lower-class patients ran the spectrum from indigent beggar, landless day laborer, servant, peddler, and artisan, to well-off peasant.[80] Most typically, they came from families of poor or small-scale farmers who combined agriculture with a trade, a home industry, or part-time work as hired laborers. In addition, Eberbach housed a substantial minority of patients from the middle and upper-middle classes (the new

Wirtschafts- and *Bildungsbürgertum*). Indeed, these patients, forming as they did 20 percent of the asylum population, were hugely overrepresented when compared to their numbers in the German population at large.[81] Many (about one third) came from other parts of German-speaking Central Europe—from places like the Prussian Rhineland, Frankfurt, Heidelberg, and even from the Austrian Empire. They were government officials, military officers, jurists, physicians, apothecaries, teachers, university students, pastors, and businessmen. Their presence at Eberbach, which deserves further study, is not only evidence of this institution's reputation; more importantly, it suggests the extraordinary optimism and faith in the curative abilities of the asylum in this period, a circumstance that would change radically by the last decades of the century.

Madness in lower-class patients was often closely related to the economic and social dislocations outlined above. The psychic toll of wrenching poverty can be seen in those patients terrified and in despair over their future livelihood after the loss of a home or the family's breadwinner. It can be seen indirectly in those patients whose psychological troubles revolved around the inability to marry for lack of property, in those patients who lost their social moorings as they were reduced to beggars roaming the countryside, and in the enormous level of alcoholism. There was, however, no simple, causal relationship between mental trauma and its social context. The links between the two were always mediated by the cultural and symbolic framework in which personal problems were experienced. Whether or not an individual was committed to the asylum was also dependent on a variety of external factors: the degree of economic independence of the individual, social and economic status within the family, and even community politics.[82]

Prior to commitment, many patients had been involved in extreme conflict with their families and/or communities, often for very legitimate reasons. Such conflicts could center around inheritance or land-use issues. Asylum patients were typically the losers in these battles—those people who had been in the weaker position to make their claims. It was very rare for a patient to be incarcerated directly against the will of his or her family. Almost all of the patients at Eberbach had been committed because people in their immediate surroundings—family, neighbors, local officials—had desired it. Communities had perceived many of the patients as dangerous, either physically or symbolically. But it was higher authorities and educated culture that translated local and familial troubles into medical problems and mobilized the state apparatus. The intertwined strands of these interests and viewpoints, as they operated in asylum and society, is examined in the following chapters.

I

Religion

2

Religious Madness in the Vormärz

Culture, Politics, and the
Professionalization of Psychiatry

In 1849 Germany's leading psychiatric journal reported a curious "illness" that, "like a plague," had swept through a number of rural Swedish communities[1]: young girls subject to an "involuntary drive to preach." The "preaching illness" began with symptoms of a "strongly-felt awakening towards repentance and improvement," headaches, and burning in the chest. It then progressed to "automatic convulsions" and visions, which the girls "imagine are the effects of God's spirit." In this state, they preached a message admonishing against sin—against dancing, drink, card-playing, and other depraved behavior—and prophesied the coming destruction of the world. Whole communities had been infected, believing in the girls' message and in their connection to God.

Identifying new forms of religious "madness" (and other mental illnesses) was a learning process, and one important venue for this was the collegial exchange of case histories in professional journals. In a postscript to the article, Carl Friedrich Flemming (1799–1880), an editor of the journal and one of Germany's leading asylum psychiatrists, appended his own recent treatment of a case in Prussia that remarkably matched the symptoms of the Swedish preaching illness. A young village girl took to falling into "epileptic fits" and, in a trance state, would admonish people in her community about their sins. She attained "great respect through her preachings and prophesying"; "listeners streamed" to hear her, even paying money for the privilege. A doctor was called in to examine her; she was ultimately removed to an asylum where, through Flemming's successful cure, she "never again made the least attempt to preach," and was able to be returned home without any further "public nuisance."[2]

The preaching illness was but one variant of a larger epidemic of religious madness that physicians, asylum alienists, and others were convinced plagued their society. They saw patients troubled by anxiety, guilt, and terror over real or imagined sins; people who were bewitched or possessed by the devil; prophets and mystics whose diseased imaginations led them to believe themselves endowed with divine powers. This was the heyday of religious madness, an illness discussed at length in the professional literature and registered in asylum statistics across Europe and North America.[3]

The notion of religious madness—that religion was either the cause of madness or that pathological religiosity was the result of madness—was not new to the nineteenth century. The idea had been in circulation within educated culture since the late seventeenth century, and in the German late Enlightenment had become a topic of wide discussion and debate. The pathologies of "false" religion—superstition, enthusiasm, fanaticism—had been a staple theme of enlightened pastors and administrators in the pedagogical campaign of the *Volksaufklärung* (popular Enlightenment). It had also been central to the self-probing project of uncovering and mastering the irrational aspects of the self that accompanied and helped shape an emerging bourgeois identity in the late eighteenth century—a discussion carried on by laymen, philosophers, theologians, doctors, and educators in the likes of Karl Philipp Moritz's *Magazin zur Erfahrungsseelenkunde*.[4]

What was new in the nineteenth century was the extent to which medicine had taken over this discourse and harnessed it to a new institutional response: the insane asylum. Flemming's preaching maidservant was dealt with not by the village pastor or schoolmaster, but by the alienist and the insane asylum. The social ramifications of this historical phenomenon have yet to be explored in depth. With few exceptions,[5] the secondary literature has treated religious madness as at base a natural, not a social phenomenon. In the early nineteenth century, religious madness, it is asserted, was an epidemiological fact, caused primarily by the wave of fundamentalist evangelical movements, such as the Awakening.[6] Adopting much the same views as their medical sources, the works argue that such religious movements, with their moral rigorism and preachings of hell and sin, drove people to despair, terror, suicide, and madness.

By assuming a pre-existing "reality," which medical diagnosis merely recorded and reflected, this approach fails to grasp the constructed nature of religious madness and the social relations that underlay its application. The religious madness diagnosis was applied specifically by educated, male, bourgeois physicians to primarily rural and lower-class (and, to a lesser extent, middle-class female) religious beliefs and experiences. It was a concept deriving from a medical discourse that fundamentally modified and redefined the phenomena it described, and in so doing turned forms of popular religious experience into pathological entities. This is not to deny the existence of the symptoms doctors described, phenomena such as religious despair. It is rather to attempt to disentangle such social phenomena from their interpretation and (re)constitution in medical discourse, and in this way to begin to gain access both to the world of popular culture and to that of educated physicians. I begin with an examination of the cultural, political, and medical components that formed the thinking of physicians and many of their educated contemporaries on religious madness.

Bourgeois Culture

Carl Wilhelm Ideler (1795–1860), director of the psychiatric section of the Berlin Charité, opened his *Versuch einer Theorie des religiösen Wahnsinns* (1848) as a battle cry against madness (*Wahn*) and darkness (*Finsternis*) in the defense of the "highest ennoblement of a progressive consciousness" and the "forces of reason."[7] Religious passion and superstition, he argued, posed one of the gravest threats to reason. In the past, they had caused untold cruelties, wars, and mass psychopathology in the form of witchhunting and inquisitions. Now, at a time of heated and bitter "religious controversies," their effects were plainly visible in medical practice—in the religious delusions of patients whose lower-level mental functions have driven out of consciousness the "real world, with all of its objective relations, requirements, and laws." The consciousness of these patients has been transferred into a "supernatural world" filled with "imaginary things from fantasy" and "delusional ideas."[8] Although not every alienist subscribed to Ideler's theory of passion, almost all would have agreed with the historical and epistemological terms in which it was framed.

Religious psychopathology could be labeled with a variety of names— *religiöser Wahnsinn, religiöse Melancholie, Daemonomania, Teufelswahn, religiöser Trubsinn,* the preaching illness—some, like religious melancholy, reaching back several centuries,[9] others of more recent origin. Religious madness also had various disease classifications according to the particular nosology a writer used: it could be treated as a separate disease category or as a subspecies of melancholia, insanity (*Wahnsinn*) or enthusiasm (*Schwärmerei*).[10] Beneath the differences in naming and classification lay the deeper division in German anthropological psychiatry: that which lay between psychicists and somaticists. The division surfaced most clearly in the debate (not specific to Germany) over etiology, in particular, over the question, as Friederich Bird posed it: "[I]s religion the cause or effect of insanity?"[11] The question was a loaded one: to argue in favor of the causal role of religion was to accept the psychicist position that insanity stemmed from disturbances of the mind (soul). This is precisely the sort of argument that the psychicist Ideler made in locating religious madness in deranged and overwrought passions. And this position is what Bird, a somaticist and assistant physician at the Siegburg asylum to the leading somaticist of the day, Maximillian Jacobi, set out to dispute, arguing that there is a physiological base to religious madness. "[I]t is not political or religious views that make one crazy; rather the cause of insanity is the continuously exalted condition of agitation affecting the physical habitus. . . ."[12]

Whatever their theoretical position, German physicians were not hostile to religion per se. To the contrary, theology and metaphysics ran deep in German Romantic medicine, and anthropological psychiatry was suffused with religious concerns. The school of psychicists defined insanity in religious terms (or, a secular version of them). Heinroth's "sin-theory" of mental illness saw the project of restoring the disordered to "reason" as leading man back to God.[13] Somaticists repudiated the union of medicine and metaphysics of psychicists, but their purpose in so doing had a religious motive: to preserve the sanctity of the immortal soul by strictly separating body and soul. Bodies became diseased, not the soul.

Physicians associated mental pathology not with religion as a whole, but very specific types of religious belief and piety—those referred to as superstition, enthusiasm, and fanaticism. Definitions of religious pathology here reveal a body of shared religious views that transcended the divisions between psychicists and somaticists. The pathological tropes of the mystic and the melancholic reveal the sorts of beliefs at issue. Mystics suffer from "delusions" of holiness, believing the self to be endowed by God with special divine powers—the power to perform miracles, prophesize, and commune with higher powers. Religious melancholics live in fear and despair, believing themselves forsaken by God and damned to hell for a life of sinfulness. Tormented by every real or imagined offense, the lives of such people unravel as the struggle for the soul becomes all-consuming: they lose interest in, indeed come to "despise" worldly affairs and personal interests. They retreat to an internal world, consumed by praying, singing, and reading the Bible. Its most extreme stage may take the form of "demonomania"—belief in the literal possession of the body by the devil.[14]

The beliefs targeted here drew from a number of sources: neopietism, popular culture, and, less obviously, religious orthodoxy.[15] In the view of the critical physician, these religious currents shared in common pre- or anti-Enlightenment qualities. In one form or another, they posited a cosmos of delusion and superstition, in which supernatural powers (ghosts, spirits, angels, God, the devil) interacted directly with, and exercised control over, nature and human activity. Belief in such a world prior to the late seventeenth century had been shared by educated and common people alike, and it had been on this basis that, as Michael MacDonald has shown for early modern England, Europeans had held a very eclectic view of psychological distress, one in which mental maladies could be ascribed to any number of supernatural (or natural) causes, including devil possession, divine damnation, and witchcraft. Likewise, healing involved an eclectic mix of medical treatment and the manipulation of supernatural forces (astrology, exorcism, and "religious healing").[16]

While, as we shall see, such an eclectic framework continued to exist in the countryside of the early nineteenth century, the culture of educated elites had undergone over a century the profound changes associated with the scientific revolution and the Enlightenment. The "desacralization" of the world that these movements brought about involved the substitution of science and rational inquiry for the supernatural. A world in which spirits, witchcraft, devil possession, and religious healing had been possible and meaningful had become anathema to the rationalist, scientific minds of a nineteenth-century educated middle class. For while that middle class in Germany remained believers, the notion of God and Christianity had been transformed. And it was this transformation that paved the way for the possibility of the very notion of religious madness, based as it was on naturalistic and medical, rather than supernatural, explanations of mental maladies.

This cultural transformation had occurred most radically among religious rationalists, whose stronghold in the early nineteenth century lay precisely within the urban *Bildungsbürgertum* to which alienists and physicians belonged. Rationalist theology—a religion of reason and morality—had purged itself of much of traditional Christianity, and this included the doctrine of original sin, the divinity of Christ, miracles and prophecies, and the existence of Hell and the devil. Such traditions were at the heart of centuries of human enslavement and darkness, teaching the faithful blind obedience to authority and the renunciation of this world in favor of the afterlife. Against such traditions, rationalist theology posited a world of natural law, watched over by a loving and benign God who was knowable through scientific observation, and a Christ who was a moral teacher. As such, rationalists posited a world susceptible to change and reform through the actions of responsible human beings.[17] Even orthodoxy had not remained immune to the currents of Enlightenment and secularization. While maintaining its faith in Christian tenets, it rejected outright or vastly downplayed belief in supernatural forces and mystical experiences (pacts with the devil, witchcraft, and miraculous visions).

Religious pathology was seen then through the lens of a shared bourgeois culture, one of whose building blocks was formed by this long-term shift towards a secular and scientific worldview. There were also a number of other beliefs and concerns embedded in the religious madness concept and specific to bourgeois culture of the early nineteenth century. The problem of excess and immoderation was one such concern. Ideler's litany of historic mystics presented the image of a piety whose intensity breaches the bounds of civilized life, driving its victims to extremes of bodily self-punishment and even social extinction. Deprivation of the body and withdrawal from daily life led early Christian mystics downward socially to the very bottom—to lives as "beggars, vagabonds, peasants, ruined artisans . . . slaves [and] thieves . . . ," who formed an "army of people deprived of all the occupations and comforts of life, suffering hunger, need, affliction, and torment, and becoming madmen. . . ."[18] The religious melancholic, infected by evangelicalism or religious orthodoxy, suffered a similiar fate in the literature: tormented by sins of the flesh, the person withdraws from daily life, seeking salvation in an obsessive and self-depriving regimen of prayer and reading Scripture.[19] Excess could also take the form of self-indulgence and sexual promiscuity—as in images of the baroque mystic Marie Alacoque, who, after ripping out and offering her heart to Jesus, takes Him "in her arms and cuddles him."[20]

What comes through here is a bourgeois *Biedermeier* sensibility of orderliness, moderation, self-discipline, and *Gemütlichkeit*. The baroque piety of pain, ecstasy, and physicality was just as foreign and abhorrent to this mindset as medieval inquisitions and the flaming torments of a Dantean hell. Self-mastery over an internal "other"—over the irrational forces of the ego—was a quintessentially bourgeois value, closely connected, as has been suggested, to the insecurities and aspirations of a social class forming itself outside of and against the traditional corporatist order.[21] Yet the self-mastery they aimed at in the early nineteenth-century literature was defined not only in terms of control, but in terms of the freeing or maintenance of feeling, energy, and "natural drives."[22] The pathology of excess in the religious mystic and melancholic was more than anything a pathology of repression and self-denial—of both the body and the social person. Frustrated and needlessly guilt-ridden sexuality appears over and over again in this literature as the cause of deep, pathological anxiety, depression, and the downward spiral into insanity.[23] The denial of the body also had its social component, leading the person who "completely devot[es] consciousness to a supernatural world" to the "denial of all earthly interests."[24] Those "earthly interests" were based on the values of work, achievement, and sociability, as Ideler makes clear in his summation of religious madness as "loneliness, avoidance of all work, repose and idle daydreaming, seeking to rid oneself of all life interests."[25]

What was being formulated in the discussion of religious pathology was a bourgeois ethos of individual responsiblity, achievement, productivity, and "earthly" happiness, informed by the reevaluation of passion and feeling in the Enlightenment and Romanticism. Against the guilt-inducing iron hand of Christian morality, medical writers formulated a conception of the healthy individual with "natural drives." Based on the assumption of the person as a composite of various discrete and identifiable drives, health depended upon the prevention of disorders of excessively weak or strong "natural" instinctual drives, that is, upon ensuring that those drives were allowed to serve the "natural ends for which the drives [e.g. eating and sex] are intended."²⁶ For, where the "*Lebenssinn* is disturbed, obstructed or overstimulated, there is . . . [a] disordered consciousness."²⁷ The definition of what constituted "natural" drives and their proper balance under the rational mind reflected a class-specific set of values. Writing without a trace of irony, one contemporary medical report explained that essential to a healthy "free will" were the natural drives for "property," "honor," "status," and "power."²⁸ A properly balanced economy of natural drives would serve and further the individual's bodily and social needs, ambitions, and duties. There is no better example of the naturalization of bourgeois values within contemporary medical categories of insanity.

The literature on religious madness thus substituted a medico-moral discourse about the maintainance of the healthy, balanced, and rational life for the religious experience of sin, expiation, and the miraculous. At the core of the former was the construction of a new individualist subject: rational, autonomous, and responsible, who embraced the norms of self-promotion/achievement, sociability, and self-cultivation towards the goals of prosperity and worldly happiness. In this way, the discourse of religious madness participated directly in the formation of a new set of norms, behavioral codes, and experiences of selfhood within an emerging enlightened bourgeois public.²⁹ Presented as natural and universal, this model of personhood expressed instead the norms of a particular class and, more specifically, a particular sex within that class: bourgeois men. Heinroth, for example, implicitly worked with such a model in his critique of the mystical piety of the neopietist writer Jung-Stilling: "where other people think, reflect, choose, and act . . . , [Jung-Stilling] abandons himself to blind chance, which he calls divine guidance." Heinroth presented this reprehensible "lack of will" as female. It showed "passivity" and was described with reference to the feminine: ". . . his entire life, he was driven about by external command [*Bestimmung*] . . . and changed his supposed profession as often as fickle women change their clothes."³⁰ If religious madness could be symbolically gendered as feminine, its epidemiology, as I will show in chapter 3, also had a strong class component.

The Politics of Religion

The discussion of religious mental pathology was shaped by and inseparable from political currents and debates. It was first via the politics of religion in the late-eighteenth-century *Schwärmerstreit* that the notion of religious madness became a focal point of public discussion. In this literature, the trope of the religious melancholic and enthusiast was a polemical tool used by enlightened writers in the struggle against obscurantism, superstition, and despotism.³¹ The power of religious madness as political critique took on renewed intensity in the increasingly polarized religious environment of the Vormärz. And the terms of the debate—between rationalists and liberals, on the one hand, and the exponents of orthodoxy and neopietism, on the other—were retained as the writers and practitioners of mental medicine took over this discourse. Some understanding, therefore, of the politics of religion in these years is essential to grasp what religious madness meant, and the socio-political agenda that underlay the employment of this diagnosis in the medical community.

Vormärz society was riven by religious divisions that were highly politicized.[32] Those divisions involved confessional tensions between Catholics and Protestants that emerged with force in the late 1830s. More important for this study were the highly charged disputes that crossed confessional lines: between religious rationalists, on the one hand, and neopietism and orthodoxy (neoorthodoxy), on the other. Rationalist theology, as its eighteenth-century precursor, was closely identified with and a driving force in the rise of political liberalism—its theology of natural religion providing the undergirding for a politics of opposition to bureaucratic absolutism and feudalism, calls for freedom of thought and expression, representative government, and other liberal reforms.[33]

Liberal rationalists (both Protestant and Catholic) faced off against an array of conservative religious traditions and movements within both Christian confessions, and the piety and beliefs of the latter were precisely those that figured so prominently in the literature on religious madness. Within Protestantism, there were the adherents of orthodoxy and neopietism (the Awakening movement)—two former enemies now united against liberals and the forces of change associated with the Enlightenment and the French Revolution. The former expressed their opposition in the firm support of Christian dogma, while the latter did so as an "undogmatic religion of the heart [and] of inner feeling." In radical rejection of the Enlightenment worldview, the Awakening not only embraced the Bible as the literal truth of God, but posited a human nature of depravity and sinfulness in which grace and salvation were to be found through a deeply emotional conversion experience and a life thereafter of strict moral purity. It proscribed all earthly enjoyments, and advocated discipline and suppression of physical desire, and dedication to a life of good works.[34] With its stronghold in southern and western Germany in the middling to lower strata of small-town and rural society, the Awakening drew its strength from the social and economic crisis of the countryside, as it was able to provide the suffering and displaced with a sense of community, feelings of self-worth, and the ability to express in their own religious language the "painful experience of . . . everyday life."[35] The "preaching illness" described at the start of this chapter was no sickness at all to the communities where it appeared; it was part of a revivalist religious movement.

Finally, liberals clashed with a Catholic church in which ultramontanism was making steady headway in the 1830s and 1840s, thus sharply intensifying liberal hostility to an institution long identified with authoritarianism and superstition.[36] Ultramontanist opposition to state interference in church affairs was only one facet of a combative, antimodern movement that sought to stamp out all traces of rationalism and liberalism in order to return the church to "rigid hierarchy . . . discipline," and centralization of authority in Rome.[37] Demanding absolute obedience to church dogmas and the suppression of all modern tendencies, it sought to purge the universities of all such influences and increase its control over education and other affairs, which brought it into open clashes with the German states. Just as ominous in the eyes of liberals and religious dissenters, it encouraged a religious revival of traditional, baroque piety—pilgrimages, processions, the Marian cult, religious brotherhoods.[38] As Anderson puts it, ". . . a gradual 'resacralization' of religious life, beginning around 1820, replaced the rationalist, utilitarian ethos of the Catholic Enlightenment with miracle, mystery, and authority."[39]

The concept of religious madness drew its force and a good deal of its meaning from the nature of these religious differences and the way they overlapped with political divisions. In the hands of oppositional and enlightened groups (rationalists, liberals, radical democrats), the attack on neopietism and other pathology-inducing religious beliefs was code for a broader assault on political conservatism and cultural traditionalism. As such, religious madness was a contested concept that pitted the exponents of science, rationalism, and liberal reform against adherents of orthodoxy and, especially, neopietism. A stir erupted, for example, around a 1826 administrative report of the Hamburg *Allgemeines Krankenhaus*, which had claimed that "a dark, creeping mysticism" was causing insanity and suicide among the patients.[40] This report generated an angry denunciation in defense of the neopietist "reaction against . . . natural religion [and] Deism" by the Hamburg senator Martin Hudtwalcker, which was widely publicized in the press.[41]

Liberals saw clear links between the mental derangement of that "dark, creeping mysticism" and political tyranny. The liberal leader Karl von Rotteck spelled out plainly this political critique of supernatural thinking in that central compendium of Vormärz liberal thought, the *Staatslexikon*. For Rotteck, superstition, which he identified with mental imbalance, had to be seen in historical and political terms—as a "natural propensity" that has been purposefully cultivated and manipulated by the deceptions of both "priestly dominance" and "worldly despotism"—by church and state—in the interests of political domination. It is for this reason that he called the superstitious "slaves." Superstition also provided Rotteck with a focus for delineating the proper relationship between state and society in the *Rechtstaat*. State power is a necessary tool for eradicating superstition when it is a question of combatting criminal acts (e.g., the "miracle doctor" prescribing harmful medication), but the state should

never be allowed to interfere in matters of personal belief, however false and ignorant those beliefs might be. For a state wielding such powers, even in the interests of enlightenment, poses a potential threat to all beliefs and freedoms.
The solution to superstition is more freedom, not less, which one achieves
through education and the healing power of "reason and truth."[42]

When the forensic physician and democrat Gustav Blumröder (who would
later be imprisoned for his political activities in the 1848 Revolution)[43] singled
out pietist "private conventicles" and the Catholic confessional as forms of "ter-
rorism" and disseminators of "contagion,"[44] it was the oppositional political
critique of Rotteck and others that endowed his and other medical attacks on
religious conservatism with a special force and meaning. It was also politics
that could lay behind what on the surface appeared as purely medical differences of opinion. The argument of Friedrich Bird, a liberal and somaticist,
against the psychicist's interpretation of religious madness ("it is not political
or religious views that make one crazy; rather the cause of insanity is the continuously exalted condition of agitation affecting the physical habitus") was simultaneously a defense of religious skepticism and freedom.[45] Specifically, Bird
sought to counter the assertion of the British alienist George M. Burrows that
religious madness was caused by "doubt over the truth of the doctrines of the
religion to which one belongs," an assertion that in effect pathologized religious
skepticism.[46]

As these differences of opinion indicate, the discourse about religious madness was not the sole preserve of liberals. In the Vormärz, even some conservative physicians had come to embrace the illness concept. In fact, the most pro-
lific medical writer on religious madness, Ideler, was a conservative Romantic,
whose writings were replete with attacks on liberalism and "all revolutionary
heads."[47] The deeply religious son of a Protestant pastor and preacher of religious sermons to his patients in the Berlin Charité,[48] Ideler may have agreed
with liberals about the pathologies of pietist sects, but he also stressed the dangerous "egotistical passions" of the present, a reference that managed to link
neopietists to liberals, democrats, and capitalists in a suspicious and anxious
view of the modern world. Pessimistic about human nature and fundamentally
authoritarian in outlook, Ideler, unlike Rotteck, saw the need for strict governmental authority (including censorship) and traditional morality to battle the
pathologies and chaos of passion: "one vainly seeks in enlightenment alone for
a bulwark against enthusiasm . . . which only firmly based moral conditions
can secure."[49]

A conservative political agenda went hand in hand with a more repressive
and traditional way of construing the nature of illness and the norms of personhood. Liberal and radical democratic physicians stressed in their analyses of
religious madness the need to liberate the individual's "natural drives" from the

guilt and repression of pietist and orthodox morality. That repressive morality could in turn be construed in terms of a social and familial order that inhibited the free choice and development of youth in matters of marriage and romance. Claiming that "unsatified sex drive" was one of the most common causes of religious melancholy, Bird explained how one male patient lapsed into the illness in a state of extreme guilt and anxiety from the "pollutions" and "dirty fantasies" he was plagued with since his youth.[50] For Bird, the cause of the malady lay in the patient's upbringing—in the "strict orthodox faith of his father" and the obstacles that prevented him from marrying the girl he loved.[51] The inability of the patient to realize his desires in the natural and proper state of matrimony had devastating results: "for since his vigorous body and his fantasy (which made him susceptible to images of sensual pleasure) required contact with the female sex, thus the lack of physical pleasure in his life had a highly detrimental effect." When the patient finally did marry later in life, "the woman was so old, as he himself, and in no way able to fulfill his fantasies and divert them from other subject matter [i.e., "dirty" fantasies].[52] The mental hazards of sexual repression could even apply to women. Indeed Bird, as others, claimed that women were more likely to suffer from religious melancholy "because on the whole the female more than the male sex must let [the sex drive] remain unsatisfied."[53]

The conservative Ideler, on the contrary, bemoaned the pathologies arising from too much liberation and challenges to established authority ("immorality," "egotistical passions," etc.). Accordingly, he focused attention on the need for repression of the body, particularly in the case of women. While acknowledging the medical problem of "frustrated sex drive,"[54] he held up the mystic Catherine of Siena's self-sacrificing asceticism (fasting, sleeping on wood planks, and wearing iron chains) as the "purest example" of spiritual love of God.[55]

The liberal Bird, starting from the position that religious truth is to be found through rational inquiry into the natural world, linked treatment of religious madness to training in individual responsiblity. He explained to one patient: "[I told him], he must blame himself, not doubt God's grace, who no longer performs miracles. I asked him how he came to the idea of praying and *Wachen* as a remedy, and he named me numerous biblical reasons. I referred him [instead] to earthly measures. . . ."[56] Ideler's view of the religiously rational, on the other hand, would not have excluded the teachings of Scripture, just as his rhetoric stressed obedience to established authority more than individual responsibility and critical inquiry.

Given the deep political divisions and animosities between liberals and conservatives at this time, it is remarkable that on the topic of religious madness the two sides converged to the extent they did. One factor working to unify medical practitioners was the shared cultural framework they brought to the problem of religious madness. Another was the implicit social agenda of both conservatives and liberals in the matter of religious madness: the disciplining of lower class religiosity. Condescension and anxiety toward the lower classes, and the need to control their religious beliefs, pervaded this literature. Mental incapacity makes the lower classes vulnerable to all sorts of "dumb [religious] stuff."[57] Blumröder related a story told to him of a twenty-one-year-old *Bauernsbursche* consumed with anxiety after hearing the admonishing words of his pastor at communion: "Whoever unworthily takes of this body and blood, takes to his damnation."[58] Misunderstood words, and especially the egregious effects of pietism on vulnerable and ignorant minds, not only causes untold mental anguish, it disrupts work.

But mostly, the real, barely veiled, danger of misunderstanding in lower-class religious madness came from those claiming spiritual empowerment. Dr. Biermann, *Königlichen Hannoverischen Land- und Stadt-Physikus* in Peine, treated one such case: H.L., a fifty-three-year-old village day laborer who, through his association with the Moravian Brethren, came "to imagine" that he had "direct [contact] with the Creator" and was divinely endowed with such powers as "the sword of justice. . . ."[59] The "limited mental powers" of the patient made this "fanaticism" all the worse: his "misunderstanding of some passages from the Bible, e.g., 'I live, but not I alone; rather Christ lives within me'" had caused full-blown insanity. H.L.'s real crime (using the author's own juridical language) was daring to step beyond his assigned lowly mental, spiritual, and social position:

> This punishment [i.e., insanity] occurs when people of limited mental powers, as H.L., abandon the purely practical path of faith to which they have been assigned, and try, with the sophistry of a hidden conceit, to attain what is concealed from the intelligent [i.e., divine truth].[60]

H.L. was incarcerated in an insane asylum, by recommendation of Dr. Biermann, where he was later declared "incurable."[61] In the case with which this chapter began, Flemming, a liberal, used the institution to deal with a similar case: the female peasant-prophet who, in invoking her religious authority, asserted a spiritual status wholly at odds with her social place (as both peasant and woman), the hierarchy of the church, and, potentially, the laws of the state. There were similiar cases at Eberbach. The threat of lower-class religious madness was entangled in the "social question." And physicians across the political spectrum invoked their medical expertise in the policing and disciplining of lower-class religiosity. On this issue, conservatives and liberals differed only to the extent that the former included in their sense of social menace not only peasant prophet-mystics and neopietist enthusiasts, but, of course, liberals and democrats as well.[62]

The Professionalization of Psychiatry

It is no accident that the heyday of religious madness coincided with the early attempts of medical practitioners to create the field of mental medicine with an institutional base in the insane asylum. The "epidemic" of religious madness was closely connected to the professional struggles of these early psychiatric practitioners and writers to legitimate mental medicine and to forge a professional identity and ethos. Professional interests constituted, then, along with the other factors identified above, a strong force uniting physicians of otherwise widely differing views behind the drive to medicalize religious madness.

The problem of religion for mental medicine was, first of all, an institutional one: the problem of wresting from churches, faith healers, and other "quacks" a monopoly over the care of mental maladies. The attainment of a monopoly over the "market in services" has been identified in the literature on professionalization as one of the key prerequisites for the establishment of a profession.[63] For the medical profession as a whole, this monopoly in the early nineteenth century was still far from the case, for university-educated physicians still contended with competition from numerous illegal and legal healers—from licensed surgeons, bathkeepers, and midwives, to illegal quacks of all kinds.[64] In this respect, Nassau's unitary state medical system was an anomaly: it had officially abolished all "nonqualified" medical healers, though it did not thereby succeed in doing away with the use of quacks, to which the many complaints of physicians and officials testify.

The stiffest competition to the new speciality of mental medicine seemingly came from those associated with organized religion and the supernatural—churches, pietist sects, and miracle healers of all varieties. Monasteries, Catholic lay orders, and clerical pastoral care had long involved the churches in caring for the mentally troubled. While the consolidation of the state had diminished this role of the churches, religious and supernatural involvement with sickness and madness had far from disappeared. On the contrary, physicians were faced with a renewal of belief within both religions confessions, in the form of the Awakening and Catholic ultramontanism, both movements that not only made ideological claims of an ability to heal the sick, but provided strong organizational support for these activities. Organized by the Catholic Church, the 1844 Trier pilgrimage, which drew half a million pilgrims to the supposed healing powers of Christ's holy tunic, provides only the most spectacular example of how closely masses of the population remained wedded to religious answers to illness and personal suffering in the Vormärz.[65]

Goldstein has analyzed the "boundary disputes" between church and mental medicine in the French context, showing how the professional claims of expertise brought psychiatry into direct competition with the Catholic Church and religious orders.[66] An important factor in the fierce medical hostility to

Church involvement with the mad was in fact the closeness and indebtness of the new moral treatment to religious healers. Philippe Pinel, the founder of modern French psychiatry, incorporated the pastoral care of the Church while secularizing it and turning it into a tool to wrest medical jurisdiction and expertise of madness from the Church in a campaign to exclude the religious orders from the care of the insane. While French alienists were never entirely successful in ousting the Catholic nursing orders from asylums (they were needed as caretakers), they were able in many cases to severely circumscribe the use of priests and religious services.

The issue of religion and church played an equally important role in the professionalization of psychiatry in Germany. However, the very different medical, political, and religious circumstances in the German context meant that there were some differences in the way in which early psychiatry situated itself institutionally vis-à-vis religion and church. The pronounced anticlericalism that played such an important role in the views of Pinel and other French alienists did not apply to Germany, where anthropological psychiatry saw itself, in one form or another, as a supporter of religion. In France, the fault-line drawn between religion and science since the eighteenth century was one that pitted a conservative, royalist Catholic Church against the critique of a generally anticlerical and materialist scientific community; in Germany, by contrast, the crucial fault-line was not that separating science and church, but that between the adherents of rationalist religion and neoorthodoxy. German psychiatrists (primarily rationalists) saw religion not as a corrupting force, but in its proper rationalist form as a bulwark against mental and social disorder. For these reasons they did not seek to the same degree as their French counterparts to create strict boundaries between religion and medicine. They tended to envision a positive role for religion in the institutional care of mental illness. Accordingly, the employment of clerics, who performed regular religious services and pastoral care, was common practice in German asylums.[67] At Eberbach (and elsewhere), the clergy were viewed as useful, indeed indispensable, adjuncts, not rivals, to medical treatment.

Yet, in the managment of asylums and treatment of patients, German alienists were adamant that the role of clergy and religion was to be limited and strictly subordinated to the authority of the medical staff/director. They also opposed the use of nursing orders as attendents. Even the epitomy of "theological psychiatry," Heinroth, raised his voice in support of expanding the expertise of specialist alienists at the expense of the clergy and other nonmedical professionals. Heinroth's claims, however, were made within, not against, a religious framework. For Heinroth, what distinguished the psychic doctor, a healer of "soul disorders," from other nonmedical professionals was the way he combined in himself both medical knowledge of somatic illness and the personal qualities of other disciplines, theology among them, concerned with the mind:

whoever takes upon himself to be a doctor of the psyche must be specially schooled by the psychologist, by the cleric, and by the educator; . . . he must develop in himself the gift for psychological observation, must adopt a religious point of view, and must himself attempt to live the life of a cleric . . . to lead a life of reason, or in the words of the Holy Writ, a life in Christ.[68]

If in Pinel's moral treatment, pastoral care was appropriated and assimilated to a scientific method, in Heinroth that scientific method itself remained deeply embedded in a religious worldview. This religious framework (although not shared by all German alienists) as well as the lack of clear demarcations between the terms and methods of mental medicine, on the one hand, and those of the nonmedical professions, on the other, suggests the very different scientific context in which German medicine, deeply influenced by Romanticism and *Naturphilosophie*, engaged in its "boundary dispute" with church and religion.[69]

The diagnostic category of religious madness was itself a factor in this dispute and in the larger claims of alienists to scientific expertise and legitimacy. Religious madness furnished an immensely useful tool, enabling medicine to cast itself in the role of enlightened liberator bearing the tools of rational science to free those souls thrown into terror, despair, and finally, madness by the forces of darkness, superstition, and fanaticism. After dramatically invoking the mental and physical destruction wrecked by religious fanaticism through the ages, Ideler's solution appeared eminently sensible: mental medicine. Insane asylums provide the possibility of "objective research" into the nature of "religious consciousness." Indeed, the benefits to society, he claimed, would extend beyond the cure of the mad themselves: the knowledge developed from such studies would help solve the age-old problem of religious fanaticism, as manifested in the bitter *Streitigkeiten* between "dogmaticists and pietists."[70]

On the basis of its "natural scientific standpoint," the Coblenz Medical Board was able to make itself useful to the Prussian government in the matter of a Bavarian faith-healer peasant who in 1821 began drawing large numbers of Prussian pilgrims to be healed by his religious-miracle cures.[71] Drawing upon their knowledge of the close relationship between body and mind, the physicians explained to the government that what appeared to "more limited minds" to be miracle cures could be ascribed to a purely "natural phenomenon"—one of scientific interest that could provide "new proof for the great significance of psychic medicine."[72] The Board actually ended up recommending against banning the pilgrimages. This could be taken as evidence of medical "tolerance" of nonmedical healers, as Loetz has recently argued for Baden.[73] Yet the more significant point is the very existence of the report itself: it reflected and helped solidify the relationship of academic medicine to the state and enabled medicine to assimilate religious healing on its own terms, as a natural phenomenon. The

miracle healer was allowed to practice, but medicine had won the more important battle: the (re)formulation of what constituted reality and truth.

As a state-formed accrediting institution, the Coblenz Medical Board knew
perfectly well that the audience that mattered most in medical claims to expertise was the state. In Germany, the state was a key factor in the professionalization of occupations; this included the psychiatric profession and the problem of
religious madness in particular. The Vormärz presented a particularly oppor-
tune moment for the extension of medical expertise into the realm of religious
madness, given that the illness meshed so well with the broader aims of state
policy. Most of the period was dominated by the attempts of the German states
to extend their influence over the churches, to propagate in the interests of
order and progress forms of rationalist religion in the churches and schools,
and to eliminate or control religious fanaticism and superstition in the form of
pilgrimages, pietist conventicles, quacks, mystics, and lay preachers.[74] While
the medical rhetoric was one of liberation, tolerance, and enlightenment, religious madness helped forge ties between an emerging mental medicine and the
authoritarian states of the Vormärz. These ties promoted the status of psychiatry while involving it directly in a broad assault on popular culture in attempts
to reshape the beliefs, values, and, experiences of the self in rural and small-
town Germany.

3

Religious Madness and the Formation of Patients

If religious madness was integral to the professional interests of early psychiatry, its significance went beyond the goal of attaining institutional control over madness in "boundary disputes" with religious healers. For underlying the problem of the continued consultation by the sick and needy of nonmedical healers was the broader problem of culture: those masses of people whose supernatural understanding of mental afflictions remained far removed from the secular and naturalistic terms of mental medicine. It was this supernatural thinking that fed the continued use by communities of religious and magical "quacks"; and it was also this that made it sometimes impossible, as the Eberbach cases will show, to medically treat the religiously insane, since they refused to even see themselves as sick.

Religious madness was thus a point at which two fairly distinct cultures of illness collided, where the "superstitions" of the masses met the new thinking and practices of medicine, the state, and the bourgeoisie. Given the continued presence of the supernatural within popular understandings of madness, physicians and alienists, in making new claims of expertise in the curing of madness, were faced with an extraordinary task vis-à-vis the first generation(s) of asylum inmates: not only developing methods of curing but also forming the psychic and cultural preconditions of illness—namely, the modern, secular experience of illness. The religious madness diagnosis formed one important moment in the historical development of the modern mental patient. Its application by medical practitioners involved attempts to transform religious and supernatural experiences of mental trauma into mental illness and to insti-

51

tutionally reorient communities and individuals away from church/local healers and towards medicine, state, and asylum.

Mental Trauma and the Supernatural

Religion and the supernatural were pervasive themes in the Eberbach cases: a conservative estimate shows their appearence, in various guises, in at least ninety-three cases, both male and female, that is, almost one-fourth of the surviving files. These cases contained the range of characteristics seen in the literature: self-proclaimed Gods and Jesuses, mystics, people possessed by the devil, the bewitched or magically maligned, and sinners fearing eternal damnation. Class was an important social factor in these cases, with lower-class religious lunatics far outnumbering those from the middle classes. In treating such people, medical officials and asylum staff encountered a world that had failed in significant ways to undergo the secularization that had occurred in educated culture. They found a world steeped in "superstition" and pre-Enlightenment or anti-Enlightenment forms of piety, such as the Awakening.

There is by now a large literature documenting the persistence in the countryside well into the nineteenth century of a religiosity that combined elements of Christianity with pagan, magical beliefs, despite the efforts by authorities since the Reformation to eradicate the latter.[1] Nassau was no exception. One medical official railed in an 1832 report, for example, about how "superstitious" the people in Amt Wehen were: "When a sick person does not instantly get better from a regular doctor, he resorts to all sorts of quacks, sorcerers, and the like."[2] When a medical official in Amt Meudt detailed the belief of his maidservant patient that she was bewitched and damned, he was quick to place this fact in a larger cultural context: "Very bad religious education was for years characteristic of this area, manifesting itself especially in prejudices of all kinds, the greatest one-sidedness [*Einseitigkeit*], and crassest superstition."[3] The Awakening was also a force in Nassau, particularly in the Westerwald and in some southern areas, where it attracted not only peasants and laborers, but also some skilled artisans and a few Protestant clergymen.[4]

Just as religion and the supernatural remained central to popular culture, so its imagery pervaded the experience of personal distress. The alienist Ludwig Snell (1817–1892) understood this perfectly well in his own way. As late as 1855, the then director of Eberbach's successor asylum, Eichberg, commented that "common people have not the slightest rational idea of insanity . . . Uneducated people have the idea that an evil spirit, as it were, takes possession of an insane man and drives out his being with altogether new and perverted elements."[5] In fact, "uneducated people" in Nassau held, like the well-studied seventeenth-century patients of Richard Napier (the English pastor and healer),[6] a very eclectic view of insanity that embraced a range of explanations, from physical illness to social and psychological stress to supernatural forces (demonic possession, witchcraft, ghosts, and spirits). The supernatural, let alone the notion of an evil spirit capturing the soul, was not an all-purpose explanation of insanity, as Snell implied. It would be more accurate to say that it formed one important element of the cultural framework—a kind of language system—that people had available to them to make sense of their emotions and life events. Personal troubles and feelings were symbolized with the use of supernatural imagery—the imagery of bewitchment, devil possession, ghosts, sin and damnation—drawn from both popular and elite culture. As such, the narratives of religious madness in these patients joined together, through metaphor and imagery, the private and personal with a broader social field of meaning.

In present-day psychological terms, one could say the supernatural functioned as metaphor for both internal and social experience, which were projected onto supernatural forces. There was, for example, the baker's son whose life had been tormented by a harsh and abusive autocratic father.[7] The son had come to believe that an evil spirit had kidnapped his soul. "Chosen" out of a wide range of supernatural beliefs in popular culture, the metaphor of a soul kidnapped by an evil spirit articulated, it seems, an intensely personal drama—that of the soul-destroying relationship between son and father—within a broader, cultural field of meaning. The peasant woman Lucia T. killed her four-week-old baby in a fit of what today would be called postpartum depression.[8] She, on the other hand, said she had felt possessed by the devil during her pregnancy, and after the infanticide pleaded to be "burned" as a terrible sinner.

At a time of mass pauperism, there were those whose fantasies sought to reverse and compensate for an unbearable reality of financial crisis, destitution, and shattered self-esteem by transforming the self into heroic, powerful, and divine figures. This interpretation fits almost all of the self-proclaimed Gods, Christs, mothers of Christ, and other divine figures. They included the desperately poor joiner Georg M., who, out of shame, had sought to hide from his neighbors the true extent of his poverty and indebtness. Immediately preceding the outbreak of his insanity, all of his belongings had been auctioned off, thus making public his shameful secret. Georg M.'s insanity consisted of the belief that he was "God and very high-class [*vornehm*]. . . . He asserted he was all-knowing and all-powerful and very rich."[9]

Belief in the literal divinity of the self has to be seen at the extreme (and no doubt delusional in the eyes of the community) end of a spectrum of beliefs about links between humans and the supernatural world within popular culture. This was, after all, a world in which a simple peasant girl, as in Flemming's patient (see chapter 2), could attract followers as a prophet and mystic. Such people also appear in the Eberbach cases. The miner Veit H. believed himself called by God to found a new religious sect. At the time of his incarceration, he had been preaching and prophesying as part of a pietist-influenced group at the mine where he worked, and had at least one devout follower (who was also incarcerated).[10] The Awakening played a role in a number of other cases, manifesting itself either in prophesying or in the classic symptoms of religious melancholy: depression, anxiety, and fear of damnation.

Religion also provided a powerful social language of protest and reproach in both public and private matters. In 1847, at the peak of the price inflation and economic crisis, the tailor/day laborer Johann S. sat quietly listening to an afternoon sermon in a Wiesbaden church. When he saw the bishop step to the altar wearing a golden cross, "a strange combination of ideas immediately developed" in his mind. As the bishop proceeded out of the church after the service, Johann S. rushed at him, tearing off the cross. Arrested and finally interned in a hospital (not yet Eberbach), Johann explained the motive of his attack: "The gentleman at the altar ought not to wear a golden cross, because Jesus bore the cross on his back"; at another point he said simply that "he liked the cross so much that he could not resist the desire to just hang it on himself and possess it." He was transferred to the asylum.[11]

Medical writers generally believed that women were particularly vulnerable to religious madness, given the link made between this illness and "unsatisfied" or "frustrated" sex drive. Such was the diagnosis of Elisabeth M., a forty-one-year-old single servant and day laborer, who was diagnosed with nymphomania and religious melancholy. As the medical report put it: she suffered from "nymphomania . . . hidden behind religious melancholy," caused by an "unsatisfied sex drive" [*unbefriedigten Geschlechtstrieb*] as well as insufficient religious education.[12] Poor and no longer young, she had been spurned by a lover, a fisherman of means, who had given her hopes of marriage; after this, she was maliciously encouraged to pin her hopes of marriage on another well-off and eligible fisherman and vintner, who in fact wanted nothing to do with her.

Elisabeth's failure in love paralleled the economic disaster of indebtedness that befell she and her mother with the failure of the wine harvest. The two came to merge in her mind: the unproductivity of the soil and her failure to marry. She now blamed the two men, and "all men," for the harvest failures and her family's indebtedness. Pained and enraged, she turned to the church, and finally entered the family home of one of the men who had rejected her, bearing a Bible from which she read aloud a passage "to prove how bad it is that [he] does not marry her." Increasingly marginalized, teased by children in the streets, she took to the "public street" to preach, recite from the Bible, and sing. Though she herself began to feel that she had "lost her mind" [*Verstand*], she firmly refused all medicine, asserting that "only Heinrich [the first name of both the men she wanted to marry] can help me." In this she recognized that her condition was not medical, but social and economic in nature—her desperate need for financial support and social position from the only source it could come from: marriage, preferably to a well-off man.[13] The medical report made this social drama into a simple narrative of frustrated sexuality and ignorance; in fact, it was a complex story of class and gender relations within village culture, in which a financially and socially desperate woman in search of marriage reached for religion as a higher authority and sacred body of beliefs to legitimate her claims and reproach her enemies.

What were the reactions of communities to the "superstitious" beliefs of patients? Could those beliefs be interpreted by families and communities as signs of mental illness? These questions are not easy to answer given the limitations of the sources. Many of the ideas of patients drew upon beliefs that were still pervasive in rural communities and, by themselves, would not have seemed out of the ordinary. On the other hand, the belief systems of those communities had not remained untouched by recent (and long-term) historical developments. Religious rationalism was taught in Nassau's schools and preached from its pulpits (see pages 63 ff.).[14] Both the Eberbach sources and the complaints of officials about widespread "superstition" suggest, however, that the reception of religious rationalism by rural communities involved selective assimilation (and modifications of) "official" religion into preexisting popular ("unofficial") traditions.[15]

There are scattered pieces of indirect evidence suggesting that certain superstitions of patients could be interpreted in communities as signs of mental aberrance. In an investigation of the mental state of Anna W., a peasant woman who had murdered her three children, the report used testimony of neighbors and relatives attesting to her belief in witchcraft.[16] The brother of the "religiously mad" and "nymphomaniacal" Maria L. testified that she had seen a ghost.[17] These statements, however, appear much more ambiguous when the sources are read "against the grain." The comments by relatives and neighbors occurred in the context of official investigations of individuals who had committed acts that had already established them as mentally deranged in the community. Retrospectively, witchcraft and ghost beliefs assumed, presumably, a different aspect. Further, since both women were diagnosed with religious madness, it is likely that the investigators themselves, looking for evidence of superstitions, played an important role in eliciting the statements of community members. Other cases suggest how, in the midst of family conflicts, families sometimes strategically employed beliefs associated with religious rationalism against a member in order to see that person locked up in the asylum.[18]

It appears that "superstitious" beliefs alone did not make an individual mad in his or her community. Eberbach's religiously mad became outcasts and vulnerable to incarceration only when their beliefs combined with certain aberrant behavior that had already marginalized them. Patient beliefs in their own divinity were probably a different matter, especially when combined with erratic and unproductive behavior. Yet such beliefs were not far removed from those of any number of self-proclaimed prophets and seers, including the ill-fated Eberbach inmate Veit H., who gained followings in the nineteenth century.[19] Unfortunately, the sources do not allow access to those elements of self-presentation and social context that differentiated the delusional (in the eyes of communities) from "real" prophets.

Religious madness was not an exclusively lower-class or rural phenomenon. Among the middle classes, however, this "illness" and the theme of religion in general, disproportionately appeared in females. At points of crisis in their lives, women readily turned to religion, and they were much more likely to experience trauma within a religious framework: self-loathing and depression, for example, were experienced through the imagery of sin. Class and gender overlapped in interesting ways in these cases. Middle-class women were positioned differently (and more ambiguously) than men to rationalist, bourgeois culture: they shared many of its tenets by virtue of their class position, but at the same time, they remained outsiders (in this case, more religious, less "rational," and largely shut out of those institutions where a scientific outlook was disseminated) by virtue of their sex. Anna S.'s "madness" in the 1820s resulted from a furious hatred and jealousy of her rector/professor husband, who was a proto-typically enlightened and scientific man. For years she had considered herself ill and had sought out the help of a number of doctors. There were times, however, when she claimed she was in communication with higher spirits under God's protection and refused all medical advice. In a letter to her young son, Anna expressed pride in his progress at school, but, in the same sentence, hastened to admonish him not to forget God and prayer. For his part, the husband wrote contemptuously of the association between Anna's "insanity" and her religiosity, "to which the patient [Anna] has had predilections since childhood" and which led her into "wrongheaded reading."[20]

There were strikingly few religious madness cases among male, middle-class patients, and the theme of religion in any form appears much less frequently than in the female cases. This fact seemingly reflects the changes in bourgeois culture outlined above and the gendered, specifically male nature of those changes. There is some qualitative evidence, however limited, to support this conclusion; it indicates how secularization could furnish educated, middle-class men with an experience of religious madness very different from that of the lower classes.

A recent medical dissertation provides an intriguing, but wholly unproven, explanation for the mounting incidence of religious melancholy in this period: the torments of the religious melancholic reflected the broader "spiritual struggle" between the Enlightenment and the counter-Enlightenment movement of evangelicalism.[21] A similar idea can be found in the contemporary medical literature, formulated as the problem of religious "speculation" and "skepticism." Yet only one Eberbach case fits this description, and, not suprisingly, it is that of a male, middle-class patient—a young chaplain who had been forced against his will by his strict schoolteacher father to enter the ministry. Raised in a religiously "pious" home, Alois F. was sent off to the orthodox Catholic seminary in Mainz and later studied theology at university (Würzburg and Freiburg). The young chaplain's tormenting doubts about himself revolved around the fact that "towards religion he is entirely indifferent." The assumption of his first position as chaplain in Niederlahnstein therefore threw him into internal crisis: terrified, overwhelmed by feelings of inadequacy, and wracked by guilt, he began to be visited by nightly apparitions. A man entered his room at midnight declaring "you are damned"; he glimpsed fiery figures from the churchyard of his hometown; God, Jesus, and the Holy Ghost fought at his bedside. He was convinced that God had sent the apparitions to convince him of His truth and punish him for his religious doubt.

Alois explained his psychological and moral state in a letter to his priest requesting to be released from his position as chaplain:

> All spiritual functions that I performed up to now occurred without conviction, without soul . . . mechanics is my characteristic . . . I feel completely certain that I am not only unfit for the spiritual estate, but for every other; for I truly lack reason. I can't get myself to believe in the slightest thing.[22]

Torn between the orthodoxy of his upbringing and education, on the one hand, and the secular and rationalist influences at university[23] and in the life of Mainz (a stronghold of religious rationalism and later political radicalism), this man classically fits the image of religious despair resulting from the clash of intellectual movements in a "modernizing" world. In his ultimate resolution of the conflict, however, Alois chose the past—both his own and that of his culture. In a sermon he wrote during his sixteen-month stay at Eberbach, he railed against "the false Enlightenment," those "enlightened people that make religion into an object of reason." The word of God, he pronounced, was "more a thing of the heart than that of reflection."[24] Placation of the terrorizing father-apparition won out over religious doubt in the fervent embracing of neoorthodoxy.

There is no such comparable case among the large number of lower-class religious melancholics. These people struggled with the daunting and often unattainable goal of living morally pure and upright lives. They could be overcome by terror after hearing the fire-and-brimstone sermons of evangelicals (especially perhaps because, as some historians have claimed, "sinning" in the form of high illegitimacy rates, drinking, and low church attendance was indeed widespread and related to the weakening of church authority).[25] Yet it would be inaccurate to characterize the inner struggle of the lower classes as a clash between an enlightened, secular culture and neoorthodoxy, for the fact was that religious rationalism had either made little headway in these communities or had been selectively assimilated and modified.[26]

Another middle-class case, that of the apothecary Anton R., indicates how bourgeois culture had transformed the very experience of religious madness. Anton R.'s symptoms revolved around the supernatural and its power over his life. He was "in communication with demons and spirits, had premonitions of events that refer[red] to himself, his friends and family."[27] Yet he experienced these beliefs in a way not present in any of the lower-class files. The commitment report explained,

> he is not yet freed from [his] idée fixe, but is changing and he himself is conscious [*das Bewußtsein hat*] of his insanity [*Irrseyn*]. He tries to suppress his fantasies, and he likes to be instructed by people, to heed their opinions and confide in them. He thus seeks out company in order to distract himself and get rid of his idée fixe.[28]

Anton's receptivity to medical interventions was surely connected to his occupation as apothecary, but other middle-class patients demonstrated a similiar attitude. Not unrelated to this receptivity is the extent to which a bourgeois secular and scientific culture had penetrated the very experience of madness itself. At a very early stage of his "illness," Anton experienced the very appearance of supernatural thoughts as signs of mental derangement, as witnessed by his efforts to "suppress" those thoughts. In Anton R., the supernatural had become a *symptom* of madness.

To this extent, Anton R. was "ill" in a way unlike the vast majority of the religiously mad at Eberbach. To these lower-class people, the supernatural was not a symptom; on the contrary, it was an *explanation* for madness and personal trauma. Accordingly, these people did not necessarily turn to the medical profession for help. Indeed, some, like the tailor apprentice Heinrich F., were adamant that help could come only from nonmedical sources able to manipulate the supernatural powers at the source of their troubles. Having recently returned to his hometown after many years away on the *Wanderschaft*, the forty-nine-year-old Heinrich F. was first brought to the attention of the local authorities because of his drinking and "irregular manner of life." Under medical examination he firmly rejected any notion that he was ill, asserting that he required "only the help of a clergyman, who would know how to drive out the evil spirit dwelling in him."[29]

In both an existential and sociological sense, people like Heinrich F., who understood and experienced their personal problems in supernatural terms, who therefore sought out the help of magicians, clergymen, miracle healers, and resisted both the thinking and practices of medicine and asylum, were neither ill nor yet patients. This fact is of great significance for an understanding of the rise of the asylum and the profession of psychiatry. In its initial phase, the modern profession of psychiatry developed from its institutional base in the insane asylums that were founded in this period. And the patients of these asylums, the people who formed the backbone of the asylum system, were overwhelmingly from the lower classes. But if the Eberbach cases are in any way representative of asylum patients—and the medical literature on religious madness shows that they probably were—then this nascent profession had before it a formidable task, one to which historians have given scant, if any, attention. The formation of psychiatry into a modern profession required not only the standard institutional and intellectual criteria set out in the secondary literature (specialized education, monopoly over the care of the mad, official licensing requirements, and professional organizations); psychiatry, of course, also needed patients, and this was not a given. The Eberbach sources suggest that many of the first asylum patients needed in fact to be taught to be ill and shaped into patients. More broadly, a cultural shift was required of whole communities, that they cease their "superstitious" use of magicians and quacks, turning instead to medicine and the asylum for help.

The religious madness diagnosis wielded by a newly created state medical system and asylum was central to the project of transforming bewitchment, demonic possession, and divine damnation into psychopathology, and people like Heinrich F. into patients. Given the rootedness of these supernatural beliefs in popular culture, however idiosyncratically expressed in individual patients, the use of the religious madness diagnosis had broad social implications. Its use in such cases involved less curing insanity than the cultural recoding of the supernatural into medical terms. The pathologizing of popular experience that occurred through the religious madness diagnosis has to be seen not simply as an unfortunate by-product of the asylum system, but as central to the spread of that system and to the formation in the same period of psychiatry as a new medical specialty.

The Medicalization of Religious Madness

The transformation of the possessed and divinely damned into patients involved, at the most basic level, the recoding of those beliefs into mental and physical symptomotolgy, into markers of illness. This involved the scripting of a wholly different narrative of pain and madness from that of the person under medical observation and treatment. Lucia T., a thirty-four-year-old Catholic peasant wife of a shoemaker, killed her four-week-old child in 1835, cutting its throat with a tool from her husband's work table, in a fit of what would come to be seen as "temporary frenzy" [*Tollheit*]. During her initial incarceration in prison, a medical investigation of Lucia's mental state was requested by the *Criminalamt*, and what resulted was an eighty-three-page medical report proving the existence of insanity and providing the historian at the same time an extraordinary document on illness and madness in the Vormärz.[30] The narrative Lucia provided of herself and the infanticide was one of sin and damnation, conceptualized in the terms of impurity, dirt, and bodily possession.[31] Before the killing, in a period that appears to have stretched back to her pregnancy, she saw her household as contaminated [*verunreinigt*], dirty, full of vermin. She saw herself as a sinner, eternally damned, because she had wanted to drown herself. In response to her husband's hope that the birth of the child would make things well again [*wieder gut werden*], she let him know: "You believe I am pregnant with a child in my body; [no] I have the devil in my body." After its birth, she distanced herself from the baby, claiming it did not belong to her and, like the cases of infanticide studied by Regina Schulte, even denying its very humanity: "They took out of my body a piece of raw flesh."[32] A widowed housemate was the first to discover Lucia in the room right after the killing. Asked why she had done it, Lucia replied simply: "I killed my child, burn me immediately." While the examining doctors found Lucia perfectly able to speak clearly and lucidly about her past life, they could not get much of anything out of her when she was asked to explain the motive for the murder. To this question she would answer only: "I have been forsaken by God; [and] without God I can say nothing." Later, she explained how "through punishment, the crime will be redeemed and so [I] will be able to find God's grace again."

Lucia's reticence was probably not unrelated to the futility of communication with her interlocutors, the physicians to whom she chose to invoke the word of God. For the physicians did not simply reject her explanations of divine damnation and devil possession; they considered the explanations themselves symptoms of underlying mental illness. Like their patient, the physicians located the problem within her body, but this was a body of a different sort. If for Lucia the body was a site for supernatural intervention and divine punishment, the physicians perceived it as a natural, organic mechanism, a site of internal interactions of physical and mental life between the nervous and the sexual system, between nervous energy and the movement or stoppage of fluids (milk, blood, bowels). This body had a history of malfunction internal to itself that could be traced through external signs: the "excited nervous system" from her sanguine, choleric temperament and shifting, easily excitable moods; full-bloodedness from her frequent nose bleeds; milk and bowel stoppages after the birth, and so on.

The medical conception of Lucia's body accorded with traditions shared by both laypeople and physicians, lower and upper classes alike.[33] As such, its idiom would have been familiar to and probably shared by Lucia T. in the understanding of illness. But Lucia T. did not believe she was ill; she considered herself a sinner who must be punished. While Barbara Duden's study demonstrates the shared vocabulary of physical illness between doctor and patient in the mid-eighteenth century, one century later that communication had begun to fracture—not yet in the rejection by medicine of many of the earlier terms of bodily functions, but in the way those old terms were being put to use in a new professional and institutional context: that of mental medicine and the asylum. Citing the leading European authorities in the field (Esquirol, Heinroth, Friedreich, Jacobi), the authors of the medical report on Lucia integrated the old humoral body of fluids and stoppages within the latest theories of mental dysfunction, arguing that if insanity is defined as a "dream state when awake," caused by disturbances of the "imagination," then Lucia's delusions constituted insanity (*"fixen Wahnsinn"*). Since, however, insanity does not by itself affect the faculty of "will," the act of murder was the result of temporary frenzy.

There was, finally, a number of ways in which the entire conception of the self was reconceptualized in this case along secular, individualistic lines and in accord with bourgeois values. The medical narrative placed Lucia's acts as a mother within a broader cautionary tale of faulty gender relations and deficient motherhood, naturalized in the sentimental, bourgeois version of the ideal of motherhood. Lucia's treatment of her baby as a "piece of raw flesh" and the subsequent murder were only the most horrendous and extreme acts of a pattern of defective motherhood, now seen as a form of madness:

> In her dream world, [her] scarcely awakened motherly tenderness is soon suppressed, and we find the lovely image of a mother, which is bestowed [upon women] with the first child, is here entirely effaced. While [Lucia] . . . at first expressed pleasure with her child, she soon manifested great indifference to it, neglected its care and cleaning. She cannot even attend to the swaddling of the child, and her husband must take over [its] entire care . . . the [parish] priest noticed an incredible coldness and lack of feeling from her [toward her child].[34]

In the contemporary literature, medical writers were at pains to work out the distinctions and boundaries between simple superstition and religious enthusiasm, on the one hand, and full-blown religious madness, on the other—a crucial problem because of the very important political issues at stake (religious freedom and tolerance) in definitions of religious madness.[35] The problem was solved, as Ideler characterized the debate, in the general agreement that the boundaries between the two were indeed very "broad" and contained a "number of transitional stages."[36] Yet placing the two—superstition and religious madness—on a single spectrum of pathology already potentially blurred the distinctions between them.[37] The Eberbach cases show that those distinctions in practice were indeed blurry, allowing the pathologizing of what otherwise could be conceived as simple peasant ignorance and superstition. Those people harboring "superstitious" and "fanatical" religious beliefs were most vulnerable to being medicalized and institutionalized when their beliefs were combined with socially disruptive and aberrant behavior. The following case illustrates that the path by which this occurred was anything but simple, with medical officials forced to negotiate between several ways of interpretating their patients and between the alternatives of religious or medical forms of treatment.

The case begins in 1824, when a medical official, Dr. Frangel, went on request of the Nassau government to the town of Camberg to examine a miller, Heinrich M., who was suspected of having gone mad. Heinrich at the time was in the midst of a bitter court case with his wife. It is not exactly clear what the court case was about, but one aspect of the marital problems involved Heinrich's belief that his wife was unfaithful, and this had led to his physical (and sexual) abuse of her.[38] A considerable sum of money, 2,000 florins, had recently been "withdrawn" [*aufgekundet*] from Heinrich. It had originally been "family members" who had notified the authorities about Heinrich's "crazy behavior" and "ideas." Finding no outward signs of insanity, Dr. Frangel suspected the family of having used the claims of insanity as part of their court battle against Heinrich. The doctor therefore remained noncommittal in his assessment of the case. On his third visit, however, Frangel was finally able to get Heinrich to talk, and something of significance began to emerge: Heinrich had expressed the idée fixe (obsession) that his mill and home were "disturbed" by ghosts. With this new information, Frangel began questioning his patient closely: "What does this disturbance consist of [what is the evidence for it]?" Heinrich would only answer that "he can't say and doesn't want to say, because he lacks proof and because he has no *science of ghosts*" (emphasis mine). The doctor then tried instructing Heinrich on his misconception. But the latter would have nothing of it, telling the doctor repeatedly: "I will not let myself be made into a simpleton" (by you).

This fateful encounter between Dr. Frangel and Heinrich M. was more than a medical examination; it was an encounter between two fundamentally different outlooks—between the scientific culture of an educated, middle-class doctor and the "superstitious" oral culture of the miller. The encounter was also between fundamentally unequal partners, and culture was a crucial factor in this power inequality—a state of affairs understood by the patient and highlighted in his (sarcastic?) reference to his lack of a "science of ghosts." The doctor's authority flowed directly from his mastery of a language of science, empowering him to instruct, diagnose, and ultimately recommend incarceration. The miller, lacking such a language, could only express his beliefs at the risk of seeming a "simpleton." No communication, no defense of belief was possible across this cultural divide.

The ghost idea—seemingly a symbol of domestic conflict within Heinrich's home—would play a central role in his incarceration at Eberbach for the rest of his life.[39] One year after his incarceration, Windt explained that Heinrich's symptom—a belief that he was "under the domination of a spirit or ghost," manifested in visions and voices—"would not have drawn the attention of the authorities if [Heinrich M.] had not caused it as a result of his . . . suspicions of his wife's unfaithfulness," and his "mistreatment" of her. The ghost belief was the central factor in the perception of Heinrich as ill, and this belief, together with the pressure on the patient's chest before the visions, indicated the diagnosis: "the pathological moment is solely physically determined in disturbances of the abdominal economy. . . ."[40]

Yet it is noteworthy that Dr. Frangel had not initially considered the ghost belief sufficient grounds for incarceration. As part of the well-known "superstitious" beliefs of ignorant peasants, incarceration of such a person did not occur automatically. There were especially practical matters to consider. "[The ghost idea] in no way dominates him to the extent that it prevents correct mental connections; rather, with respect to his business and household affairs, his ideas are totally understandable [*verständig*]."[41] The doctor thus initially recommended "instruction" by the local pastor. Frangel explained several days later that Heinrich M. "suffers from an idée fixe," but is to be considered "more wicked [*boshaft*] than mentally ill. At least his illness is not yet of the type that he could be treated as a full-blown lunatic [*vollkommenen Wahnsinniger*]."[42] Yet in this very same report, Frangel was now recommending incarceration: the required "correctional and consistent psychic treatment . . . cannot take place in his present condition" (i.e., at home, where he was free to resist and posed a potential threat to his wife).

The utter vagueness and confusion over what precisely constituted mental illness, how it should be treated, and by whom, is striking. Frangel differentiated full-blown insanity from a mere idée fixe, the latter of which could be dealt with through instruction, and even overseen by a pastor. But at the same time, an idée fixe was already itself considered a form of mental illness, even if the patient was to be considered "not insane," only "wicked." It was the existence of the asylum itself, together with pragmatic concerns of social order, that were ultimately the decisive factors effecting the transformation of superstition into illness. Yet the mere placement of superstitious ideas on a continuum of mental illness, though it did not label the person as mad per se, was crucial in the events of incarceration and, once in the asylum, became the very basis for diagnosis and treatment.

State and Asylum

The medicalization of religious madness was closely linked to long-standing attempts by the absolutist states, together with middle-class, enlightened reformers, to reform the peasantry in the campaign of the *Volksaufklärung*. In the name of "humanity," "progress," and economic productivity, the "common man" was to be freed from his magical, superstitious thinking and practices, and shaped into a morally accountable, rational, and industrious citizen. The campaign was pegagogical, including the distribution of enlightened reading material; it also took the form of a legal crackdown on religious processions and pilgrimages, the Catholic cult of saints, and other practices of a baroque religiosity that encouraged disorderly behavior (drinking, dancing, etc.) and the squandering of money and work days. In Nassau, where, as elsewhere in Germany, rationalist theology predominated within the clergy of both confessions throughout most of the first half of the nineteenth century, state and church worked closely together in enforcing the (chronically resisted) new laws.[43]

State support of the *Volksaufklärung* in Nassau was, in turn, closely connected to the politics of state building and the formation of *Staatsbürger.* Church and educational policies were key fronts on which the state sought to establish control over and integrate its highly diverse population after 1806. The subordination of churches (*Staatskirchentum*) and schools to the state was crucial and a major impetus behind the 1817 union of the Calvinist and Lutheran faiths within a single Evangelical church. It also involved the propagation of religious tolerance and rationalist theology in the schools and churches; indeed, it is no exaggeration to say that such a policy lay at the very heart of state formation.[44] Under the reformist course of *Regierungspräsident* Karl von Ibell, it was essential to combat the intolerance and prejudices of religious fanaticism and "Schwärmerei" in order to meet the challenge of unifying a state formed out of extreme religious, social, and political fragmentation. A cornerstone of this policy lay in the school reform of 1817: the reorganization of the school system in which the state consolidated (at the expense of the churches) and centralized its control over education. The reformed *Simultanschule* of the 1817 decree created mixed confessional schools, while also "protecting the parity" of the Christian confessions in education.[45] Religion was envisioned as the most important element of the curriculum—at the core of forming *Staatsbürger*— and that religion to be taught was adopted directly from rationalist theology and the enlightened, pedagogical ideas of Heinrich Pestalozzi. It consisted of ecumenical religious instruction (*allgemeiner Religionsunterricht*) in a "positive" religion of reason, which would imbue children with the moral teachings of Christianity in order to make them into virtuous, disciplined, industrious, and obedient citizens.

The institutionalization of religious madness in Nassau functioned as the medical arm of these state policies, setting out to accomplish in the medical realm a transformation of mind not unlike that aimed at within school and church. The asylum's explicit and unabashedly pedagogical measures were not merely devised to enlighten its patients in religious belief. The fashioning of inmates into patients involved medicine in training a new experience of the self— in reinterpreting supernatural experience in "rational" terms—which paralleled and drew from the discourse and practices of the *Volksaufklärung* and the political agenda of the state.

The issue of religious belief at Eberbach was far from confined to the religious services and pastoral work carried out by its Protestant pastor and

Catholic priest. Religion was an immensely complex and ever-present set of daily practices and interactions between patient and staff, and religious instruction was inextricably bound up with medical treatment. It is almost always when pedagogical interventions were frustrated (which was often) that the staff recorded such matters, thus giving us access both to what precisely they were attempting to accomplish in the first place and how it was resisted by the patients.

The baker Mathias D. spent two stints in Eberbach. At least one of these admissions was caused by his conviction that several women in his community with "magical powers" used worms to "bewitch" him.[46] The medical log on him noted at one point that the patient "still believes in witches and ghosts."[47] The key word here is "still." Mathias D. and other such patients were routinely subject to "instruction" to rid them of superstition. The cooper and peasant Friedrich B., who believed himself and his cattle bewitched by the devil, provides a further example (out of many more that could be cited) of the pedagogical program of the asylum and the resistance it met with over and over again. The log noted: "Stupidity [*Dummheit*] and simple-mindedness [*Einfalt*] manifests itself [sic] in his conduct and speech, and allows him to persist in his assumed certainty in [the existence of] witchcraft."[48] When instruction and other "medical" measures refused to dissuade the tailor-journeyman Heinrich F. from his belief that he was possessed by an evil spirit, the asylum organized an (undescribed) "event" (*Veranstaltung*), bringing in the pastor for this purpose. It had, however, "not the slightest effect . . . he [Heinrich F.] indicated that he stands firmly by what he believes, and that one can do what one wants [to him] but it will never dissuade him from his thoughts".[49] (Two days earlier he had been put in the lockup room with the windows covered to block out all light, and doused with vinegar and water.)

Along with the eradication of pagan and magical beliefs, training in religious rationalism and tolerance involved rooting out religious "enthusiasm" and "fanaticism." These latter cases included pietist-influenced disciples as well as such Catholics as the schoolteacher Philipp O., who believed himself "called [by God] to return the Lutherans back to Catholicism and convert the Jews." "His hatred towards those of other confessions," it was noted, "was so strong that he would have liked to engage in bloody acts against them."[50] In 1843, when religious tensions were rapidly mounting, with the Bishop of Limburg moving the Church towards ultramontanism, the Catholic bookbinder and vintner Joseph H. was admitted to the asylum with the belief that he was an apostle called "to introduce a general reform of religious services" and "to destroy what to him appears not Catholic, for example, to cut out the word 'Duke' from a church prayer [book]."[51]

In an age before mass politics and mass media, the indoctrination of Christian morality and belief, however updated in its moderately enlightened form, remained an indispensable tool of political rulership. Despite its origins in the Enlightenment, rationalist religion in the new elementary schools, as adapted by bureaucratic states like Nassau, was never intended to stimulate free thought; rather, it was to provide a modern, rationalist set of values and attitudes to underpin economic productivity, social order, and political obedience. Basting complained about a rebellious and delinquent patient: "Religion is totally foreign to him; thus for him *nothing* is holy" (emphasis mine), echoing thus the conception of religious belief as a foundation of social order and obedience.[52] The use of religious indoctrination for purposes of power and rulership was self-consciously adapted to the medical setting of the asylum. As Lindpaintner explained it,

> Industrious religious exercises provide support for the [idea] of the domination of the invisible, awaken the sense for humility and obedience, and both, in this way, for the external law and the . . . humane will of [the patients'] superiors."[53]

Lindpaintner's was a rationalist God—universalistic, all-powerful, abstract, and benevolent. A direct parrallel was to be set up in the minds of patients between this divine authority and the "humane" secular authority of the asylum, with the patients learning the lesson of submission and obedience to the will of their keepers as they learned the lessons of religion. Such an approach pragmatically served the interests of both medicine and state. As all alienists agreed, the *sine qua non* of mental medicine was, after all, the physician's ability to wield absolute mental authority over the patient in order to win the latter back to rationality. At the same time, the related long-term issue of rehabilitation to the outside world was never far from mind. The inability of patients to grasp the equation of divine and secular (medical) power boded ill for their proper adjustment to life outside the asylum, as the following remark about the peasant/cooper Friedrich B. makes quite explicit:

> Demands to go home. Confused views about civil life, based on religious opinions he formed from reading the Bible. He believes he must fear God more than the world, and he considers it permitted to be in dereliction of secular authority.[54]

We have seen that the theoretical distinction between superstition and religious madness often blurred in practice. In the incarceration process, this could occur when the former was accompanied by behavior perceived as dangerous or disruptive. Within the asylum, the Eberbach sources make clear (as the contemporary literature does not) that issues of power, authority, and obedience were central to the daily practice of distinguishing the merely superstitious from the religiously mad. Unlike many medical officials, the asylum staff treated superstitious ideas as a sign of mental derangement. Yet the degree to which the asylum focused upon and made those ideas a cornerstone of treatment and medical evaluation—particularly in the matter of releases—differed radically among the patients. On the one hand, there were cases like the peasant Friedrich B., whose first admission was brought about from his belief that he and his cattle were possessed by the devil. The asylum noted that "he has no enlightened religious notions and is therefore in this respect not in clarity [*nicht im Klaren*]."[55] Yet, just three months later and mentally "unchanged," he was released as "cured." At the other extreme, there was Heinrich F., the tailor journeyman possessed by an evil spirit, who, with no other apparent signs of mental derangement, was forced to spend the rest of his life in the asylum.[56]

The decisive factor in such cases was the extent to which the patient displayed the proper behavior and attitudes for the outside world, and respect for authority was among the most important attitudes the asylum looked for in a recovering lunatic.[57] Friedrich B. had made substantial progress—in his interactions with his wife, whose visits with her husband were closely monitored, and in his relations with the asylum itself. Friedrich B.'s records noted that he was "significantly improved . . . more modest and content," and "thoroughly orderly and gives no occasion for complaint."[58] In stark contrast, the tailor journeyman Heinrich F. passionately resisted the authority of the asylum, refusing for thirty-five years to relent in his belief that he was possessed and that he had been unjustly incarcerated. He did learn to avoid punishment by outwardly conforming, but the asylum staff, to their great irritation, was never able to get to the inside of the man:

> The lunatic so far has been quiet and calm, works at what he is given, and seemed externally to comply with the regulations. But one perceived from his whole demeanour how powerful a deeply rooted, preconceived idea worked in his inner self . . . when he was asked about it by the directors of the asylum, he burst into angry, wild utterances related to his residence here and the way he is treated; was, however, highly uncommunicative about his secrets and truths [his belief in spirit possession], as he calls them.[59]

The interests of the state in consolidating its power through legislating against religious intolerance and superstition paralleled and complemented the professional interests of mental medicine in wresting the sick and needy away from their attraction to quacks and religious healers, and in curing illness. The influences between the two—medicine and asylum, on the one hand, and the state, on the other—were reciprocal and mutually reinforcing. The asylum did not simply reflect and carry out in the medical sphere state policy; the medical theories of religious madness and the existence of the asylum in turn worked their influence on governmental actions and attitudes. In at least one case, the asylum itself took direct action in initiating police measures against missionary preachers and other "unauthorized healing prophets." As Lindpaintner explained, such action was necessary to combat the pathologies of mind "spread" by pietist reading material and *"Tollkräute."*[60] The case in question was that of

Margarette K., the wife of an innkeeper and brewer in the town of Caub, whose "religious insanity" and "demonomania," the commitment report opined, was caused by her contact with the Moravian Brethren.[61] Like the medical official who authored the commitment report, Lindpaintner understood the devastating affects of such "theological quacks" who prey on the ignorant and vulnerable with their mystical tracts, and he took it upon himself to investigate and cut off the means of contact between her and the religious sect. For this purpose Lindpaintner questioned the husband carefully on how his wife had gotten hold of Moravian Brethren tracts, and on the name and whereabouts of the missionary who distributed them. He then sent this information off to the Nassau government. For his own part, the husband promised, on his wife's release, not to allow "the guy from Neuwied [the missionary] to slip her spiritual books [ever again]." "I'll grab him and give him over to the authorities."[62]

Reshaping the Self

If the medical treatment of religious madness complemented and supported broader state policy toward the social problem of superstition and religious enthusiasm, that problem itself took on new meaning specific to the institutional context of the asylum and the broader context of the professionalization of psychiatry. At the most basic level, alienists and physicians were faced with the daunting problem of how to successfully treat patients who not only resisted the advice and authority of the asylum, but whose very form of thinking was at odds with the very philosophy of the asylum—those people who understood their problems in religious and supernatural terms. These patients fiercely resisted the asylum or were incapable of even seeing themselves as ill. Incarcerated for "frenzy," the aforementioned tailor Martin M. stood frightened, as if in a daze, crossing himself and begging for "mercy."[63] Punishment and painful treatment measures did not rid the religiously mad Johann S. of belief in his own divinity; those measures were simply assimilated into his fantasies, such that he now felt that he "suffers for God's honor and for the salvation of humanity, the pain from the tartar emetic applications conforming [*erfüllend*] to his calling as martyr."[64] The bewitched Friedrich B. "longs to go home and does not grasp what he is here for."[65] The possessed Heinrich F. wrote desperate pleas for an official hearing to examine his case, while for thirty-five years refusing to relinquish his beliefs.[66]

Christianity itself formed a barrier to treatment, as the asylum confronted in the religious politics of institutional life the age-old problem of governments: Christian belief could provide subjects with an empowering set of tools to resist worldly authority. The peasant Maria H. fiercely resisted the asylum and its claims that she was mentally ill; at the same time, she asserted that she was "under spiritual [as opposed to secular-medical] rule" and "must marry the Pope."[67] Peter M. was "industrious and rational. Only the Bible confuses his head and [he is] therefore . . . still considered dangerous." That sense of danger on the part of the asylum surely had to do with the fact that Peter had killed his younger brother. But perceptions of his "confusion" were certainly related to Peter's demands for his release and for a "fixed punishment for his crime."[68] The one true rebel in the asylum was a Catholic priest, who tried to organize an uprising of the patients.[69] Other patients took less confrontational paths, trying with varying degrees of success to hide their beliefs from the asylum. The asylum only observed the "bigotry" (*Frommelei*) of a "religious visionary" knife-grinder "when [he] was alone and believed that he was not observed."[70]

This religious thinking of the asylum's patients was not wholly unproductive; it could be manipulated and harnessed to treatment, as when, for example, the asylum staged a quasi-exorcism for a female patient who believed she was possessed by the devil (in her abdomen).[71] Yet, on the whole, the superstitions of patients posed serious obstacles to mental medicine, for the asylum was here faced not simply with the task of treating and "curing" such people, but with the cultural and social problem of transforming beliefs to the extent that these people could be made receptive to and understand the terms of patienthood and illness itself. Indeed, the two tasks—medical and cultural—were inextricably linked. As such, the process of transforming such people into patients—of substituting the language of the medico-psychological for that of the divine—required a fundamental reshaping of the experience of selfhood and subjectivity.

The patient experience of the self that comes through in these cases is one of nonboundedness and penetrability between the internal and the external world, between the body and the divine. The feelings and events of the most intimate aspects of the self—in mind and body—could be influenced by and interact with such external forces as God, the Devil, demons, and ghosts. Madness and personal trauma could thus be experienced as an invasion of the self by outside powers, as opposed to a condition emanating from a bounded, internalized self. The lack of fixed boundaries between self and world was in part rooted in conceptions of the supernatural world and its relationship to human life. Unlike the distant, omnipotent, and benevolent God of rationalist theology, God to these people was a very intimate presence, constantly intervening in life to punish sinners and reward the faithful and good. God was also not an abstract principle: He possessed human traits, which, as Heinz-Dieter Kittsteiner has shown for eighteenth-century Prussian peasants, drew from the social world of lord-peasant domination. Possessing both human "strengths and weaknesses," God was at once an angry, punishing "despot"—capable of revenging Himself with illness, droughts, storms—and on the other hand, inexplicably, "boundlessly benevolent" and merciful when He so chose. Finally, God was not omnipotent in a cosmos populated by spirits, the devil, and witches, who, like God, could be manipulated and "bought off" by various magical and ritual practices.[72]

This nonbounded self was also the product of a still predominately preindustrial society in which dependency on and obligations to family and community norms formed the basic fabric of social existence and physical survival. Notions of freedom—freedom of action and of the mind—and of morality could not be separated from the constraints and embeddedness of this self in a social world of duty and obligation. Lucia T., the peasant woman who murdered her child, made very clear that her "crime" was not simply the act of killing, but the social act of bringing "disorder" and "misfortune" to her "household," both before and after the infanticide.[73] The examining doctors shared with Lucia the belief that she was not "free" in her actions and person, but their notion of freedom rested on a wholly different idea of the self. The physicians replaced the unfreedom of the supernatural (devil possession) and the social (the duties to household) with a conception of the individual as an abstract principle, composed of "drives" (for self-possession, sex, property, honor, power, etc.), who was free only when able to balance and control those drives.

The subject of popular culture contrasted radically with the individualized self that physicians experienced and expected as a sign of health: unitary, autonomous, responsible, and cut off from direct divine intervention in a cosmos ruled indirectly by God through the laws of nature. This was the rational and virtuous "man" of liberal thought, internally guided by reason, able to control passions, and hence "free." The construction of such a subject was both a prerequisite of the work of mental medicine and one of its goals, as the asylum reached beyond external behavior into the recesses of the psyche to reconstitute its internal processes.

On a fundamental level, the person at the mercy of supernatural forces was someone who lacked personal responsibility, since behavior and thoughts did not necessarily emanate from a bounded self, but in connection with an external and uncontrollable world. Responsible citizens required, in turn, not only a new understanding of the divine, but a degree of self-reflection and awareness that would enable the individual to monitor and master the irrational inside the self. Yet precisely some of the most superstitious patients lacked this capacity, a deficit that was not simply personal (related to mental trauma and confusion), but also cultural. The peasant Maria H. was perfectly capable of conversing "rationally" on topics of "everyday life," so noted her commitment report. But when asked to engage in "[self]-reflection," she manifested "almost true craziness": there was a significant "lack of logical thought" and inability to "pursue [logically] an idea," as she would abruptly shift the conversation to all manner of "heterogeneous topics."[74] The maidservant Maria L. also displayed the paradoxical combination of simultaneous rationality and utter mental confusion about her own person.

Duchy of Nassau, 1816. Designed by Jackie Beukelaer

Eberbach Asylum. A nineteenth-century view of the asylum, correctional house, and chapel at Eberbach. By permission of Hessisches Hauptstaatsarchiv, Wiesbaden.

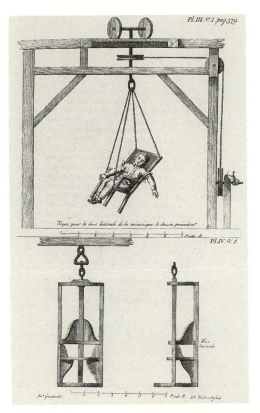

Rotary Chair. One of the "therapeutic" contraptions used at Eberbach and other contemporary asylums. Such machines assumed a close interconnection between the mind and body. Rotating at very high velocities, the chair's curative affects supposedly came from the shock to the nervous system induced by severe physical discomfort and fear. Courtesy of the Wellcome Institute Library, London.

Restraint instruments used in nineteenth-century psychiatry to restrain, punish, and calm violent and recalcitrant patients. By permission of the American Psychiatric Association.

Drawing by the patient Maria G., a servant from Rheingau, who was incarcerated at Eberbach in 1830 and later transferred to Eichberg. Translated, the words read, "Eichberg, October 4, 1858. Third evening after mealtime, until 8:45. Song: Great honor to God in his loftiness. A safe stronghold is our God, a trusty shield and weapon. Solemn moments of examination. Man shall examine himself and thus partake of this bread and drink from this goblet" (derives from a hymn by Luther). Juxtaposed, image and words depict the amibiguity of of asylum authority and the conflation in this patient's mind of church and asylum (see Chapter 3). The image shows a pipe-smoking man—presumably the asylum's director—who is both armored (sporting a medal instead of a heart) and all too human (the leaf-veins and sad or frightened eyes). He is at once scientist-observer, military man, and spiritual protector. By permission of Hessisches Hauptstaatsarchiv, Wiesbaden.

When questioned, she "answered well, yet she has no insight into herself."[75] The problem was not lack of rational thought; it was her lack of "clarity with herself"[76]—namely, the incapacity for the kind of self-reflection that would enable her to curb the sexual passions and irrational thoughts that had caused her incarceration as a nymphomaniac and religious lunatic.[77]

The asylum was able to command a degree of order and obedience from Maria, but her external conformity fell considerably short of the change it sought to effect. "She does what she is ordered to do, but when left to herself she indulges in indolence." The rules and laws of authority, as long as they required external enforcement and hence constant surveillance, could always be broken. The solution to both the impracticability of external surveillance and the social dependency it engendered was, as Foucault argued, a reformulation of the methods of discipline such that external law was internalized within the self. As the asylum put it in this case, she needed to "act[ ] from within herself. . . ."[78] Another term for this self-disciplining was *Selbstbeherrschung* (self-mastery). As the alienist M. Jacobi explained, self-awareness and Selbstbeherrschung—key liberal concepts—could be fostered by "exercising and strengthening the memory, attention, [and] the faculty of judgment. . . ."[79] These were far from abstract principles in the asylum; they were concretized in "microtechnologies" of power that pervaded the minutiae of daily activities, including the most mundane bodily movements. The asylum noted that Maria L. "constantly looks around her, but can not state why, although her thinking is not confused. . . ."[80] Even the tiny movements of her head and eyes were subject to questioning, an interrogation that problematicized the (probably nonplussed) response of blankness from the woman, and whose very question aimed at a level of self-consciousness hitherto uncultivated and presumably unknown in this maidservant.

Instilling Conscience

The self-awareness and self-mastery demanded of Maria L. and other patients had certain repressive functions insofar as they were qualities of mind aimed at self-censorship, control, and conformity to and within the authoritarian structures of asylum and society at large. Yet, as Foucault rightly points out, the power wielded by the asylum was not merely repressive, but productive, producing a new type of subject, one who learned to internalize within the self the external laws and rules of the institution. Foucault was describing the formation of a specific sort of conscience, which Freud named the "super-ego": the splitting off of one part of the self (ego) to monitor and control the other parts of the self. As Freud put it:

one part of the ego sets itself over against the other, judges it critically, and as it were, takes it as its object. . . . What we are here becoming acquainted with is the agency commonly called 'conscience.'[81]

The Freudian conscience posits an innate and universal structure of the mind, the product of the psychic development of early childhood. Foucault provides a radically different view of conscience and the self: the modern subject-patient on which Freud based his theories is not given by inherent structures of the mind, but is the historical product of a lengthy development by which new conceptions of the self are formed through novel "technologies" of power that, within a wide range of institutions (family, school, prison, asylum), replace such purely externalist approaches as corporal punishment for acts aimed at the mind.[82] But it is Heinz-Dieter Kittsteiner who has set out specifically to challenge the universalistic Freudian super-ego in a fascinating work that fully historicizes conscience and thereby one of the essential components of selfhood and subjectiviy. The "antecedent conscience" (the equivalent of the super-ego) of the experience of guilt and internalized law that directs action, preventing beforehand proscribed acts, is, according to Kittsteiner, a very late development in the history of self, a formulation of liberal and enlightened thinkers of the seventeenth and eighteenth centuries. The Lutheran and pietist-influenced pastoral had long been directed at the formation of an internalized conscience, but it conceptualized this conscience as a subsequent experience: after committing the sin, the guilt-ridden sinner atoned for his or her sins in the attainment of grace. With its new goal of creating the free and moral citizen of civil society, the Enlightenment replaced the subsequent conscience of grace with the antecedent conscience of virtue—an internalized, normative structure whose constant self-surveillance would provide the basis of a life of virtue, responsibility, and hence intellectual and civic freedom.[83]

On the basis of eighteenth-century court protocols and church reports on the conversion experiences of criminals, Kittsteiner found in stark contrast a psychic structure in peasants that failed not only to conform to the new Enlightenment conscience of virtue, but even to that earlier antecedent conscience of the church. In its attempts to inculcate morality and virtue in peasants, Enlightenment reformers, as their clergymen predecessors, were confronted with people who lacked the "bipolar internal control mechanisms" that would allow for an internalized moral sense.[84] Sin and immorality were not experienced as internal events, generating feelings of guilt and remorse (to the frustration of the church and enlightened reformers); they were external acts equated with punishable and dishonoring offenses for which one could always atone and receive mercy after the fact by an eminently bribable God (one paid services to Him in church rituals, just as one performed services to one's lord). Given the qualities of God and the larger supernatural world (as outlined above), the soul was not an internalized site of conscience, but "merely the point of intersection of [the] battle" between the forces of good and evil.[85] Against this psychic structure, the Enlightenment sought to construct in peasants the internalization and "integration of evil into the self"—to create that bipolar structure of mind that would provide the basis of "the life-long exercise of virtue."[86] This was the pedagogical principle underlying the new disciplining practices in areas ranging from child-rearing, education, criminal justice, to the pastoral work of the (enlightened) clergy.

Kittsteiner's model of peasant conscience (or lack thereof) is not entirely borne out in the Eberbach cases, but his historicization of conscience provides a very interesting and useful framework for thinking about the restructuring of subjectivity that took place in the early nineteenth-century asylum. In large part, the asylum can be seen as an institution that incorporated into medical practice the pedagogical principles and aims of the Enlightenment, just as it medicalized and implemented the theology of rationalism of both state and churches. Many of Eberbach's patients did indeed manifest a kind of pre-Enlightenment psychic structure and subsequent conscience very similiar to the eighteenth-century peasants Kittsteiner analyzed. Examples Kittsteiner provides of this mentality, such as the woman who blamed Satan for her own murder of her child, or the woman turned prostitute who claimed that the devil seduced her,[87] could just as easily have been taken from the Eberbach sources.[88]

Eberbach's medical records made explicit mention of issues directly related to conscience, and in some cases, to the illnesses and mental deficiencies associated with the lack of (an antecedent) conscience. About a seventeen-year-old boy (Peter L.), whose out-of-control behavior included physical assaults ("mistreatment") on his mother and siblings, the commitment report complained of the boy's insufficient understanding of morality, on the basis of which he was to be considered suffering from "idiocy":

> Although he knows why he is blamed and that his behavior must be punished, yet, he knows only the *externals* [*das Aüßern*] of punishable words and acts, but (sic) he has no clear consciousness of the magnitude [*die Größe*] of his moral offenses against his mother . . . for he admits all of his acts with the greatest naïveté and the greatest indifference . . . without denying or [trying to] cover up his behavior.[89] [emphasis in the original]

That this boy's ingenuousnous and honesty (not just his lack of emotion) should be considered a sign of mental deficiency and faulty conscience provides an ironic twist to the moralistic pedagogy underpinning the rehabilitation of the delinquent patient. The contradictory intellectual stance of making dishonesty a measurement of moral depth and progress appears to have proceeded from the institutional context in which the assessing of conscience in delinquents like Peter L. took place. This occurred in situations of punishment, where an authority figure confronted the delinquent with the threat of a punishment which, it was presumed, the latter would seek to avoid with denials and lies. As such, it shouuld be noted that this physician's notion of conscience implicitly derived as much from the normative behavior of prisoners and delinquents in the everyday and expected resistance of power, as from the normative principles of psychology.

Neither asylum measures vis-à-vis conscience nor the patients' own thinking on this matter, however, neatly conform to Kittsteiner's (and, in another version, Foucault's) paradigmatic shift from the Christian pastoral of grace to the enlightened inculcation of virtue. For one, the measures directed at the problem of conscience displayed that characteristic manifested across the board in Eberbach and the Nassau medical system: the intermingling of models of action taken at once from the authoritarian state, on the one hand, and from liberal thought, on the other.

For more than two decades, the petty "thief" Johann K. taxed the nerves and expertise of Nassau's penal system (during which time he was transferred in and out of prison, the correctional house, and the asylum), as a man with extremely strong passions and a very low tolerance for the everyday slights, abuses, and punishments that were the lot of someone of his lowly and criminal status. The asylum described him as a "crude, immoral, depraved person," with "unbridled drives" and "wild passions," for whom "every form of constraint is intolerable."[90] The greatest of his "wild passions" appears to have been tobacco and respect, the deprivation of either of which could rouse him to fury. But the deeper problem with the man, from a psychological and moral perspective, as the prison doctor Kleinschmidt explained, was his lack of an internalized conscience:

> Reason [*Vernunft*], the moral principle of humans which is manifested most distinctly by conscience, became [in him] ever more [*noch und noch*] subordinated to the will and dominated by his . . . lower feelings. He knows that stealing is forbidden, his reason, his moral feeling, is however too subordinated to his faculty of desire . . . and thus he is not able to state the reasons why stealing is morally bad, unjust. Therefore *he does not refrain from stealing because he sees it as a morally bad act, but only because he knows he will be punished* (emphasis mine).[91]

And to dispel any doubts that the man's thievery came not from real need, but from a faulty psychic structure, the doctor added for good measure that "he commits theft not to secure his existence, but in order to satisfy his carnal appetites [*niedere Begierde*]." In fact, as Dirk Blasius has shown, petty forest theft (poaching and illegally cutting down trees), for which Johann K. had been convicted, was widespread and on the increase in the hunger years of the 1840s among the very poorest rural groups, caused by poverty, the loss of customary rights to the commons, and the tightening of state forestry laws and enforce-ment.[92] Within the "moral economy" of the rural poor, forest theft was per-fectly justifiable; what was immoral was the lack of economic protections and the loss of common lands.

Dr. Kleinschmidt's report, in emphasizing the psychological issue of external obedience versus internalized conscience, stands in stark contrast to the purely externalist and coercive approach articulated in an asylum report on Johann K. two years later. Windt, its author, explained how a combination of work, "strict treatment," and punishment (the asylum did not shrink from using in this case its full arsenal of coercive and pain-inducing measures, including forced stand-ing and cold douches on the head) had achieved a degree of success: "A regu-lated and active manner of life and fear of punishment gradually awakened in the lunatic the sense for obedience, docility, and industriousness."[93] Dr. Klein-schmidt had made Johann's fear of punishment (as opposed to internalized moral sense) a symptom of mental deficiency; the asylum, to the contrary, in-tentionally sought to cultivate this very quality—fear—in its patient as the goal of treatment. The asylum staff felt content when the patient learned to obey out of fear, whereas Dr. Kleinschmidt felt this was precisely the point at which treatment should begin and against which it should be directed.

It is not that the asylum was more authoritarian and traditionalist in its thinking; numerous cases (some discussed above) demonstrate the concern of its staff with the internalization of conscience and the reshaping of psychic structures, not merely external obedience and conformity. These sources demonstrate the (co)existence of both absolutist and liberal models of discipline and conscience. The logical question following upon this observation, then is: what determined the differential use of the two models of practice in the asy-lum? This is a complex question. The case of Johann K. suggests at least one de-termining factor: the pragmatic choices made in the dynamics of institutional life itself. At his first admission twelve years earlier, the asylum had in fact pro-ceeded with the very same psychological premises and goals expressed by Dr. Kleinschmidt. The log on Johann K. noted, for example: "This week, [he] was calm and behaved industriously and rationally. But he lives in fear and [only] this holds him in check. He is indescribably crude and conscienceless. . . ."[94] The later shift towards an approach of purely external coercion and intimida-tion developed over time as the asylum (and other institutions) came up against the recalcitrance of a patient who was mentally inaccesible to more subtle psy-chological techniques.

A fascinating (and tragic) thing occurred when nineteenth-century discipli-nary institutions adopted and applied the new psychological principles of en-lightened pedagogy to influence the internal state of its lower-class inmates: in producing the desirable "guilt" and "remorse" over past crimes, they also pro-duced madness—often religious madness. The best example of this is the story of Johann M., the son of a well-off peasant family, who landed in prison in 1840 on suspicion of murder by arsenic poisoning of his lover's baby and the later attempted murder (by the same means) of the woman herself, who had since become his wife. It all started when, in 1837, his lover Maria F. got pregnant and successfully sued him for child support when he sought to avoid responsibility by denying his parentage of the child. Several months later, the baby mysteriously died immediately after a visit by Johann M. and his friend (later known as his accomplice). At the time, it was believed the baby had died from an apoplectic fit, and there things would have remained if Johann M. had not once again gotten Maria F. pregnant. Presumably seeking to avoid a lengthy and hopeless court battle, he finally married her. But this was only a stopgap measure; Johann M. had other, more sinister plans for his wife. He once again seduced his friend into a murder plot (this time against the wife). This time, their plan backfired: the attempted poisoning of the wife left only a pig and a cat dead, and the two suspects were sent off to prison while a criminal investigation got under way.

Not bright enough to lie convincingly, the friend was forced to confess almost immediately. Johann M., on the other hand, held out for a year under intense pressure, as he was absolutely convinced that he could not be convicted without a confession; indeed, he was so convinced of his ultimate victory over the criminal justice system that he even refused a defense lawyer. When, as a result, the court assigned him a court-appointed *Official-Defensor,* the seriousness of his predicament began to sink in: the trial was going forward and he faced conviction and punishment. It was at this point that Johann M. began to break down. He began to believe that his soup was poisoned. The prison doctor found this to be of "great psychological interest," since its mimicking of the original crime bespoke "a bad conscience."[95] That night, as Johann explained the next morning to the prison doctor, "the devil was on him," causing him such torment and terror that he said he would hang himself before he went through another such night. He needed to confess to the *Herrn immediately,* or "he [would] die in the night." After his three-hour confession, Johann appeared "calmer and freer," but the relief lasted but a few hours. That night his agitation reappeared, and he began also to speak incoherently and act crazy, at times withdrawing under his covers, at other times raving. He was finally to be transferred to the asylum.

Johann M. began the lengthy, intentionally psychologically grueling period of investigation in the prison as a mentally "healthy," if criminally suspect inmate; he left a tormented man living a nightmare of devil persecution and imagined impending death, which in turn was interpreted by the physician as the very essence of "mental alienation." Here we have a perfect illustration of the literal institutional "production" of mental illness. Yet no understanding of how and why this process worked is complete without the inclusion of the patients. It was the peculiar structure of Johann M's "conscience" and morality in interaction with the structures of authority in prison, which, as a result, produced the madness symptoms that landed him in the asylum. Johann M's conscience functioned remarkably like the subsequent conscience of Kittsteiner's peasants. His conscience was not guided by an internalized norm; but was one in which immorality and sin were equated with criminally punishable acts and revenged by a punitive, wrathful God. Hence Johann M.'s conscience was triggered precisely at the point where he was to face punishment, as the punitive secular criminal justice system merged in his mind with the punitive supernatural forces come to avenge his sins.

A very interesting piece of evidence corroborating this interpretation is Johann's state of mind after his transfer from prison to the insane asylum: when the threat of punishment was removed, the symptoms of both madness and a "bad conscience" seemed to instantly disappear. The asylum found him suddenly free of both insanity and his earlier conscience. Asked how he was doing, Johann responded happily "I don't notice anything [of the former symptoms] any more and am glad that the things are gone."[96] Several days later when "reproached for his crime," he blithely responded: "I can't do anything about it when someone else is bad." He denied the crime and, to the disgust of the asylum, "showed not the least [sign of] regret or feeling."[97]

Johann M.'s case was only one among many where madness, in the form of a tormented conscience and religious melancholy, surfaced precisely at the point when the accused was undergoing a psychologically grueling criminal investigation or after conviction—in other words, when the person was faced with the threat of discovery and punishment.[98] In this way, a kind of feedback system was set up, where the more strictly punitive institutions of prison and correctional house produced the symptoms of madness, which the asylum then set about curing. The asylum, thus, was brought heavily into the business of not only inculcating conscience, but of curing its pathologies—the pathologies of peasants caught up in an unforgiving punitive system that, unlike that of God and lord, could neither be bribed nor evaded. The extravagant displays of bad conscience in these instances—the perpetual praying, singing, citing of Scripture, and begging for mercy—were coded as "illness symptoms"[99] by the very same prison officials, physicians, and asylum staff charged with instilling morality and conscience in the delinquent, criminal, and mentally troubled. In this way, the new disciplinary system paradoxically reenacted and superimposed itself on the old rituals of confessor-sinner, both, as we have seen in the asylum, encouraging and using those relations for its own secular purposes (pedagogical and medical) and, at other times, proscribing them through their medicalization (in the transfer of prisoners to the asylum as religious lunatics).

Together with the secularization and (ideally) internalization of conscience and morality, the application of medical models worked to individualize this area of experience, thereby redefining matters of social duty and norms as ones of personal responsibility. This emerges most clearly in a closer examination of the circumstances triggering conscience and the understanding of conscience by the patients and their communities. Contrary to the single model of conscience of peasant society that Kittsteiner found—subsequent, externalized, and rooted, above all, in conceptions of the divine—the Eberbach sources reveal substantial variations among the patients. If Johann M., the callow arsenic poisoner, whose "conscience" was activated only when faced with punishment, represents one extreme in a spectrum of experience, the other extreme might best be represented by Jacob W., a single, twenty-four-year-old journeyman from a poor, Catholic family of the village of Ransbach. By his own and his family's account, Jacob's mental troubles were closely linked to the issue of conscience, but the conscience that emerges from their account, paraphrased by a medical offical, operated quite differently from that of Johann M. Jacob W. was thrown into terror and a "struggle with his conscience" by the mere thought of a possible transgression, and that transgression was, on the surface, incomparably minor compared to the act of murder. A "blooming woman," whom Jacob saw daily at work, made "illicit propositions [to him] for love and sexual satisfaction." His "conscience offended," Jacob's urge was to flee—to give up his position—but he was prevented from doing so by his parents. Now, forced to remain in daily contact with the woman, Jacob "struggle[d] with his conscience" in an unsuccessful attempt to repress the "sensuality and passion" that the woman had ignited in him. At this point, the woman (and, perhaps others) began to make fun of him, even accusing him of having propositioned her. Fired from his job as a result, socially disgraced, his mental condition deteriorated from there.[100] By his admission to the asylum, he was hearing voices that put him into "supernatural connection with the Catholic church," which he believed had "taken his honor due to his melancholy condition."[101]

In sharp contrast to Johann M., Jacob W.'s conscience was a severe, self-censoring mechanism, an internalized norm with great preventive power, for the very thought of its contravention threw him into severe crisis. As such Jacob W.'s conscience appears very much like a modern super-ego, conforming to the model of the antecedent, internalized conscience of virtue. Indeed, this was precisely how the physicians involved interpreted his internal struggle. To the medical officer writing the commitment report, it was clear that Jacob's trouble lay in the sexual stimulation of contact with the woman, which, far from being satisfied, became the source of taunts and disgrace (*Schande*). Basting's view took the sexual interpretation even further, placing Jacob's sexual fantasies about the woman within a broader personal history of masturbation and unsatisfied sexual drive. The themes of shame and "dishonor" were thus cast as purely sexual matters, a psychological struggle between desire and morality, generating guilt when the latter was not able to hold out against the former.

Jacob W., the village journeyman, thus appeared in the medical narrative to suffer the sexual torments and scruples of a bourgeois obsessed with the dangers and immorality of sexuality. As such, the medical interpretations tell us much about the psychology and morality of the physicians, but very little about their patient. If Jacob was troubled, it was not, from what is known of peasant sexuality in the historical record and from the facts of this case, the sexual urge itself that disturbed him, but the object of sexual desire, namely, a woman whose social status made any sexual contact between himself and her "illicit" and forbidden. The real danger for Jacob in desiring a woman of higher status in the village hierarchy was borne out in the loss of his job and the dishonor, shame, and contempt heaped on him when his "conscience" failed to prevent the socially forbidden feelings.

If the consciences of Jacob W. and Johann M. radically differed, the difference seems closely related to their respective social identities within village life. Jacob W.'s poverty, low status, and economic and social dependency within village life as a journeyman artisan appear to have required a more powerful and internalized conscience than that of the well-off peasant Johann M. Indeed, the conscience of this lowly and poor journeyman held striking similarities to that of women, for whom social honor and sexuality were deeply interwoven and for whom thus the need to guard one's reputation was closely connected with adherence to village sexual codes. The Eberbach cases are strewn with examples of the high social costs to women of a damaged sexual reputation. They included women like Katharina S., a widow whose mental equilibrium was shattered when a jealous wife found her husband visiting Katharina's home and caused a "public scandal." Katharina, with her "lost honor," was so "ashamed before all people [that she] no longer [wanted] to go out." The woman's internal struggle as described by the asylum—a struggle between "moral feeling, honor, and sensual desire" in a "guilt-ridden conscience"—matched precisely that of Jacob W.[102]

What Jacob W. shared in common with Katharina S. and other women was his subordinate and dependent social position in the village hierarchy. The degree (and, perhaps, kind) of conscience in villagers appears in these cases to have been in inverse proportion to the degree of power held by the person, and as such structured by both gender and class position. David Sabean found something similiar in his analysis of a murder case in eighteenth-century Württemberg. Conscience, as he phrased it, was embedded in "the everyday practice of power." "The operative word in the structure of domination between the propertied peasants and the marginal landholders, artisans, and day laborers was 'fear,'" and it was this "economy of fear" that necessitated, on the one hand, a more "active" conscience in the dominated, and, on the other hand, the "conscienceless" brutality, violence, and intimidation of several members of the village elite in Sabean's case study.[103]

If conscience was structured by relations of domination, it was also inseparable from the notions of duty and obligation that composed the web of social and familial relations of village life. In attempting to restructure along secular and individualistic lines the subjectivity of its patients, medicine attacked ignorance and "superstition" in the lower classes, in particular their nonenlightened conceptions of the divine. Yet the barrier against a modern experience of subjectivity raised by village culture extended beyond the problem of "superstition" to the fact of its social embeddedness in the familial and social duties and norms of village life, a self that contrasted radically with the autonomous, rational individual posited by liberal thought.[104]

No case better illustrates this self and its contrast with the liberal model of medicine than that of Johann W., a thirty-three-year-old laborer from Idstein.[105] Partial access to Johann's notion of conscience comes from a lengthy confession of murder he gave to the asylum. One night in 1824, in Eberbach's convalescence hall, Johann blurted out to the guard: "I don't belong in the madhouse, but in prison . . . With two [others] still living in Idstein, I killed Frenchmen and a woman in 1813 and my conscience allows me no peace [of mind] . . ."[106] With this statement and an ensuing six-hour confession taken by Lindpaintner, the burden of guilt Johann had lived and struggled with for eleven years was, as he had hoped, "lifted from my heart."[107]

The Napoleonic retreat of 1813 had offered an irresistable opportunity for a bit of easy plunder, as not only French soldiers, but officers and their servants bearing finery and gold, made their way home through the forested area surrounding Idstein. Thus it was that one morning, after a schnapps at the local tavern, Johann W., together with his brother-in-law and a friend, met two French officers and a "beautiful young woman . . . [in] elegant clothing" on the same forest path where minutes before the former had already relieved some other French soldiers of their belongings. In the ensuing robbery the officers were beaten to death. There remained the woman, sobbing and pleading for her life. As Johann, feeling pity for the woman, attempted to save her, his friend, the leader of the group, jumped the woman and slit her throat.

Despite community suspicion and two official interrogations, the truth of that day could never be proven and the three accomplices thus escaped criminal punishment. Yet Johann's life would never be the same, as the weight of a terrible guilt bore down incessantly on him:

> Since this act I did not know how to find peace again; that same entire winter I drank dreadfully. As long as I was drunk, the melancholy thoughts were gone. But when I again became sober the sorrow returned. I often went to the place where the murder was carried out; I called to our *Herr* God and prayed that he would forgive me the sin. I was not like other people anymore; I could no longer enjoy anything. When listening to music, I felt well as long as the whirling [*Taumel*] lasted. But *it was all only external.* At night the murder appeared in my dreams. I was always afraid. Mornings and evenings especially, I was drawn to the murder spot. I felt relieved when I was there. (emphasis mine)[108]

Memory—the repetitive replaying in the mind of the crime that included repeated visits to the murder site—was at the heart of the suffering Johann experienced in his guilty conscience. He spoke of that memory and its pain as an enslavement: of a burdening of the "heart," in which, as he told Lindpaintner, "I [am] not completely free . . ." Only confession, Johann felt, could free him from both memory and guilt, to, as he put it, "relieve" his "heart" *internally* in contrast to the merely "external" relief of music and other palliatives. In so many words, Johann explained that he had, however, forced himself over eleven agonizing years to block his "internal" need to speak the truth in confession in the face of a powerful external constraint: the bonds of familial loyalty and an obligation to protect his complicit brother-in-law. To the earlier interrogations of the *Kirchenrath*, who had "appealed to [his] conscience," Johann now, in his asylum confession, explained why he had remained silent earlier: "So I may halfway have given [the *Kirchenrath*] to understand that I knew myself to be not entirely free, but I confessed nothing, due to my brother-in-law, who has a lot of children." In other words, the exposure and subsequent imprisonment of the brother-in-law, who already "since this murder business suffered from epilepsy," would have brought financial ruin to Johann's sister and her children.

Neither the operations of memory and conscience nor Johann's suffering from a guilty conscience can be understood outside of this fundamental struggle that the murder triggered, which pitted against each other the demands of two conflicting moralities: between, on the one hand, the religious and psychological experience of guilt with its demands to save the soul and relieve the conscience and, on the other, a morality of social and familial obligation, with its demands of loyalty and duty to save and protect the family. A sense of the intensity and desperation of this inner struggle comes through in the words Johann used to describe the problem of confession: the need to confess, as he told Lindpaintner, had become an "urge" that had to be constantly "beat[en] back," but had "become stronger and stronger so that I could no longer hold out." For "it must be lifted [*weg*] from my heart and then I'll be in my right mind again [*wieder geschied*]. The others may now also suffer! It can then go as God pleases."

Johann's "internalized" conscience was embedded in a decidedly nonliberal experience of the self, a self in which issues of freedom and guilt were defined through and inseparable from the social bonds and norms of village life. Such a self stood in stark contrast to the ideal person on which both state and medical practice were constructed at this time: the autonomous, self-determining individual for whom freedom is, on the one hand, a legal and juridical category linking the individual citizen (*Staatsbürger*) directly to the state, and, on the other hand, a psychological category—a state in which reason prevails over the lower functions of passion, imagination, and will. This case also highlights the ultimate limitations and problems of carrying over into historical analysis the dichotomous categories of internal vs. external conscience and self (Kittsteiner) that were historical products of contemporary political, pedagogical, and medical agendas. If there was such a thing as a "peasant" conscience or experience of the self, it is not best understood within the terms set up by the very authorities (church, state, medicine, school) seeking to reshape that self, but rather as it was mediated by and expressed through the relations of class, gender, and familial positions within village society.

Religious rationalism was critical to the consolidation of the state and the political integration of its citizenry in the formation of rational and moral *Staatsbürger*. It is probably fair to say that religious rationalism left no person's life untouched: its institutionalization in church, education, and, as we have seen, in such disciplinary institutions as the asylum, meant that even the poorest and most mariginal peasant had at some point heard it preached from the pulpit, sang its hymns, or found his or her favorite religious procession now banned.[109] The process of substituting a rationalist view of life for old superstitions required a profound shift in the mentalities of ordinary people and an attack on firmly held beliefs. Yet the ordinary person in Nassau seemed to quietly and passively accept all of this. Alfred Adam thus concluded that Nassauer agreed with the changes.[110] One implicitly gets the same impression from Wolfgang Jäger's structural approach (modernization theory) to the issue.[111] The local view from "below" in the Eberbach sources paints a very different picture—of a population steeped in a religious worldview far from the ideals of policy makers and educated bourgeois; of deep, but prepolitical resistance to those ideals; of wrenching struggles, not passive acceptance, surrounding the redefinitions of self, God, truth, and the supernatural that accompanied the formation of the *Staatsbürger* and the modern mental patient.[112]

II

*Sexuality
and Gender*

4

Medical Representations
of Sexual Madness

Nymphomania and Masturbatory Insanity

Nineteenth-century science played a critical role in the formulation and legitimation of modern gender norms and the subordination of women through naturalizing gender difference—representing as "scientific" and universal in the supposedly biological makeup of the sexes what were in fact social and prescriptive beliefs.[1] Feminist studies in the history of psychiatry and on the hysteria diagnosis in particular have been groundbreaking in opening up this line of analysis.[2] In stark contrast to the topic of hysteria, nymphomania has received almost no attention in the historiography.[3] It played no role in the creation of famous psychiatric careers, as did hysteria in the work of Jean-Martin Charcot and Sigmund Freud.[4] Rather, nymphomania was one of those vague, all-encompassing, but all the more ubiquitous, terms for female sexual deviancy that floated in both medical and popular culture.[5]

Yet, in the Eberbach case histories, it was nymphomania, not hysteria, that predominated in medical representations of female sexual maladies, its symptoms or diagnosis appearing in the case files of almost one-third of the female patients.[6] Its prominence in these cases, as I shall argue, was related in complex ways to the primarily rural and lower-class social background of these patients, a group which, while typical of early–nineteenth-century asylums, has received no systematic treatment in the study of gender and madness. This class dimension is probably one reason for the paucity of studies on nymphomania: hysteria was classically, though by no means exclusively, an illness of precisely those elite Victorian women on whom the historiography of hysteria and madness has hitherto focused.[7]

Gender, as feminist scholarship has shown, is a "symbolic system" that "sig-nif[ies] relationships of power." Gender categories are also relational: defini-tions of femininity are developed in opposition to those of masculinity.[8] These elements of gender are important for understanding the medical construction of sexual pathology in the Eberbach files. Nymphomania had its male counter-part, masturbatory insanity, and both these "illnesses" can only be understood properly in relationship to each other, as two gendered sides to the coin of sexual pathology. This chapter begins with the medical representations of sexual pathology, showing how nymphomania and masturbatory insanity par-ticipated in the formulation of polarized gender norms underway in bourgeois culture. Chapters 5 and 6, which explore the links between class, gender, and sexual madness in "nymphomaniacal" women, move outward from the nym-phomania diagnosis to examine the ways in which medical constructions of fe-male sexuality intersected with, acted upon, and transformed the meaning of the sexual lives of lower-class women.

Nymphomania

For a century obsessed with sexuality, it should come as no surprise that Eber-bach's case histories are saturated with the theme of sex. What is surprising is the specificity of the medical narratives, which distinguish them quite drama-tically from those of the later part of the century. Unlike the late nineteenth-century sexologists, who were preoccupied with "perversions" in sexual object choice and "inversions" of sexual identity, sexual pathology in the Eberbach files revolved around the themes of energy and control: the intensity and de-gree of sexual desire, the relationship between mind and body in the control of desire, and the (re)establishment of the proper balance between reason and the sex drive. Nymphomania and masturbatory insanity, each in their own way, were illnesses (or symptoms) of sexual energy levels gone awry, as well as of the loss of control of the mind over the body. This way of thinking about sexual maladies derived in part from the neurophysiological model of disease then dominant in German medicine; it also reflected the social concerns with inner discipline, control, and rationality that had been a hallmark of late Enlighten-ment thought. They were also central to the bourgeois culture of an emerging civil society of the early nineteenth century.

No consensus existed in the medical community at this time about either the precise nature or the etiology of nymphomania. A relatively new disease term coined in the late seventeenth century, nymphomania could be classified as an illness in its own right, as a mere symptom of another pathology, or as a cause of illness.[9] There was a particular lack of clarity about nymphomania's rela-tionship to other female illnesses associated with sexuality, namely, hysteria and erotomania: nymphomania could be subsumed under either two of these illnesses or, as in Pinel's work, under the general category of "névroses de la génération." Theories of its etiology were likewise manifold. They included a range of physiological, social, and hereditary explanations, such as excessive pungency of the seminal fluid, excessive blood congesting in the brain, hereditary malformation of the uterus or ovaries, masturbation, sexual promiscuity, or mental stimuli from, for example, reading novels or contact with men, conveyed by the nerves from the brain to the genitals.[10]

Yet, at its base, nymphomania was a fairly uncomplicated illness concept whose symptoms and effects on women most doctors had no trouble recognizing. All understood nymphomania to be a female pathology of overstimulated genitals. It was believed that "unnatural" overexcitement of the female genitals would, if not "cured," continue to intensify until finally consuming the entire woman, making her a raving maniac and robbing her of her mind (called the "loss of shame"). At its most extreme stage, it was a state of "the dominance of lustful ideas with the unbridled striving to realize them without consideration of time, place, and circumstance."[11]

The notion of excessive sexual energy informed both the assumption that this illness was developmental and the definition of its trajectory. At least since M.D.T. de Bienville's influential treatise (1771),[12] nymphomania was believed to progress through stages of ever-intensifying sexual excitement and its concomitant—the weakening of rational control over the "animal instincts." The pathologies of Eberbach's patients could be found at various stages of development. The unmarried Marianne H., who still possessed "reason," had a relatively mild case: the "domination of sensuality" took the form of a "struggle between virtue and satisfaction of her desires," where it was "difficult for her to repress her painful desires" for her "beloved" lieutenant.[13] Elisabeth N. was among the more extreme cases, a woman in which "reason [had] lost control over the desires and the acts originating from them." At this point, a previously "moral and well-behaved housewife and mother" began "attacking men on the street and demanding marriage and sex from them."[14]

Male Masturbation

Unlike the historiographical silence about nymphomania, the masturbation phobia of the nineteenth century has exerted a fascination on the late twentieth century, and it, along with masturbatory insanity, has been the subject of a number of scholarly studies. The historical interest has seemed warranted not only by the intensity of the phobia, but also by the huge range of disabilities and illnesses ascribed to it in the nineteenth century. Beginning with an anonymous anti-masturbation tract published in the early eighteenth century, whose ideas were later given scientific legitimation in the Swiss physician Tissot's famous treatise (1760), masturbation by the early nineteenth century had come to be seen as the cause of a huge range of physical and mental illnesses, including epilepsy, consumption, digestive disorders, impotency, hypochondria, imbecility, hysteria, and nymphomania.[15] Its pernicious effects were believed to derive from the "unnatural" loss of semen (considered the body's most "precious" fluid) and the weakening of the nerve fibers from overstimulation.[16] Medical and pedagogical works focused primarily on children and youths—supposedly the primary self-abusers. Masturbation supposedly stunted and weakened the body and mind of the young so that, as Tissot put it, "young people look like old men: they become pale, womanish, languid, dull, sluggish, dumb, foolish . . ."[17] Robert MacDonald describes the "archetypal masturbator" of this literature as "the sallow youth with sunken eye, weak muscles and clammy hands, the pasty-faced degenerate, stunted, solitary . . . already set on the downhill slope . . . to becoming a driveling idiot. . . ."[18]

Interpreters of the nineteenth-century masturbation obsession link it in one form or another to the bourgeoisie—its anxieties, values, and identity. A number of historians have noted the connection between the quintessential bourgeois values of thrift, self-control, and prudence—so essential to bourgeois class identity and success—and the "deviant" characteristics of the onanist: he succumbed to sensual enjoyment, and became lazy, ennervated, and unable to work. Further, economic metaphors of "wasting" or squandering the sperm were constantly used to describe the immorality and danger of the act.[19] Foucault (and those following him) has argued that the pathology of the "masturbating child" was part of a broader strategy of self-legitimation by the bourgeoisie in its struggles for political and economic hegemony. Against the sexual excesses of the aristocracy, the bourgeoisie asserted its virtue and morality; against their descent and blood, which had legitimated aristocratic power, the bourgeoisie focused on the health, vigor, and longevity of their bodies.[20]

The Eberbach sources support the contention that masturbation fears were specific to the bourgeoisie, but they also show the strongly gendered component to those fears.[21] Alone, the diagnostic statistics of the asylum suggest the overwhelming identification of men with masturbatory insanity. From 1825, when Eberbach began listing the causes of insanity by gender in its yearly reports to the government, through 1844 (the later reports are missing), not a single female patient was listed under the heading "onanism" or "self-defilement" (*Selbstbefleckung*). By contrast, masturbation stood consistantly near the top of the list of causes of insanity in male patients beginning in the mid-1830s;[22] and the issue of past or present masturbation was standard in the evaluation of male patients, particularly in those cases of single youths.

What made masturbatory insanity gender-specific was not the assumption by physicians of its greater incidence in males. The act itself was noted repeat-

edly in many female cases, and it was considered a common element in the etiology of nymphomania. Not only did men not monopolize the act, but they
were not necessarily considered more vulnerable to its deleterious effects. In
much of the literature, in fact, little or no distinctions were made between male
and female masturbation, and the idea of nervous exhaustion and enfeeblement was supposedly applicable to both male and female physiology.[23] What, in
practice, made masturbatory insanity a male disorder was the set of symptoms
attributed to masturbation and seen only in men.

In the nymphomania cases, masturbation caused excessive and aggressive
lust; in males, it produced precisely the opposite set of symptoms: enfeeblement,
weakness, listlessness, passivity, and idiocy. In other words, in the Eberbach
cases, the "archetypal masturbator"—the stunted, exhausted, solitary youth—
that historians have remarked on was almost exclusively male.[24] Nymphomania's male counterpart—satyriasis—was almost never diagnosed at Eberbach.[25]
The real counterpart to nymphomania in male patients was masturbatory insanity, with its wholly opposite set of symptoms.

Gendered Models of Sexual Pathology

Nymphomania and masturbatory insanity thus suggest the employment by the
asylum of gender-polarized models of sexual pathology. In the female cases,
sexual pathology was thought of in terms of surfeit—not only of sexual desire
but of a whole range of emotions, including physical strength itself. Nymphomania was envisioned as a concrete presence in the body; sexual desire was an
occupying force, imagined alternatively as an erupting physical energy or
nerve force ("nymphomaniac excitement pulsates through her body,"[26]) or as a
hungry animal ("[Her] sex instincts . . . have remained unsatisfied [due to
her] physical infirmities and form"[27]). Usually the possession of sexual desire[28]
was conceived in the imagery of fire: "fiery," red, and hot faces; wild, "gleam-
ingly animated" eyes; bodies in violent and uncontrollable movement as
nymphomaniacs threw themselves to the floor, laughed, danced, jumped,
lashed out, smashed objects, tore their clothes. For centuries a metaphor for
sexual passion,[29] the image of internal fire encapsulated essential features of
nymphomania: its uncontrollability and danger, its explosive quality, and its
fluidity. Nymphomaniacal desire, like fire, might rage or be partially extinguished only to flare up again at a later time. "[Her] sex-drive is very active,
sometimes visibly increasing to true nymphomania."[30] Such women were in
effect read as thermometers: they registered, through all the outward signs, the
flaming and subsiding of desire. Of one patient it was said that "the nymphomania often stages a lively appearance." The patient underwent treatment and
subsequent observation, but "the medicine has brought about no change."[31]

About another patient, it was noted that "with fixed and flashing eyes, she grabs at every man who comes before her, and the caressing and other fondling reveal the love flames flaring up in her."[32]

Since nymphomania was defined not in terms of specific acts but as a state of being—of overexcitement—it had the effect of bringing together the most disparate behavior into a causal unity and sexualizing a vast range of seemingly contradictory symptoms. This can be seen in the asylum's description of a nineteen-year-old nymphomaniac, Kresschen L.:

> Previously [she was] well-behaved and modest. Now she is in a state in which there is no sign of shame or morality. She takes her clothes off, throws them to the earth, rolls on the ground, hits out, disobeys the attendant, and shows in all her actions great senselessness.[33] In conversation she lapses into convulsive laughter or breaks out into the most frightful swearing. At the sight of a man she goes into raptures, approaches with great trust and betrays here all too well the fire that has ignited the passions.[34]

The "fire" was the physiological process occurring in the genitals, and it was this condition that unified the wildly different acts and moods of the patient— rage, insubordination, humor, and seduction. Thus, nymphomania was only partly about sexuality as we now see it. In actuality, it ascribed to the female genitals a huge range of behavior, much of which contained no overt sexual content. This behavior included the open expression of raw, unrepressed emotion—tearing the clothes, screaming, hitting, and ranting. "Sensuality and nymphomania have broken through all of the limits [*Schranken*] of morality. She is unclean, rips her clothes, and is highly dissatisfied with her stay [at Eberbach]. . . ."[35] In another case, the medical log noted: "intractably wild, no straitjacket holds her back. Pure raving and nymphomania."[36] In fact, no sexually overt behavior in raving women was necessary if "unnatural" sexual activity was known to have occurred in their past. Masturbation, bearing illegitimate children, extramarital affairs, and employment in a bordello—all fell within this category.

In sharp contrast to the nymphomaniac's excesses and explosions, the consequences of sexual indulgence for the male masturbator were portrayed in terms of decline, fall, deterioration, and loss. If fire and possession best characterized nymphomaniacs, "weakness" and "dullness" were the operative terms for male masturbators. The bodies and minds of these men appeared exhausted and enfeebled from the ravages of the draining away of their semen and the harm done to the brain nerves. Their symptoms ranged from the inability to concentrate their thoughts or even get out of bed, to idiocy, from paleness to defective genitals. The asylum described the masturbator Ferdinand W., a forty-seven-year-old former state official as "physically weak, sunken in full passivity [with] a particularly weak memory"; his walk was unsure and stumbling, and every one of his movements exhausted him. He could sit or lay around all day "indifferent to the outer world," and "without the will to raise himself out of the base slavery of his disgusting habits."[37]

Unlike the female cases, raving behavior in males was only rarely attributed to the genitals.[38] Sexual meaning was not attached to such behavior as tearing the clothes or rolling on the ground. In fact, even stripping or running around naked were not read as sexual in men. The examining doctor of the vintner Anton B. noted, for example, how in front of his family and the doctor, Anton "stripped himself entirely naked with the most impudent shamelessness." The diagnosis, however, was simple "raving," not satyriasis or any other sex-based illness. Even Anton's earlier "excessess" and "promiscuity" figured in the diagnosis only insofar as they caused marital troubles.[39] In the case of a farmhand, Heinrich G., the doctors typically did believe that his "excesses with the female sex" contributed to his later insanity, but this behavior was grouped together with his other excesses, such as drinking, under the broader category of "disorderly manner of living," and the diagnosis was accordingly "insanity" and "raving."[40] Physicians, state officials, and communities alike were certainly concerned with raving and out-of-control men, but in the male sex such behavior was associated with alcohol, not sexuality. Over and over again in these cases, it was drinking that led to "excess" and the need for incarceration. Not the satyr, but the alcoholic was the trope for male loss of control.

Public versus Private Symptoms

There was always something public about nymphomania: it occurred in relation to others (doctors, attendants, officials, community) and was defined in terms of the "scandal" posed by the loss of "shame." If medical practitioners asserted physiological and mental explanations for its symptoms, they never disguised the fact that they saw the disease as well in moral and social terms as an affront to and violation of morality as they knew it. Those feelings were expressd in a plethora of morally charged adjectives: "scandalous," "shameless," "indescribable," "beyond imagination," adjectives that referred to any number of public transgressions of sexual propriety, from running after men on the streets to the asylum patient who "looks at every man with lust, approaches with great longing and friendly smiles, [as if] she is expecting her bridegroom and wedding finery."[41] Female patients had to be prevented from masturbating not only because it was ruinous to their health, but because it caused "scandals."

The problem with male masturbation, to the contrary, was its privacy.[42] For a variety of reasons—anxiety and shame, the desire to masturbate, and the consequent lethargy and loss—male masturbation causes a turning in on oneself and a withdrawal from society and family.[43] Masturbators tend to want to lie in bed all day, are anxious and embarrassed, and seek solitude. Such was the case with Ludwig J., a dyer, whom the asylum regarded as a "person weakened and *cowardly* from onanism" (emphasis mine).[44] The peasant Johann V. was "serious, brooding," and "stayed away from social contact." The association of these symptoms with masturbation in the medical case history is clear enough when, after listing them, the doctor noted, "No one noticed if [Johann V.] practiced onanism."[45] On being informed of the symptoms of Adolph H., a twenty-year-old law student, the doctor immediately surmised onanism. Those symptoms were fearfulness, embarassment, shyness, and the inability to concentrate.[46]

Aggression versus Passivity

In the female cases, desire, once aroused, became insatiable; unable to control themselves, nymphomaniacs aggressively "demanded" sex. In male masturbators, what was often striking to the doctors was the lack of demand, the passivity and indifference, even contentment with one's lot. Windt remarked about one alleged masturbator: "*no desires* or special preferences, rather great indolence and indifference" (emphasis mine).[47] Except in those advanced stages of the illness when the patient was dominated by the basest drive for "food and self-preservation" and "all intellectual light [was] extinguished,"[48] the male masturbator's sensuality was a passive enjoyment of the good life, not an active drive for a sexual or other object. Lethargy, passivity, indifference, dreaminess, a "partiality for living well," such as the enjoyment of smoking, drinking, and eating, were the pathologies of the male onanist. Gustav V., a thirty-five-year-old state official, was suspected of masturbation due to his mental "distraction, laziness, [and] indolence." He liked living well, and "[could] sit all day by the oven smoking and dreaming," displaying an infuriating "indifference" to his fate, and remarking only with a laugh, "If I had a wife it would help me."[49] Serious matters indeed, Gustav's "silent smiling" and "cheerful mood" required medical intervention and explanation. The asylum noted how the patient was always distracted, worked uncommonly slowly and without attention, and seemed to be incapable of the necessary reflection for employment. "The patient [himself] seems to feel this weakness."

The pathologies of depletion and loss in these masturbation cases related not only to strength and will, but to sexual desire itself. Basting commented with amazement that the peasant Johann R., despite having become "weakened" from onanism, "is however still dominated by a prevailing sex-drive"; Basting went on to point out that "if he continues to masturbate, he will for sure become a victim of idiocy."[50] In the case of the twenty-three-year-old journeyman dyer Ludwig J., the examining medical official considered masturbation to be the cause of his lack of desire for the opposite sex. Noting the patient's onanism since age twelve, the physician explained that Ludwig's relatives had been struck for a long time by his "indifference to the female sex," adding that the family, however, never suspected the "real reason" for this condition, i.e., onanism. The symptoms of its pathological effects were clear: sensuality, indolence, and a "proclivity to a life of pleasure."[51]

The Gendering of Brunonianism

The construction of these medical narratives of sexual madness in terms of over- and underexcitation largely derived from the medical system that predominated in early nineteenth-century Germany: Brunonianism. The theory of the Scottish physician John Brown (1735–1788) posited a fundamental life force—"excitement"—produced by a "combination of . . . stimulation [from the environment] and intrinsic excitability [of the organism]."[52] Disease was caused by an imbalance between stimulus and excitability, and thus took either of two forms: asthenia, the result of insufficient stimulation, or its opposite, sthenia, caused by excessive amounts of stimulation. This "dualistic theory of disease"[53] found its most enthusiastic reception in Germany, where it was assimilated to the vitalistic theories of Röschlaub, Blumenbach, and Schelling's *Naturphilosophie*.[54] As such, it was used to spearhead a reform movement of Germany's medical system that sought to displace the older humoral medicine and with it the entrenched position of non-university trained healers (*Wundärzte, Bademeister*, etc.) who had been mainstays of the corporatist order. Against the therapeutics of humoral medicine—cleansing the body of impure fluids—, which any practitioner could and did apply, the neurophysiological model of Brunonianism required trained physicians able to assess the level and kind of neurological imbalance and apply a therapy of stimulation ("drugs, strengthening diet and psychical stimulation")[55] or, less frequently, of depletion (the withdrawal of stimulation through bloodletting and other measures).

Brunonianism was thus intimately involved in the simultaneous critique of the established corporatist order and the new claims of university-trained physicians to an enhanced professional status and monopoly over medical care. Not surprisingly, Brunonianism found great favor within the emerging field of mental medicine and was embraced by the likes of Johann Christian Reil, Johann Christian Heinroth, and numerous other German experts in the field. With the superimposition of Brunonian theory upon existing nosologies, "mania" and "raving" were now classified as states of "overexcitement, hence a sthenic illness, caused by a cerebral defect or excessive stimuli (passions)." Melancholy and hypochondria were, on the other hand, seen as states of "underexcitement"—an asthenic illness.[56]

In theory, there was nothing gendered about how the disease process worked in, as it were, the Brunonian body. The physiological process affecting the nerves in masturbatory insanity was considered the same for both men and women. In both sexes, the original damage of masturbation was caused by the overstimulation of the nerves; the later enervation and weakness (which would ultimately take place in both sexes) derived supposedly from the increasing in- elasticity of the nerves (together with the loss of semen). Overexcitement in Brunonianism "[could] increase so greatly as to destroy excitability and thereby bring on an asthenic state in the form of weakness."[57] In other words, overex- citability and understimulation were conceived in medical thinking about mas- turbation not as two different gender-specific illnesses, but as two different stages of a single disease process.

This fact makes all the more interesting the wholly gendered way in which Brunonian thinking was applied in practice. What is so striking in the Eberbach cases is that, to use the language of contemporary medicine, sexual madness was perceived in women at its sthenic stage (nymphomania), whereas in males it was seen in a later asthenic phase of "weakened" and "deadened" nerves.

Repression and the Production of Desire

The therapeutics of curing women and men of sexual madness differed sub- stantially, given the way in which their respective illnesses were represented on opposite poles of the sthenic/asthenic dichotomy. Most historians of the mas- turbation phobia have focused on the perceived threat posed by masturbation to a bourgeois culture of self control and repression.[58] However, the Eberbach cases show that this paradigm was really only applicable to females, where sexual pathology was defined in terms of excess and overexcitement. Accord- ingly, therapy was aimed at limiting, controlling, and eradicating desire. As a sthenic disease of overstimulated "sex-drive," treatment of nymphomania re- quired the withdrawal of all external exciting stimuli, both mental and physi- cal. Described as "cooling," treatment began with separation from the male sex, the key stimulant in such cases. Methods for quenching the fire could also in- clude the use of cold douches over the head; an array of "antispasmodics," such as bloodletting and vomiting; a bland diet that excluded such "irritating" and "inflaming" substances as meat, spicy foods, coffee, and alcohol; and strait- jackets and solitary confinement for the most recalcitrant and raving. In addi- tion, there were the standard "indirect" treatments to distract and redirect the thought process, such as work and reasoned talks.[59]

Training in self control as well as the use of restraint mechanisms such as the straitjacket were also important in the treatment of male masturbation. However, the definition of male pathology as depletion and weakness called for a therapeutics of strengthening and invigorating the body and mind with a stimulating regimen of, among other things, physical exercise and a "strength-ening diet" that might include meat, coffee, and alcohol—the very diet that was deemed so pernicious to the overheated passions of the nymphomaniac.[60] In other words, attainment of self-control in males was focused not on repression, but on the freeing and production of energy, will, strength (mental and physi-cal), and desire itself.[61]

The former law student Adolph H. had been one of the best students in his *Gymnasium*. Onanism, however, had led to "hallucinations" and his failure at school (he left before taking the final exam). In the asylum, he "practiced onanism openly and shamelessly," and thus needed to learn how to "master his passion." Yet the cure for the passion of onanism (of a "weakly constitution," failed exams, and mental confusion) did not involve suppressing his desire so much as stimulating and reviving his strength and vigor: "exercise in fresh air, physical work . . . a *strong* and easily digestible diet . . ." (emphasis mine).[62]

The Construction of Femininity and Masculinity

In identifying and treating nymphomania and masturbatory insanity, medical practitioners were implicitly engaged with the extramedical questions of femi-ninity and masculinity. Pathologies of opposites, these illness categories re-flected and helped reinforce a new normative ideal of gender based on separate spheres. Emerging first in the late eighteenth century, historians agree that ideal was closely associated with the bourgeoisie. Many link its emergence to the structural changes in work and family that resulted from state-building, the spread of capitalism, and, in the nineteenth century, industrialization.[63] As larger-scale and centralized enterprises and bureaucratic offices gradually di-vorced work from the household, so the normative roles of women and men were increasingly polarized: women were expected to lead domestic lives as wives and mothers in the "private" sphere, while men claimed a monopoly over the "public" world of work, politics, and learning.

Ideological justification was required for the fundamental gender inequality which, as a result, lay at the heart of the capitalist, liberal order of the nine-teenth century. Thus, demands for the social and functional polarization of the sexes were accompanied and underpinned by a redefinition of the "essences" of masculinity and femininity as complementary opposites. Women's innate de-pendency, emotionality, nurturing, and weakness, so the argument went, suited her for the roles of domesticity, whereas the male qualities of rationality, aggressivity, strength, and activity made men natural actors in the public sphere. Medical representations of the (gendered) body played an important role in the justification of separate spheres.[64] Thomas Laqueur shows how in this period (the late eighteenth century onwards) the hierarchical ordering of the sexes in the Galenic medical model was replaced by a physiology of opposites: women's bodies, particularly because of the newly elevated role of the ovaries, were no longer seen as similar but inferior versions of the male body; rather, it was asserted that women and men had fundamentally different physiologies and that a female's physiology prescribed her confinement to the private sphere.[65]

The notion of separate spheres pervaded medical constructions of nymphomania in both theory and practice. The contemporary literature explained the vulnerability of women to sexual illnesses and the greater frequency of sex obsession in women (as compared to nymphomania's male counterpart, satyriasis) by their special nature and domestic function: their attachment to family and thus the great importance of love in their lives; their weak nerves; and the dominance of the reproductive organs over their bodies and minds. Bienville claimed that the female "genitals . . . are much more easily and sooner aroused and ignited than in men" because "the nerve fibers in women are much more fragile . . . and taut." Thus, "they must be more intensely aroused or more sensitive, from which it is easy to conclude that the sensations and demands of lust [are] likewise much stronger [in women when they have been improperly aroused]."[66]

Writers also pointed to the psycho-social differences between males and females. "If in the man the physical need [for sexual satisfaction] is greater, so by contrast is love endlessly more powerful in the female, and the female alone is capable of a true self-sacrificing love. The need for love is deeply rooted in the feminine personality and stands in the closest relation to [her] intended purpose, that of becoming a wife and mother." The fulfillment of the "need for love," by which a woman's femininity could "develop and unfold," could only occur through the relationship with a man, and its loss could give rise to nymphomania. While "excessive sex drive in men occurs much more frequently," it was less likely to lead to mental disturbance: the more purely physical nature of the male sex drive allowed men sexual satisfaction without love and attachment.[67] A series of normative and precautionary statements on gender and the social role of women were thereby embedded in the concept of nymphomania. Weak-nerved and delicate women at the mercy of their reproductive lives and emotions belonged at home as wives and mothers, and required protection and surveillance to ensure against the potentially disruptive forces of their latent sexual voracity.[68]

In medical practice, we can see how nymphomania and masturbatory insanity pathologized precisely those traits in women and men that were gradually being excluded from the norms of femininity and masculinity in bourgeois culture. The public sexual immoderation of the nymphomaniac was the most obvious violation of "feminine" modesty, chastity, and sexual passivity. But the gender deviancy of nymphomaniacs went far beyond the transgression of sexual norms: nymphomaniacs were not only immodestly overt in their sexual desires, they were women who expressed a range of emotions openly and force-fully. Nymphomania was a disease of loud and foul mouths, unruliness and open defiance, of "coarse," "uncouth," "impudent," and "insubordinate" fe-males. On one nymphomaniac servant girl and her foul mouth, Basting com-mented: "Her speech is coarser than is typically the case with the female sex." "Coarse," we learn, meant "endlessly loud" and "cursing." The medical log noted these examples: "'You devils, get out of my sight,'"; and, "You devils, what do you want, let me go."[69] Adjectives of aggressivity—such as "demanding," "pushy," "forward," and "fresh"—constantly appear in these cases. Elisabeth G., the adulterous wife of a poor boot cleaner, not only engaged in an affair with a former employer; she "obtrusively approached him" herself.[70] Sexual arousal in women was set against the duties of wife and mother. It led women to focus on their own needs and desires, and therefore destroyed the ideal of self-sacrifice enshrined in the bourgeois concepts of "modesty" and female "honor." Of a "proud" and "sensual" middle-class nymphomaniac, for exam-ple, the medical log noted: "Is reckless. Decorates her cap with flowers, seeks to please and does not demonstrate the least attachment to her children."[71] On the other hand, the asylum described a recovering nymphomaniac as "a good woman who is deeply interested in her household affairs."[72]

Above all, the body images of nymphomaniacal women metamorphosing into men indicate the extent to which the transgressions of this illness were imagined as a collapse of the gender order. Such images included that of the cli-toris enlarged to the size of a penis.[73] One also finds in the literature the case of a woman who has grown a beard and become "thoroughly like a man in speech, manners and movements."[74] In these images of masculinized nymphomaniacs, one senses the male observer's own fears of emasculation and castration anxiety—fears that included but were not unique to circumstances in the early nineteenth century. For images of sexual gender metamorphosis and similiar male anxieties of the sexually voracious, devouring female are well documented in the ethnographic literature (and theorized by psychoanalysts).[75]

Strength, aggression, vitality, and desire—the presence of these qualities in fe-male patients could indicate (though on their own did not necessitate) an illness of the reproductive organs. In male masturbation cases, on the contrary, it was precisely the absence of these qualities—qualities associated with masculinity—that appeared pathological to the medical profession. Male masturbators—weakly, passive, mentally incapacitated, and socially withdrawn—underscored by virtue of its absence in them an ideal of masculinity: strong in mind and body, virile, aggressive, and self-disciplined, an ideal that rested upon the assumption of men as active social achievers and producers. Masturbatory insanity thus did not proscribe an act per se so much as a deviant gender type: effeminate, weak, so-cially isolated, privatized males. In an otherwise non–gender-specific literature,

Tissot's use of the term "womanish" to describe the masturbator was neither accidental nor irrelevant to the deeper social concerns with the "vice."

The most telling evidence linking masturbatory insanity with masculine identity and fears of emasculation is its bodily symptomatology. This included not only paleness and rings around the eyes, but also effeminate traits indicating an arrested development into manhood and the femininization of the male body. Such traits ranged from flabby muscles and lack of facial hair to small penis size. Regarding the seventeen-year-old onanist August H., Basting pointed out that "[his] development is not yet progressed enough. The beard hair has barely grown, his voice is weak and high . . . and [furthermore] his muscles are very flabby.[76] The asylum described the twenty-nine-year-old goldsmith Johann V. as a: "small, slight figure, still [lacking] a beard, a simpleminded and weakly [person], who, according to his own confession, still masturbates daily."[77] In other words, masturbatory illness was concerned in a very direct way with a norm of masculinity and the proper development of adolescent boys.

Medical examinations of the male genitals were routinely performed, and their condition, including size and strength, could indicate whether or not "selfabuse" had taken place. The outbreak of insanity in Phillip K., a twenty-year-old mason, directly occurred after two shattering events: he was inducted in the army, and his employer suddenly fired him. The medical official who wrote the commitment report had indicated the causes of insanity to be this latter event together with the prior existence of insanity in the family. But after incarceration, where an examination revealed that "the hair growth on the genitals is weak, the testicles are small and weakly developed," the real cause of Phillip's illness began to emerge. The state of his genitals showed that his "puberty development has remained behind that of his age and is not yet completed." The fact of his arrested maturation, combined with his "purposeless, bizarre movements of almost all the voluntary muscles," became the basis for the asylum's diagnosis:

> When one contemplates the type of the ailment, it becomes very probable that it is connected to the puberty development, since the form of his spinal irritation appears almost only in this period of life. . . . Whether and in which way emotions or abuse of the genitals—which, although not admitted to, according to the description of the genitals is almost certain—determined the etiology [of the malady] must remain undecided.[78]

The male masturbator of the Eberbach files did embody the more general class fears of the bourgeoisie. This is particularly clear in the association of masturbation with laziness or the incapacity to work and, in the cases of middle-class patients, with downward social mobility. Regarding Gustav V., the languid and dreamy former state official previously mentioned, Basting recounted in horror how "in this state of mind [Gustav V.] went around the country, bothered acquaintances, relatives and innkeepers, fell into the greatest poverty, his clothes practically falling from his body, was frequently ridiculed and had to endure degrading treatment. All of this could not move him to seek employment and obtain respect from the world." Furthermore, his present "laziness, indifference, and ungrounded high opinion of himself and his fate betray a condition approaching dementia . . . One must affect him from the outside such that he discards his evil habit [i.e., masturbation] and such life hopes are awakened which will stimulate a feeling of honor, desire to work, and open up in him a bright outlook on the future."[79] Masturbation, in other words, could cause the possessor of a solid, if not high, position in the state bureaucracy to lose his job and eventually sink economically and socially to the lowest level. His clothes in tatters as he roamed the country and bothered people, Gustav became the image of the pauper vagabond.

In Gustav's masturbatory insanity, one thus sees imagined the bourgeois terror of downward social mobility and the crucial importance of work and health for preventing this disaster. But the social fears referred specifically to the male sex. Loss of honor in Gustav's case was not of a sexual nature (as opposed to the female nymphomania cases), even though its original cause was sexual. Rather, honor was gained and lost according to economic productivity and social standing. In its deviancy, masturbation referred not simply to a general, class aspiration for "hegemony" vis-à-vis the aristocracy (Foucault), but also specifically to male hegemony over the "weaker" sex. Through proceeding against the act of masturbation, the medical establishment worked to shape weaklings into men and to shore up the very basis of male privilege at a time when the entire notion of privilege was under serious attack.

Anne-Charlott Trepp's recent study challenges on empirical grounds the applicability of the separate spheres paradigm, which has dominated feminist historiography, to German bourgeois society before 1850.[80] The contemporary prescriptive literature, on which most historical analyses of gender norms are based, may have advocated separate spheres and a polarized understanding of masculinity and femininity. Trepp, however, found in the lives of the Hamburg bourgeoisie (1770–1840) a much more fluid conception of gender, in which men embraced such "feminine" values as romantic love and family life, and male work itself was not strictly separated from the home. She concludes that separate spheres only became a reality for the bourgeoisie after the middle of the century, largely because it was only in the latter part of the century that industrialization created the socio-economic conditions for the complete separation of paid (male) work from the home.

Trepp's findings make the Nassau material on sexual pathology all the more interesting. Clearly, if industrialization was the key causal factor producing the implementation of the separate spheres ideology, one should not expect to find the latter in medical practices of backward, preindustrial Nassau. Bureaucratization and the spread of capitalist enterprise, however, *were* characteristic of Nassau, and many historians believe these factors to have been just as important to the emergence of separate spheres.[81] Yet, one can certainly assume that the actual lives of Nassau's bourgeoisie no more followed the lines of separate spheres than their Hamburg counterparts. Clearly (to restate the obvious), there is no simple connection between base and superstructure, material conditions and ideology. The crucial factor in physicians' gender conceptions was a bourgeois culture that took shape in Germany well before the onset of industrialization.

Above all, the employment of a dichotomous gendered schema of sexual pathology (nymphomania and masturbatory insanity) reveals the effects on early psychiatry of a fairly recent shift in conceptions of sexuality linked to liberal thought. At the most general level, the treatment of "nymphomaniacs" and "masturbators" as ill reflected a movement underway since the eighteenth century that was gradually replacing legal sanctions against deviant sexuality with pedagogical, moral, and pychological approaches. More specifically, Hull has shown that since the 1790s the (mostly bourgeois) "practitioners of civil society"—jurists, pedagogues, philosophers, and so on—had reconceptualized male and female sexuality along polarized lines. Developing the psychosocial basis of male citizenship in a liberal state involved a new normative view of male sexuality that identified it with "egoistic energy, self-willing, and rational self-limitation." Such qualities were essential components of male claims to greater political freedom and rights.[82] By contrast, women's sexuality— passive, lacking autonomy and willed control—became the hallmark of her continued social and political subordination and her relegation to a private sphere of reproduction.[83] The anti-masturbation crusade of the late eighteenth century, according to Hull, thus became a powerful "metaphor" for working through the question of how to constitute the rational, free, self-controlled, male citizen of a liberal polity at a transitional time when the German states were moving from the political tutelage of absolutism to a freer, self-regulating, liberal society of the nineteenth century.

Thus, by the early nineteenth century, two oppositional norms of sexuality had developed: one supporting (moderate) male sexual expression, the other more than ever focused on female sexual modesty and passivity. It was this sexual schema that the Eberbach asylum and Nassau's medical officials employed when they defined and targeted the pathologies of nymphomania and masturbatory insanity. Yet, at the same time, developments of the Vormärz, including the emergence of the "social question" and the rise of the asylum, presented new challenges and opportunities for the further elaboration of ideas and practices concerning the regulation of sexuality. The Eberbach cases were precursors of a general shift in the nineteenth century that focused increasing attention and fears on the sexuality of the lower classes. If medical practitioners' concerns about healthy, male sexual energy applied to all classes of men, the main issue with regard to lower-class men was not self-development and freedom, but work capacity. In lower-class women, as chapter 6 will show, medical practitioners worked in tandem with communities to enforce the most traditionalist restraints on women's sexual expression, which linked marital sexuality with the social and economic institutions of village society.

Chapter 5 will first examine how medical constructs of sexual pathology, which posited innate feminine and masculine essences, were built upon masking and transforming the meanings patients attached to sexual behavior, and how the asylum itself often played a role in producing the very symptoms it sought to cure.

5

Doctors and Patients

The Practice(s) of Nymphomania

The peasant Margaretha D., noted the asylum log, "often suffers from hysterical attacks, with which she wants to be treated like a distinguished lady . . . She raises herself above her social position and demands great attention and care."[1] This patient, in other words, though considered mad by the Eberbach asylum, was not a true hysteric: she rather "played" the hysterical lady.[2] Two important issues suggest themselves from this description of feigned illness. The first has to do with the connection between class, gender, and the representation of illness. Madness, it seems, had its class and gender codes. Certain symptoms of hysteria—which in the eighteenth century had become a fashionable illness of privileged women, signifying the pathologies accompanying luxury, leisure, and "civilization,"—appeared suspicious in a poor, peasant woman. Secondly, the "playing" of illness suggests (inadvertently) a subtext, normally buried and only implicit in the asylum notes: of illness as strategic behavior on the part of the patient within the social dynamics of the asylum. Margaretha's symptoms were at least in part the result of a self-presentation to her keepers, a communicative act, with its own aims—attention, better care, and so forth.[3] Both of these issues—the link between class, gender, and illness, on the one hand, and the strategic nature of symptoms, on the other—are at the core of the following analysis of nymphomania.

Nineteenth-century physicians interpreted the behavior of nymphomaniacal women as a function of an internal state of being—as pathologically excited genitals—and in this way, they contributed to the construction of a modern conception of sexuality as an innate essence of personality. While no longer a clinical entity in post-Freudian psychiatry, the image of the out-of-control, sex-obsessed nymphomaniac remains very much alive in popular culture and continues to be grounded in a conception of sexuality as inner essence and "drive."[4] This analysis, by contrast, looks at nymphomania as acts and attitudes, which took place within very specific social contexts: the power dynamics of the asylum and the doctor-patient relationship. The sexuality of nymphomaniacs that emerges from this analysis had certain social referents and motives; it was about a range of issues—power, identity, freedom, and survival—that structured the contacts between doctors and patients. In fact, it was precisely in and through acts of patient resistance that physicians constructed the nymphomania diagnosis, even while the medical concept functioned at the same time to erase and deny this social dimension of the "illness."

Social Class and Illness

While hysteria could be (and was) diagnosed in lower-class women—at Eberbach and other asylums—its continued cultural association with privilege seemingly did not lend itself well to educated physicians and officials speaking and thinking about lower-class female sexual deviancy. Nymphomania—an illness of transgression, eruption, excess, strength, and passion—by contrast did. True, there were some women from the middle classes labeled as nymphomanics at Eberbach. This should not be surprising given the implicit orientation in the medical literature on nymphomania (and all other female nervous diseases) towards the ailments of middle-class women. Nymphomania in this literature was generally portrayed as a middle-class problem of warding off indulgence in the excesses and corruptions of an aristocratic and leisured lifestyle. The renowned professor of obstetrics Dietrich Wilhelm Busch claimed, for example, that women with a "pampered upbringing" were particularly susceptible to the disease.[5] Peter Willers Jessen emphasized the dangers of a "sumptuous" lifestyle "devoted only to pleasures and not working . . . theater, society, concerts, balls . . . sleeping on soft beds . . . lack of physical exercise. . . ."[6] In accounting for the emergence of nymphomania in the "Middle Ages" (by which was meant the proliferation of treatises on the disease in the sixteenth through the eighteenth centuries), he contrasted the pathological effects of "knightly gallantry" with the "more natural and simple conditions" of the ancient Greeks and Romans.[7] This was a literature, in other words, written by and for the middle classes, and concerned with what Foucault has called the "self-affirmation" of itself.

In practice, however, nymphomania was diagnosed disproportionately in lower-class women. Such patients, who were generally from peasant families of smallholders and the rural proletariat, were about twice as likely to be diagnosed with the illness as their middle-class counterparts; and the most extreme stage of full-blown nymphomania was also disproportionately seen in these patients. In part, the propensity to perceive nymphomania in lower-class patients was the result of the bourgeois ideals of womanhood embedded in the nymphomania concept and applied across the board to female asylum patients.[8] Peasant women simply did not conform to those ideals when they were applied by middle-class doctors. The body gestures and physical appearance demanded of women as signs of modesty, health, and femininity were far removed from those of peasant and servant women, whose lives were spent in physical toil. It is this that was seemingly reflected in the medical comments on lower-class "nymphomaniacs" as "coarse," "sensual," "ill-bred," and "without upbringing and feeling for decorum and law."[9]

The role played by class in the medical perception of female pathology can be seen in a comparison of two very similiar cases: those of a middle-class woman and a poor servant. Both cases deal with single women of marriageable age (twenty-seven and twenty-five, respectively) conflicted over the desire for a man, on the one hand, and the problem of upholding sexual honor, on the other. The emotional problems of Marianna H., the daughter of a wealthy (*Rentnerin*) widowed mother, began at the time of her approaching marriage, which she finally called off. "She expressed the greatest worry that she could not make her future husband happy." The cause of this state of mind had to do with an "earlier love-object, whose idea gradually became so dominant [in her] that . . . she was pursued by it in every occupation."[10] In the asylum, "day and night, her sexual excitation allows her no peace [of mind] . . . longing for her beloved feeds her fantasies." On the other hand, it was later stated in the medical register that the "loss of her fiancé worries her the most." And in a suicide note, we learn from the patient herself that the loss of her honor tormented Marianna to the point of taking her own life: "My soul is no longer watched over by God, nowhere in the world do I find peace!—And my honor branded for eternity!!!!!! These words contain my terrible existence."[11]

Elisabeth D. had been working as a servant in Frankfurt when the events occurred that led to her commitment to Eberbach. "Her master had promised that she would receive an inheritance [*Legate*] . . . this hope was disappointed; at the same time that her lover left her—perhaps he had only been attracted by the expectation of the inheritance. Offended pride and fear of ridicule [also contributed to her mental state], because she had already announced to her friends her upcoming marriage."[12] After her marriage plans fell through, Elisabeth showed an obsessive interest in men: she began speaking "only of distinguished gentlemen, whom she perhaps had seen or heard of but with whom there is no possibility that a sexual relationship could have taken place. Also, her attention was very easily aroused by young men." Like Marianna, but in very different circumstances and for different reasons, Elisabeth had become obsessed with men. But like Marianna, she was at the same time extremely concerned with her sexual honor and reputation. It was the shame of being left by her fiancé that had caused her mental trauma. Later, the asylum observed that "with the least suspicion of the sullying of her good name, she is brought to despair and despondency."[13]

Despite the similarities of the two cases, the asylum treated the two women very differently. It portrayed Marianna's "nymphomania" as a "struggle between virtue and satisfaction of her desires"—namely, as a problem of conscience.[14] By contrast, the asylum viewed Elisabeth, despite her desperate pleas to the contrary, as an "impudent whore." Elisabeth's desperation over the "sullying of her honor" was in fact a direct reaction to what she was assumed to be by the asylum staff. "Although in her mania she manifests the appearance of an impudent whore, yet she steadfastly persists in [asserting] the excellence of her blamelessness [*Unbescholtenheit*], and with the least suspicion of the sullying of her good name she is brought to despair and despondency."

What an "impudent whore" looks like the asylum unfortunately did not explain. But it was at the least connected with the fact remarked on in the medical register that Elisabeth "speaks a lot about distinguished gentlemen, with whom [she claims] she has kept company." According to bourgeois decorum, baldly announcing past contact with men, and hence one's sexual looseness, did make a woman a whore. In his commitment report, Dr. Küster, a more acute observer of human psychology than Windt, captured something of the motivation behind Elisabeth's statements: "It seems she likes playing this role as if she wants to arouse respect through this silliness." Many patients, both from the middle and lower classes, fantasized of intimate contact with higher personages in order to elevate their social standing, to (re)claim for themselves a position of respect and honor when commitment to the asylum or the life tragedies that precipitated commitment had robbed them of these things. Such appears to have been the case with Elisabeth D. But the fantasy that was supposed to prove her worth made her a whore in the eyes of the medical authorities.

Elisabeth's inability to convince the asylum staff of her purity had something to do with her lack of mastery of the signs of bourgeois virtue and modesty. Marianna H., on the other hand, knew exactly what these signs were and consciously used this knowledge in order to successfully get herself released from the asylum. After Marianna's failed suicide attempt, the asylum noted a significant change in the patient: previously consumed by the struggle against sexual desire, Marianna was now suddenly "calmer," "hard-working," and "rational." It seemed apparent to the asylum that the onset of menstruation had caused the salutary "crisis" of the illness and the beginning of recovery.[15] Several weeks after her release, we learn in a letter from Marianna's mother that no such medical recovery had occurred, and that the asylum had been deliberately deceived. "With our [Marianna] it is unfortunately not going as expected.

Hardly fifty steps from Eberbach, she began to insist that she must speak with the person in question [her beloved] and to hear directly from him the declaration [of marriage], and if this does not turn out according to her wishes, she says she can not live any more . . . She said she [previously] mastered her feelings in Eberbach in order to get out."[16] Bourgeois women were trained to master their feelings, a skill that was also required of recovering nymphomaniacs in the asylum.[17]

The idea that women from the lower strata of society suffered from pathological sexuality took on added force given the close association between lower-class sexuality and the social question in the Vormärz. This association became a staple theme of the pauperism debate and the basis of state public policies aimed at restricting and containing what, in Malthusian terms, was perceived as an out-of-control sexuality generating overpopulation and hence mass poverty.[18] The perception of the danger of sexual excess in lower-class women embodied these concerns, for it was precisely these sexually overexcited women whose immoral behavior was supposedly causing the rising illegitimacy rate, threatening to deplete local poor funds, and both reflecting and helping to cause the hungry, lawless, and dangerous state of the lower orders. The behavior of these women was therefore a matter of state concern, and, as we shall see, it was the financial burdens to communities of illegitimate children (among other factors) that could unite communities and the *Landesregierung* in actively supporting the use of the nymphomania diagnosis to have them incarcerated.[19]

A number of recent studies have explored the powerful ways in which images of gender difference and the body have functioned as a metaphor to articulate a range of social and political issues.[20] The gender transgressions of the nymphomaniac's disorderly genitals are a case in point. Within the context of the social question of the Vormärz, the hypersexual female could be a very potent symbol of the dangers of social disorder emanating from the lower classes. Like the specter of the hungry masses, female desire was an insatiable force that exploded in violation of social boundaries and norms. The metaphor of the sex instinct as hungry animal appeared in both the medical literature and the asylum reports under the term "lack of [sexual] satisfaction." Unsatisfied "sex instinct" could cause sexual overexcitation when the woman's husband was old and unable to perform adequately, when she had remained unmarried, or when previous sexual experiences had ignited a lust that subsequently could no longer be fulfilled. Eberbach's case histories, as we have seen, were replete with "dissatisfied" women. The *Encyclopädisches Wörterbuch* listed "dissatisfaction with oneself or with [one's] external circumstances . . . with the world" as one of the characteristic symptoms of nymphomania.[21]

What "dissatisfaction with external circumstances," its social danger, and its connection with sexual lust could mean is shown in one patient's medical case description. It describes Louise S., twenty-three years old, unmarried, and lower class (her father was a prison guard), as a "beautiful, well-built girl" who had "a taste for young men of higher standing." Her wishes were at some point "satisfied by illicit contact." She gradually began to change: she lost sleep, spoke vehemently about things and people who were far above her station, became irritable and hot-tempered, thought she was the master of the ducal palace, ran around the room with her hair loose and flowing, complained about her lack of satisfaction and poverty, and once ran away undressed. In short, as the examining physician summed it up, she displayed a high level of "mental and nervous mobility" (*Geistes- und Nerven- Mobilität*).[22]

The case description conflated sexual and social transgressions. With the notion of genital eruption and sexual longing, it succeeded in simultaneously articulating and concealing the fact of the patient's rebellious, socially dangerous behavior. The metaphor of mobility encompassed at once the image of the patient's body in space, her mental state, and her attempted movement across class boundaries. In this juxtaposition, the social and sexual trespasses in the illicit affair were implicitly fused together, and the fierce longing for a higher-class life unleashed by the taboo social contact became indistinguishable from an unquenchable sexual thirst unleashed by sexual contact: both were forbidden fruits, the taste of which could only lead to a dangerous desire for more. Class yearnings and social transgression became matters of sexual frustration and pathological nerves. The containment of the genitals—of "nervous mobility"—was the containment of the class order.

Power and Resistance: The Doctor-Patient Relationship

The interweaving of medical theories of female sexuality with gender norms and the politics of class relations in the Vormärz formed the backdrop against which medical practitioners diagnosed and treated lower-class nymphomaniacs. One can take this analysis beyond historical generalities to the concrete daily practices in which doctors confronted patients, applied their "knowledge," and constructed the medical narratives of female hypersexuality. Several notable dynamics characterized interactions between doctors and their nymphomaniacal patients. First, an extreme power differential in the relationship of doctor and patient was determined by class, gender, educational, and occupational differences that composed the vast social distance between semiliterate female servants and peasants in confrontation with male, middle-class, educated physicians and civil servants wielding the authority to decide the fate of their patients. This power inequality reached its pinnacle in the asylum, where the interactions between male staff and their lower-class female patients, who were locked up and completely dependent upon the wills of their physicians and attendants, entailed not only the extraordinary inequalities of class and knowledge but, literally, those between the free and the unfree. Second, this power dynamic formed not only the immediate context in which the staff labeled female patients as nymphomaniacs; it played an essential role in actually producing the very symptoms of nymphomania.[23] Finally, all this occurred in a situation where sex became one medium of a (miscommunicated) dialogue between doctor and patient about a range of issues—power, identity, freedom, and daily existence within the asylum. From this perspective, the alleged lust of nymphomaniacs had a certain meaning and aim, one that had very little to do with bodily sexual urges as such.

Katharina J., a poor, widowed, peasant woman, had been incarcerated both in prison and in Eberbach for her intransigent and violent demands for the return of her home, which had been auctioned against her will to a local official (the *Schultheiß*). In 1827, when a medical official went to examine her at home two months after her first release from Eberbach, he encountered an unexpected display of affectionate and seductive behavior:

> I found her at home alone. Immediately at my entrance she received me, as earlier, with her wordless smile, and to my question where and how she has been living up to now, I received no other answer than this senseless smiling. All of a sudden, she saw my signet ring and asked me for it. My silver-studded whip likewise appealed to her. I let her take hold of it in order to see what she wanted to do with it; and with amorous glances and smiling countenance, she drew it softly over my back. To the question [of] what she wanted on the 25th and 26th in G., particularly at the government office, she smiled at me, and before I knew it, embraced and kissed me with the answer: "that's what I wanted to give him." This embrace and kiss was supposedly not meant for me but for a certain individual in G. at whose home she explained she will live in the future. . . . It clearly follows from the above that the widow [Katharina J.] has fallen into insanity which seems to have taken on an amorous [*verliebt*] tendency.[24]

The detailed and densely packed symbolism of this case description provides unusual access to the meaning of female seduction outside the physician's own medico-ideological framework. From the first, Katharina was intensely interested in the doctor's signet ring and whip. The ring represented officialdom as the tool for certifying signature on official (as well as private) documents. The silver-studded whip was a tool of discipline and, as a riding crop, of mastery and control over the horse (the possession of which required wealth beyond the reach of lower-class people like his patient). As objects of elite, male power, both were aimed at generating respect and creating social and spatial distance. In an encounter between insane patient and doctor's whip, the symbolism was clear: the patient was the horse, the doctor the rider, and insanity the internal equivalent of the disorderly "animal spirits" that required the discipline and mastery of the doctor's reason and control.

By seizing the whip, Katharina grasped the doctor's power, turning it against him. In the gesture of simulating a whipping, she played the master to his beast. It was a symbolic act of aggression, whose message is the subversion and reversal of the power relations between patient and doctor. But its underlying power lay less in the act itself than in the playful tone in which she carried it out. When playing with the signs of power, they lose their fixed, inevitable quality; they become objects of joking, mockery, and commentary. Katharina's commentary made what was implicit in the situation explicit through mimicry: she acted out the meaning of the whip to demonstrate and mock the doctor's power. His is a caressing power, one that masks its force through softness and concern. The serious respect it was supposed to elicit in the patient had become, in a carnivalesque leap, that of bodily sexual desire.

In this way, the gesture also announced Katharina's own strategy, which would continue throughout the examination: seduction as aggression; the caress as whip. A loving, sexual attitude allowed her to "get at" the doctor, catching him off guard, neutralizing any fears of violence he might have had, and playing on his belief in his own desirability (as male and middle class). All this provided Katharina access to the whip, both literally and figuratively, in the crossing of spatial and social boundaries. Katharina turned the doctor into beast as a sexual animal, someone to be set out of control by desire and manipulated by female seduction. In a situation of powerlessness (after years of futilely battling the authorities for her house and being locked in prison and the insane asylum for her trouble, there was no question of where she stood vis-à-vis this representative of officialdom), seduction was perhaps the only way of exercising a measure of control over the man, by playing with the one quality both doctor and patient possessed that potentially leveled class differences: sexuality. Sexuality could be a kind of language to be manipulated for specific purposes; it was the vehicle of (mis)communication between doctor and patient, the boundaries and terms of which Katharina aptly expressed in the image of the whip and the caress.

If in Eberbach much of what was labeled "nymphomaniacal" contained components of aggressive, angry behavior (see chapter 4), it is because most of these women were extremely angry as a direct result of their incarceration. While there were indigent and formerly abused patients who were sometimes grateful for the care they received at the asylum,[25] most of the women diagnosed as nymphomanics were enraged at their incarceration and desperate to get out. They called Eberbach a "prison," complained about the "injustice" of their confinement, and issued threats of legal proceedings. These battles with the asylum could stretch over years, and there were also a number of escape attempts, with some patients exerting enormous energy and ingenuity in this enterprise.

As in Katharina's case, one of the driving forces behind "shameless," "sexual" behavior in these women was not desire but rage. Lodged as they are among notations on insubordination and escape attempts, "shamelessness," "impudence," and the provocative sexual talk and behavior some female patients engaged in appear as extensions of battles against the asylum. In a setting where "proper," "feminine" behavior was rigidly enforced, and where, for example, patients could be punished with solitary confinement for "slovenliness" or swearing, "shamelessness" was (whether intentional or not) an act of insubordination. Given the sexual prudery of the asylum staff, certain sexually explicit acts and speech of their patients—such as stripping, simulating coitus, and "telling lecherous tales"—appear as outright provocations. Certainly patients could not have failed to notice the doctors' horrified reactions—the fact that the behavior was often so "scandalous" it could "not be described." The context of the medical notations surrounding such behavior and the whole course of an individual patient's "career" in the asylum support the idea that shock value was often precisely the intent of such acts.

The behavior of Barbara N. provides a case in point. Here, sexual provocation became the medium in which a power struggle between patient and asylum—between freedom and restraint—was played out, and where sexuality was fed by rage. If there was one clear message from Barbara's behavior in her years at Eberbach, it was an unrelenting and furious desire to escape. She even succeeded once, by jumping through the window of the solitary confinement building. At admission, quiet, homesick, and worrying about her children, she began searching for ways to escape. Locked away from her home and family, forced to work and obey, and punished when she did not, Barbara became increasingly enraged—hitting the staff, refusing to work, demanding to go home, and "raving." Sexual desire appears as the second motif, running parallel to the rage. At first "liking to talk of handsome men, [by whom] she wishes to be touched," her behavior later reached, according to the doctors, the "highest degree" of nymphomania.[26] In the intervals between "running around to every door to . . . flee," she succeeded in making a great display of sexual gestures, "letting herself fall to the floor, and rubbing her bottom around on the stones to satisfy [sic] the sex act . . ."; masturbating to the point that "she injures her genitals"; or, "at the sight of men, uncovering herself in the most lecherous way."[27] Was there a connection between the woman locked away and desperately seeking to escape and the woman "plagued" with sexual desire? Dr. Windt thought so. "The constant aimed for restraint of her wild desires [with the straitjacket] roused her to the greatest wrath, and limited the sexual excitation just as little as the medication."[28]

Patients could also use seduction and flirtation to meet certain needs within the asylum world. For many patients, an attitude of outrage and absolute rejection of the asylum eventually gave way to accommodation.[29] When and if an inner assimilation occurred, the issues for patients changed from escape or revenge to negotiating their material and psychological needs within the rules and norms of the institution. These desires were practical, such as receiving more and better food, avoiding work, and, most important, avoiding punishment or any number of "therapeutic treatments" that amounted to the same thing. Negotiations were also related to meeting emotional and social needs—recognition, respect, and attention, for example. In everyday affairs, it was the attendants who had perhaps the greatest impact on patient lives, given their constant and close contact. The perpetual fighting between patients and attendants, the hostility piled on attendants by the former, attest to the tense proximity in which the two groups coexisted. However, given that the male staff had the decision-making authority (in the adjudicating of patient-attendant quarrels, meting out of punishment and treatment, and altering of a patient's daily schedule or place of residence within the asylum), it should be no surprise that female patients went about trying out the force of their sex appeal.

In, for example, the case of Christina D., a former servant, she seems to have used seductive behavior as a plea (or ploy) for attention and care. The word *"mannstoll"* (man-crazy) appears for the first time within a register entry describing Christina as "often simulating illness, full of demands to change her situation."[30] Later entries note that she "demands better care and service,"[31] and "believes she is neglected and not duly regarded."[32] Still later, the *Mannstollheit* took on new meaning as aggression and revenge—incorporated into the war Christina waged with the asylum authorities over "the greatest injustice [incarceration] that is happening to her": "raving, curses the employees of the asylum . . . quarrelsome, obstinate, haughty, man-crazy."[33]

Viewed as communicative and strategic acts taking place within a specific social context (the power dynamics of the asylum and the doctor-patient relationship), the diagnosis of nymphomania thus reveals the ways in which female patients sought to manipulate the asylum and resist its power. Indeed, nymphomania was constructed by the asylum precisely in and through these acts of resistance. The production of "sexuality" through acts of resistance is seen in a closer examination of perhaps the most common nymphomaniacal act: stripping. In the case files, the term usually used for this act—*sich entblössen*—is ambiguous and seems to have encompassed two different behaviors: uncovering the body, usually in the gesture of raising the skirt (*den Rock aufheben*), and fully removing the clothes or undressing (*sich auskleiden*).[34]

Pulling up the skirt was only noted in the cases of lower-class patients—women such as Elisabeth S. Her commitment report explained that at age forty-three she was living in a seriously disturbed marriage with her second husband, a shoemaker eleven years her junior. The husband had recently found out about the illegitimate child his wife had born at age seventeen and whose existence she had hidden from her husband. For her part, Elisabeth, who badly wanted children, was feeling "jealousy" of her husband[35] and dissatisfaction with his meager earnings. Her first husband had earned a good living as a mason in Mainz, and Elisabeth had not been happy about a move one year earlier to the second husband's village. As Basting put it, the present husband "can not satisfy [Elisabeth's] accustomed tastes." The commitment report described her condition as "raving with particular excitement of the genital system," and noted both "the filthiest talk, especially with respect to sex" and the fact that she "constantly raises up her shirt [*Hemd*]."[36]

The case of the aforementioned Katharina J. provides insight into the possible meaning of the gesture. It appears in the commitment case history as one of a list of seven acts she committed during her incarceration in prison, on the basis of which (together with her past behavior over several years) she was transferred to the asylum as mentally deranged. Katharina had greeted the prison doctor by "pulling her skirt over her head." Acting the gentleman, the doctor had responded by taking off his hat, whereupon she "scornfully laughed at him."[37] Katharina's amusement seemingly came from the utterly absurd and inappropriate response of politeness by the doctor (the removal of the hat) to her own act.[38] A sense of the act's intent begins to take shape set alongside the other moments of "insanity" on the seven point list: She 1) threatened the *Schultheiß* with arson; 2) scornfully laughed at the doctor and *Justizrath* when questioned about this behavior; 3) smashed the windows of the prison; 4) threw the flax she was given to spin out of the window; 5) after seeing the doctor and *Amtsdiener* "broke out with the words: 'Indeed! If I had water, I'd want to kill all of the guys immediately'"; 7) at the doctor's last visit, scornfully laughed and refused to answer his questions.[39]

Katharina was in a rage, having felt herself unjustly robbed of her house by the dealings of several *Schultheißen*, and subsequently locked in prison when she sought to assert her rights to the house. Unrepentant, she asserted the rightfulness of her position by rejecting its punishment and heaping contempt on the authorities. She went even further, threatening reprisals of death and arson. Regina Schulte's work has shown us that arson in peasant communities could be used as a form of revenge against an injustice done to the self or one's family. In other words, it was an act of laying blame.[40]

Over the centuries, a number of meanings have attached themselves to the display of the naked female buttocks and/or genitals. From the belief in the gesture's magical powers against demonic influences to its use as a tool for mocking and blaming the observer, it is a motif that stretches from ancient cultures into the twentieth century.[41] Raising the skirts to expose the genitals as a female act of shaming and placing blame on the observer has been analyzed in the ancient Greek myth of Baubo;[42] the act has also appeared in medieval iconography, folklore, and in modern strikes and protests.[43]

This was the sense in which both Katharina J. and Elisabeth S. used the gesture—the latter a woman actively accusing her husband of infidelity and, implicitly, blaming him for her childlessness and reduced economic circumstances. The gesture also found its way into the asylum, where, seething with anger, patients used it tactically in the battles they waged against the institution. Barbara N., the peasant woman described earlier who spent a tumultuous time in Eberbach violently opposing its order and desperately seeking to escape, used the gesture not long after a failed escape attempt. The asylum commented that Barbara was once again "nymphomaniacal in the highest degree"; the symptom this time was that she "raised her skirt up and uncovered herself [*sich entblössen*] shamelessly."[44] If the act of raising the clothes was a socially meaningful female gesture of shaming, in the medical setting it was interpreted otherwise—as sexual excitement or shameless lewdness—by middle-class physicians who did not understand this (physical) language of blame and were predisposed to view all aberrant behavior of institutionalized patients as symptoms.

The act of stripping, often combined with tearing and destroying the clothes, had a different set of meanings. While medical practitioners saw such acts in reference to the unclothed body, the sources suggest that the patients regarded the acts as referring to the clothes themselves and the symbolic meanings attached to them. In other words, the act of stripping was not about exposing the (gendered) body (as in lifting the skirt), but of ridding the self of the clothing; and its meaning was not in the theme of sex, or for that matter, a physiological process of sexual excitement, but in the social and symbolic context and function of clothing within the asylum order.[45]

This implication and the struggle surrounding it had largely to do with a patient's social identity. Clothes were symbolic of the person; they stated who one was and where one belonged within a familial and societal hierarchy. In the asylum, where the patient had been severed from his or her home and past identity, and where identity itself was called into question and reworked by the institutional regime, clothing took on enormous symbolic significance. As something closely associated with social identity, and one of the few (if not sole) possessions of patients, clothing became a focal point of (mis)communication and struggle between patient and asylum staff about who the patient was, how and who was to define her, and the place she held within the asylum.

The loss of one's past identity, and the confusion, fear, and anger that the onslaught of the asylum regime provoked is captured well in the statements of two nymphomaniacs: both poor, one a former servant and the other a former day laborer. Anna S., the former servant, "asserts that she is simultaneously in N. [her home] and here, which is however impossible," and later she stated that "she is not [Anna S.].; she [Anna] has long been buried. But who she is, she does not know." No longer being Anna S. referred to the person "who was," as she claimed, "the prettiest girl in the world and could have made an extraordinarily lucrative marriage."[46] This was at best an exaggeration, but her point about the loss of past hopes is clear. Being an inmate of the asylum made one into another person, even if one was not sure who that person was. This transformation occurred because commitment to the institution meant the loss of reputation and honor—the qualities necessary for establishing an adult social identity as a married woman in the community. The day laborer, Catharina V., used more violent images to express what occurred to her sense of self in the asylum, claiming that her "skin was removed [and] her head exchanged [*vertauscht*]." The psychologically intrusive, mind-manipulating practices of the asylum are also captured, if more prosaically, in a later remark she made to a doctor, as recorded in the medical register: "[Catharina V.] curses, 'scoundrel, swine . . . ask my father who I am.'"[47] That is, not only the event of being ripped from one's familiar surroundings, but also the specific nature of one's inmate identity—as someone who needs to be asked who she is—problematized identity.

How such feelings could come to center on clothing is suggested in the case of Margaretta K., a poor day laborer in her mid-twenties. Soon after her arrival at Eberbach, the admission report claimed that she "demonstrates her sexual lust with every man, even uncovering herself [sich entblössen]." At another point in the report, we learn that Margaretta "vehemently demands her release. She refuses to be instructed in the necessity of her stay in the asylum and about her personal circumstances."[48] Perhaps Margaretta was engaging in the very sort of aforementioned shaming/blaming behavior. Almost two years later, the issue of clothing reappeared in a different form. During the changing of her clothing, Margaretta now "always gets into fights with the attendant because she only wants to put on the clothes which she has brought from home."[49]

The asylum clothing policy helps clarify the nature and timing of this conflict. The daily attire of patients could be made up of either the asylum clothing, the patient's own clothing brought from home, or a combination of the two. An Eberbach report explained about the asylum uniform: "The clothing of the lunatics, to the extent that it is given by the asylum, is entirely uniform," consisting, for female patients, of one skirt, jacket, and apron; two bonnets, three shirts, a muffler, two pairs of stockings, and one pair of shoes.[50] To save on expenses, these garments were dispensed piecemeal over time, when and if the patient had used up her own clothes or arrived at the asylum with insufficient clothing from home.[51] Thus, where a patient may have begun her stay wearing her own clothes, as these clothes became ruined or wore out, they were replaced by the asylum uniform. There could come a point, as in Margaretta's case, where her wardrobe was made up of a mixture of the asylum uniform and her own clothing. It was at this point where fights over the changing of her clothes occurred between Margaretta and the attendant.

One need only compare the lengthy lists of clothing middle-class patients brought to the asylum with the short and meager lists of their lower-class counterparts to see that it would have been particularly (if not exclusively) poorer patients like Margaretta who were subject to wearing the asylum uniform. And it was also these poorer patients who most frequently turn up in the asylum notes detailing acts of stripping and tearing up of clothing.[52]

We know from the register notes that Margaretta had trouble feeling "at home" in the asylum ("she does not yet know where she is at home") and that she badly wanted to get out ("she is always demanding her release").[53] Margaretta's battles to wear her own clothes were directly connected with this desire to recapture "where she is at home"—if not through release, then through wearing those things of her past associated with her former identity and world. The ability to wear one's own clothes allowed a patient to retain a part of her past identity and thus avoid, if only symbolically, the complete absorption of the self into the asylum regime. By contrast, wearing the clothing of the asylum signified precisely what one refused to accept: the role and life of the inmate. It fixed the self in the identity of inmate perhaps as much as any other daily event of asylum life.

Given that nymphomaniacs tended to be adamant in their rejection of the asylum, it may well be that much of the stripping off of clothing was intended as a stripping of their inmate identities. In the medical registers, the act of "stripping" or removing the clothes is most often surrounded by notes charting a patient's rage and/or attempts to escape from the asylum. In the case of the former servant Maria L., for example, the connection seems clear where the remark, "seeks every opportunity to escape, constantly anxious and agitated," is followed by the entry, "Hitherto unchanged. Also, today she sought to take her clothes off and behaved very agitated."[54] Patients who stripped also usually destroyed their clothing.

Finally, clothes were symbols of one's class position—both in the outer world and within the asylum. Lower-class women rejected clothes "not good enough" for them, or demanded "better" clothes like those of the higher-class patients. The desire for status and material gain that clothing symbolized in the outer world also applied to the world of the asylum, where a patient's class determined the type of treatment received. Paying, middle-class patients received better and more food, were taken on special outings, and occupied with such activities as sewing and reading. This was in contrast to the menial work of cleaning and washing demanded of lower-class patients.

The significance of clothing did not just exist in the perceptions of patients. The asylum staff was well aware of its symbolic value (if not also of the meaning sketched here), and they used it intentionally to punish, discipline, and educate the patients.

> [The] cleanliness of clothes is an essential requirement not only for . . . physical hygiene but also to restore the dignity and self-esteem [as well as] the sense for order and the attention of unclean and reckless lunatics. Furthermore, that the vain and smug fool, the proud and haughty lunatic, through

the deprivation of some of these clothing pieces can be put down and . . .
punished, and that this technique is not seldom involved in the treatment
plan, follows from the [previously mentioned] principles on which they
rest.[55]

That is, as explicit asylum policy, clothes were points where the refashioning of
the patient took place, where the patient was "restored" to order and cleanliness, or rid of his or her "pride" and "vanity." Whatever additional personal
meaning it had for individual patients, by ridding oneself of the clothing—
through stripping or destroying it—one rejected this remaking of the self.

The Formation of "Sexuality"

Clothing battles between doctors and patients were mundane, everyday events.
But it is precisely their everyday quality that enables them to cast light on larger
historical questions concerning the history of sexuality and the medicalization
of female deviancy. "Sexuality" at Eberbach is best understood not as a thing or
an essence, which the staff worked to repress and control, but as a contested
area of interaction constituted through a set of events and relationships involving doctors, attendants, and patients. There were two, fairly distinct "sexuali-
ties" in the Eberbach sources: a medical version of pathologically excited female
genitals and eroticized imaginations, on the one hand, and a set of patient gestures and words associated with social aims and motives—with issues of power,
freedom, identity, and survival—on the other. The medical recoding of these
patient narratives into genital dysfunction suggests the ways in which the
nymphomania diagnosis participated in the broader story of the construction
of modern sexuality.

"Sexuality," as Foucault argued, is a creation of the nineteenth century.[56]
The discursive ferment about sex in that prudish century did not repress sex (as
the traditional account goes) so much as it produced the concept of sexuality.
The earlier understanding of sex as a series of discrete acts (whether as the prescribed form of heterosexual, marital sex or as the proscribed and sinful forms
of bestiality, sodomy, and fornication) was replaced by the notion of sexuality as
an essence (a "truth" of the self) located at the core of and defining individual
personality. New sexually deviant categories and personality types—the "ho-
mosexual" and the "pervert"—emerged as a result. These pathological types
were historical constructs tied to new forms of knowledge produced by such
sciences as medicine and psychiatry, which made the former into objects of institutional regulation, control, and treatment.

Nymphomania appears as a transitional concept in the construction of modern sexuality. Unlike homosexuality, nymphomania was not a quality of personality so much as a transitory diseased state of the genitals or, simply, a derogatory

description of female transgressions of all sorts. On the other hand, once in such a state, the pathology came to define the nymphomaniacal woman in far-reaching ways, so that a huge range of behavior was reinterpreted as signs of underlying sexual desire and genital dysfunction. Indeed, the idea of woman as being ruled by her reproductive organs meant that a bodily state of excited genitals required no outward displays of sexuality in raving women as long as some indication in their past (illegitimate children, work in a bordello, masturbation) indicated the possibility of "unnatural" sexual stimulation or frustration. As Bienville explained, nymphomania "lurks, almost without exception, under the imposing outside of an apparent calm," and frequently becomes dangerous when the woman herself has no idea "what peril she is in."[57]

A primary function and effect of the nymphomania diagnosis was to mask the fundamental power inequalities between doctors and patients that produced raging and sexually provocative acts and speech. It did this by substituting an inner context of pathological genitals for the external and social context of behavior, which stripped patient acts of their intentions and thus of any semblance of rationality. We can see this in the treatment of time and the objects of passion in the passage on Kresschen L., quoted above (page 90). Time—social time—was flattened into an eternal present. In the medical report, there is no indication that the acts and feelings of the patient constituted distinct moments occurring over a period of time. Rather, they appear to form various instances of what was in effect one drawn-out event: genital excitement. In this report, the moments compressed into one time frame occurred over about a three-week period.[58] The compression of time could, however, involve years of a woman's life when connections were made between a woman's promiscuous past and her present raving.[59]

In addition to the transformation of time, under medical examination the individual objects of passion either disappeared altogether or became one generic man. Throughout most of the passage on Kresschen L., she seems to be the sole inhabitant of her world. She screams, swears, and rolls on the ground, as if living in a vacuum. Only the mention of an attendant and later the mysterious "men" indicate that her world included people and events to which she may have been reacting. Of course, such descriptions were typical of most asylum reports. They omitted the social context of patient behavior precisely because it was believed that patient actions bore no rational relation to the world. The nymphomania cases had a specific twist to this objectless and relationless world of the insane in the use of the term "men." Typically, Kresschen was filled with desire when "men," not a specific man, were in her vicinity. One would never know from such descriptions that, if the remark was made by the asylum staff, the "men" in question were most likely the staff members themselves, given the asylum's policy of strict separation of the sexes, including the use of same-sex attendants.[60]

Given the embarrassment caused in doctors by the behavior of nymphomaniacs, one may suppose that their use of the generic "men" was a means of extricating themselves from personal involvement. There were also compelling reasons in the disease concept itself that determined the use of the impersonal and plural "men." For what distinguished nymphomania from other sexual illnesses was precisely its indiscriminateness—the generalized and nonobject-oriented nature of nymphomaniacal desire. If erotomania was a pathology of passionate love for a single object choice, nymphomania was the need for sexual satisfaction at any cost, "without consideration for time, place," or object. The idea of indiscriminateness appears repeatedly in various guises in the nymphomania cases.

Ironically, the very institution set up to cure mental pathologies served to produce the symptomatology of illnesses such as nymphomania. In the transformation of social events and relationships into symptoms, the perspective of patients officially disappeared in medical discourse. At the same time, the failure of this discourse to wholly absorb the patients themselves and their behavior is implicitly present in the very application of the nymphomania diagnosis. For it was the extent to which these women were able to resist and manipulate the signs of sexuality, however unsuccessfully in practical terms, that fed the construction of the diagnosis and the redefining of rage and sexual provocation into genital pathology. Chapter 6 turns to the broader social dimension of this process—to the families and communities where "nymphomania" often began.

6

Women, Sex, and Rural Life

T he making of nymphomaniacs occurred not only within the confines of the asylum walls, but in the wider social world that produced mental patients. Before incarceration, twenty-five of the nymphomania cases were already regarded as such (as nymphomaniacs or as sexually overexcited) in the commitment reports of medical officers, whose information was heavily dependent on family and community informants; in government reports; and even in the direct statements of community members. These women had become threats to their families and/or communities, and the latter, as a result, had desired their incarceration as much as any intrusive state or medical profession. Moreover, the sexual danger that medical science perceived in nymphomaniacs was not wholly fabricated. In many of the cases, the women were behaving in sexually aberrant and out-of-control ways, and these actions were not incidental to their communities' perceptions of insanity and danger.

Though redefining that experience, medicine worked in the first instance with the material of village conflicts, complaints, and interests in forming the nymphomania diagnosis. These interests could coincide with those of medicine and state, and it was in the cooperation of these parties (state, medicine, and community) that nymphomania initially evolved in the cases where it was diagnosed before commitment. To understand the origins of the nymphomania diagnosis, it is thus necessary to examine those communities, their norms of sexuality and mental health, and to look at the women themselves: who they were, their problems, and the language—in action and word—they used to articulate those problems.

Rural Sex Norms and "Man-Craziness"

Statements of community members in three of the cases show that a popular version of the nymphomania concept did exist in rural society, a version covered by the term man-craziness (*Mannstollheit* or *mannssüchtig*). Its meaning, in fact, overlapped in some ways with that of the more technical, medical term. This similarity, it seems, reflected less the incorporation of medical ideas into popular culture than the reverse: the extent to which the science was saturated by and drew from nonscientific sexual mores and moral codes in the society at large. The community views of man-craziness articulated in the two cases containing detailed accounts each represent, respectively, the physiological and moral meanings of the medical term.

Man-craziness as genital pathology (physiology) appears in the statements of the female housemate of Elisabeth G., who, at the time of her commitment in 1848, was thirty-nine years old and living with her "old and poor" boot-cleaner husband in a childless marriage. Basting paraphrased the statement of the housemate, a woman "who for a long time lived together with [Elisabeth] in a house, and knows her well":

> [Elisabeth G.] has always been a very hot-tempered, malicious, but upright woman, who up to the outbreak of her illness, which occurred roughly three weeks ago, always lived properly with her old husband. She is used to eating and drinking well, constantly lived in plenty, since she does not have any children; she especially ate well and a lot. The cause of her illness is a passion she conceived for a young widower in H. Due to this passion she was seized by an aversion to her husband and by a real man-craziness [*Mannstollheit*]. For some time before this, her husband had forbidden her [to go to] the house of her lover, and this gave rise to quarreling and fights. During her illness, she not only invited sex from her favored one [*Auserwählten*] but also from other men, and acted in such a way as if she had great torment [*Pein*] in her genitals. On the trip here, she in addition called out to the soldiers in Wiesbaden, beckoning them to her. The great agitations often subsided, and then she would complain of the misery her seducer brought over her. And then she would again call for her husband and speak with him right properly. She has never been physically ill, nor had suicidal thoughts, nor made attempts to flee.[1]

In a different case, a male peasant provided the view of nymphomania as a function of immoral character. A single, penniless, fifty-one-year-old woman, Veronica D., had a decade earlier been twice incarcerated in the correctional house at Eberbach for begging and vagabondage. An 1845 case history stated that after her second release from the correctional house she had returned to this mode of life and "finally was so immoral, so dangerous for the public peace and security" that a male community member (a "Bürger") was assigned to watch over her at home. Suffering from "raving and nymphomania, she often threw the entire village into an uproar from her lecherous speech, cursing, and raving. Finally no one wanted to take her in anymore, and she was brought to Eberbach." The report went on to quote the male peasant who had brought her to the asylum:

> For years, she has been a half-witted, man-crazy [*mannstoll*], lewd person, who in previous years had a little house to which all kinds of dissolute rabble were drawn, and in which she carried on the greatest lechery. In the last eight years she was hired out to a peasant for whom she made life miserable. She often ran away entirely naked, and was for all the inhabitants, especially for the children, highly offensive. Beatings were not able to bring her to order, she [would] say: "you'll have to beat ten devils into me before you beat one out of me." She is a crazy wench [*Weibsbild*] who must be locked in the insane asylum.[2]

Within a physiological framework, Elisabeth G.'s housemate saw desire rooted in a physical occurrence of the genitals and thus employed the metaphors of irresponsibility, of mind controlled by desire. The peasant describing Veronica D., on the other hand, saw Veronica's acts as the products of willful moral depravity and thus as a disciplinary problem. Both peasant views also shared with medicine the association of nymphomania with indiscriminate, extramarital sex. Elisabeth G. was not just overcome by desire for her "lover," but for other men as well, including soldiers on the street. Veronica D. was portrayed as a whore.

One need not assume that elite medical ideas of sexuality "trickled down" to the masses to understand why rural communities would have considered such behavior deviant and ill. In fact, even the "physiology" of Elisabeth G.'s housemate seems to have drawn its source more from the religious than the medical sphere. "Torment" (*Pein*), the word the housemate used for the process she imagined in Elisabeth's genitals, had religious connotations, referring in the Christian tradition to the punishment suffered by the sinner.[3] By contrast, the medical case history accompanying Elisabeth's incarceration worked with a model of sexuality as an inner drive. The medical report implicitly made the frustration of this drive the cause of her marital troubles: "Since she has been married for thirteen years to an already aged and poor man, so there was all kinds of discord [in the marriage]." This included the discord of lack of sexual satisfaction by a woman who, "rumor" said, had worked in a bordello and therefore was someone "used to sexual enjoyment."[4] The housemate, on the other hand, stressed the discontinuity between the present sexual passion and Elisabeth's former life, seeing it as an anomaly interrupting and intruding itself into an otherwise fairly orderly existence.

Indiscriminate, extramarital sex placed both women outside of and against village sexual codes and the social order that depended on their preservation. Sex in peasant society served important social and economic functions.[5]

Through marriage alliances and the transmission of property, sex facilitated the formation and continuity of the household—the basic social and economic unit of the society. Unlike bourgeois sexual norms, premarital sex was not in itself dishonoring to women, but was only condoned when it occurred within the framework of courtship for the purposes of a subsequent marriage. The sexuality of both Elisabeth G. and Veronica D. was directed, on the contrary, to pleasure seemingly for its own sake, not as a means toward, or an activity within, marriage. Such behavior would have represented a social and economic threat to the community. As Benker explains:

> The integrity of the social system, the stability of the status quo of the transmission of property and the class order were guaranteed by the interlinking of sexuality and marriage. 'Promiscuous' behavior by a woman, behavior which denied the basic unity of sexuality and economy, conceiving sexual interactions rather as purely personal and uneconomic, was suited to destabilizing and endangering this order.[6]

Sexual promiscuity in addition posed the financial problem of its products: illegitimate children. Not only the state and the medical profession, concerned with the social and political consequences of illegitimacy, but local communities as well had an important stake in preventing illegitimacy, since such children, when disowned by their fathers, became financial burdens of the community and required public support from the meager reserves of the local *Armencassen* (poor funds). The population explosion of the Vormärz and the resulting pauperism put tremendous pressure on public welfare funds, which in Nassau were already severely limited given its restricted tax base.[7] Medicine and the nymphomania diagnosis were useful tools to protect against the financial threat of illegitimacy. In recommending the incarceration of a woman who had given birth to two children whom the husband claimed were not his, one medical official argued that "since she is nymphomaniacal [*mannsüchtig*] and probably still finds occasion for extramarital, illicit contact . . . it is to be feared that she will get pregnant and have more children, which . . . will have to be supported by the *Gemeinde*."[8]

In this respect, the asylum and the medical profession found themselves incorporated into (and furthering) a long tradition, dating back to the early modern period. For the collaboration of communities and the state in matters of sexuality was nothing new. Out of a common interest in maintaining orderly familial and property relations, the German absolutist states had long worked jointly with communities in the regulation of sexual morality.[9] The medical involvement with nymphomania signaled a recent shift away from legal sanctions against deviant sexuality and toward a pedagogical and psychological approach to the matter. But, at the local level, as seen in the Eberbach sources, this development did not mark a sharp break with past practices and attitudes.

Finally, there was the problem promiscuous women posed to the honor and reputation of families and husbands. A woman's sexual honor was crucial to not only her own, but also her entire family's reputation. The disgrace of a "promiscuous" family member reflected back on the entire household, damaging its reputation and status within the community. It was therefore strongly in the interests of families to monitor and control their wives' and daughters' sexuality. We can see the damage an adulterous, "nymphomaniacal" wife posed to both the husband's honor and his pocketbook in a case involving a couple from the strata of well-off urban craftsmen. Pregnant at the time of her commitment, Margeretta F.'s condition had become the subject of rumor and gossip. "It is said that [the husband] is not the father of her children; it is also well known that out of shame he likewise denied several of her previous pregnancies during her insanity, afterwards however he admitted [to them]."[10] While Margaretta maintained that her husband, a Limburg town-councillor with a tavern and leather business, was the father of her child, the latter had been keeping his wife locked up and actively sought her incarceration in the asylum. In response to the asylum's plan of temporarily releasing Margaretta for her to give birth at home, the husband requested his wife's "lifelong" commitment to the asylum. One telling letter shows that his business and reputation were very much on his mind. "Due to [her] raging howling and wailing everyone is afraid to come into my house. Since innkeeping and the leather trade is my only means of support, and this is impossible if my wife is left here, so I request . . . the speedy decision [on the request for commitment to Eberbach]." He complained that she also interfered with his duties as town councillor in the city hall. There is no record of how his wife's absence (first in Eberbach, subsequently in a private home for the insane) affected the husband's business; presumably it picked up again. But we do know that it helped him carry out his political "duties," and his career flourished; in fact, he was elected to the office of mayor.[11]

The issue of household honor and reputation probably played a role in the different ways the community viewed the sexual deviancy of the aforementioned Veronica D. and Elisabeth G. The former lived at the very margins of society among what the peasant termed the "rabble"—presumably beggars, vagabonds, and petty criminals. The description of her was made by a male "peasant" member of the community, who stood socially and economically entirely removed from her. "Lechery" and moral depravity were terms of class difference; the discourse of protecting morality functioned here as the defense of the system against the marginal and deviant. Elisabeth G., by contrast, though poor, had been integrated into the community. Moreover, the description of her promiscuity in terms of illness and irresponsibility was made by a woman who, as a member of Elisabeth's household, shared close personal, social, and, presumably, economic ties with her. Elisabeth's behavior was thus bound up with the housemate's own identity and reputation—hence the latter's need to condemn and halt the offending behavior, and to minimize the shame through the notion of irresponsibility (i.e., illness). This desire to protect the household's reputation also may have been reflected in the housemate's omission of the "rumor" that Elisabeth had worked in a bordello.[12] Finally, one wonders whether the housemate's shared gender with Elisabeth G. did not also play a role in her ability to imaginatively enter Elisabeth's body and feel her "*Pein.*"

Medicine and Community in the Making of a Nymphomaniac

Strict village sexual codes and social norms thus informed the popular conception of man-craziness. In certain respects, rural sexual norms shared with bourgeois culture basic moral assumptions about indiscriminate female sexual behavior, just as both communities and the state shared strong financial interests in the prevention of illegitimate births. Yet the meaning of popular sexual norms and their application to deviant women drew from the structures and conflicts of rural life and, as such, could diverge significantly from bourgeois culture. The making of a nymphomaniac thus involved a complex interplay between village interests, norms, and conflicts, on the one hand, and their redefinition as illness by medical officials, on the other. In these matters, the relationship between a medical official and a community was particularly complex and ambiguous: the former was an outsider, who refashioned the meaning of local events in a different language system and helped to police the community; but he was also often an accomplice (and dupe) of the latter.

These dynamics are well illustrated in the events that ended with Christine F.'s incarceration at Eberbach as a nymphomaniac in 1841. A peasant woman of about forty years of age, Christine had one child with her husband, Johann F., and earlier in life she had raised four illegitimate children, two of whom were still living. Here is a detailed description of the events of Christine's insanity from the perspective of two community members who brought her to the asylum, and whose account was paraphrased in a report by Basting:

> The wife [Christine F.] comes from a place in Amt Braubach where her mother, an old, very respected midwife educated in Darmstadt, still lives. For many years she has been known as the crazy bull [*närrische Stier*]. She was always extraordinarily hardworking, working more than a male farmhand. She was always in the fields very early, took care of her household in an exemplary way, but always behaved recklessly and lived with her husband, who is twenty years older than she, in discord. Also, the husband is a semi-simpleton, a secret drinker who secretly spends all the money he gets his hands on on food and drink and gives his wife no share of it. She became really insane two years ago from fright: she wanted to dry flax in the room, a fire began, and the house was in danger of burning down. The *Schultheiß* and

farmers who came to put the fire out treated her terribly, even mistreating [beating] her, after she was already exhausted from the exertions of putting the fire out and was, besides, very affected by the misfortune. She became quieter, read a lot in religious books, learned entire sermons by heart, with which she harangued the people, and seems to have begun drinking. She always complained of terrible, violent headaches and rushing in her ears; she didn't sleep and neglected her household. She has been raving since three months. Especially at the beginning it went on day and night, and she couldn't be kept in her house; she bothered old people in their homes, mistreated her child and even drank up her breast milk. She took the medicine prescribed by medical officer Wuth irregularly; thus there was no improvement. . . . Lately she has shown the greatest hatred toward her husband. By contrast she has always been affectionate toward her child. But they had to take the child away from her because she picked it up by the legs and could have harmed it. She has never tried to take her own life or mistreat other people or instigate other misfortunes. Rather she has been worried about her and other people's lives.[13]

This account presented the events of Christine's insanity as a story of social marginalization and, perhaps, injustice. While her reputation was stained, and she was considered an oddball (the nickname crazy bull), Christine had been nevertheless a respected, capable worker and housewife, who had to put up with an entirely unsatisfactory husband. Christine moved from this condition via a momentous event, the fire episode, to a woman alienated from the community, who neglected and abused her duties as wife and mother.

A complex set of social circumstances surrounded the development of Christine's mental disturbance. These included marital conflicts and tensions between her and the community as a whole. Typical of most married nymphomaniacs, serious problems marked her marriage, and her unconventional sexual behavior was only one side of the story. The husband, for his part, shirked his marital duties (in his drinking, stinginess, and implicit laziness). This was a husband whose ruinous effect on the household contrasted sharply with the wife's exemplary housekeeping. However troubled her marriage and reputation, Christine had managed to survive, socially and economically, within the community. The fire event dramatically changed this situation, pushing her over the edge to become an outcast. That she felt unjustly accused of negligence in causing the fire, and from there went on to act in ways that only intensified her mariginalization, is witnessed in her public recitations of the Bible and the neglect of her household and duties as wife and mother.

A second detailed account of Christine's case, her medical case history, as written by one Dr. Wuth, presented a strikingly different narration of insanity, in which social events were replaced by a tale of erupting genitals induced by an immoral life. At school, Christine "developed good aptitudes so that she is considered particularly gifted and learned by her acquaintances." However, she is "very reckless and flighty . . . [and] does not like to work seriously and continuously." Moreover, "according to [my] inquiries the sex-drive was always predominant, which has now pathologically increased." She frequently lived in "disharmony" with her husband, for which she has been punished. "Before her marriage the madwoman had lived promiscuously [*liederlich*], which had caused fights in the marriage, especially since she persists in her promiscuity." Christine had an "attack" of insanity one month ago on the way from Ruppertshofen to Nastätten. The doctor did not explain what the attack consisted of, but on the basis of this and the above facts, he concluded that Christine was suffering from "nymphomania and frenzy":

> The illness probably has a somatic basis, the result of excessive irritation of the uterine nerves, or the malformation or chronic inflammation of the ovaries. An incorrect and neglected upbringing may have contributed to the development of the illness. . . . Through intemperance in love, perhaps also from onanism, the original predisposition intensified to illness. The latter is all the more likely since her old husband cannot sufficiently satisfy her sex-drive.

Treatment consisted of bloodletting, the application of leeches, cold douches on the head, and warm ones on the breasts "in order to maintain and increase the milk secretions." For the future, Wuth recommended "separation from the male sex" and a "dietetic" cure: a meager, cooling diet and hard physical work.[14]

The community account had made a fairly clear distinction between sexual deviancy and insanity, imputing no link between past (or present) sexuality and present insanity. Christine's pre- and extramarital sexual activities had given her a bad reputation but they were not seen, even retrospectively, as symptoms or causes of illness; instead, it was the fire incident that made her "really" insane. By contrast, the medical report made a direct link, via the motif of irritated genitals, between events of Christine's past and present; indeed, Wuth suggested that sexual promiscuity itself may have already been a pathological symptom. In this compression of time, the earlier causes of genital irritation constituted a precondition that ultimately erupted in full-blown nymphomania. The really significant events had been taking place within the inner organs, an incubation space for the developing illness; therefore, the outer context of fire and mistreatment made no appearance at all in such an account.

The nymphomania diagnosis, for Christine F., thus evolved by a process of selecting, screening out, and recoding a large assortment of "facts" about this woman and her life. The nymphomania concept itself determined in large part the relevant facts selected by Dr. Wuth, as they provided the framework for seeing illegitimacy and raving as medically relevant and related. United, the two symptoms—illegitimacy and raving—took on new meaning: sexual promiscuity became the precondition of raving, while raving was sexualized by being read retrospectively as the outcome of an immoral past.

Dr. Wuth's perception of nymphomania also entailed a certain class-based view of health and normalcy. Promiscuity in the village account related to

Christine's character and reputation, not to the state of her genitals. Illegitimacy was neither pathological nor, by itself, did it marginalize Christine in the eyes of the community. These attitudes are consistent with historical studies of peasant culture. Sexual promiscuity was ruinous to a woman's honor and reputation, but it did not rule out her ability to maintain her status as a "faithful and hard-working" woman in the community.[15] Given the financial and legal hinderances to marriage for large sections of the nonpropertied lower classes at this time, affairs not consummated in marriage and producing illegitimate children were not all that uncommon. Such compromised women seem to have remained integrated into village life, despite the damage to their reputations.

Dr. Wuth saw these issues quite differently. In his report, sexual promiscuity took on special significance as the cause of illness and a sign of an immoral life. Illegitimacy, the most concrete effect of licentiousness and the only concrete piece of "evidence" provided in the report, acted as a kind of character-framework (Christine F. as a whore or loose woman), into which the "facts" provided by his informants were placed—a framework that gave coherency and believability to the pieces of information coming his way. Here, the two interpretations of nymphomania—as a moral failing and as an illness—are so fused together that the immoral has itself become a form of pathology and vice versa. Evident as well in this medical case history are the public policy concerns that associated illegitimacy—a social pathology of the immoral and unhealthy environment of the lower classes—with pauperization, overpopulation, and social disorder. These concerns are implicit both in the pathologizing of illegitimacy and in the suggestion that "faulty upbringing" (i.e., a deficient environment) lay at the root of mental disease.

There were thus several factors—medical, cultural, and political—that made it possible and compelling for Dr. Wuth to see Christine's problems in terms of her genitals. The documents suggest how village interests also shaped his diagnosis. Like all medical officials in the position of examining a patient to be committed to the asylum, Dr. Wuth's judgment largely depended on the information he received from his informants, who, at the minimum, normally included family members and local officials (the *Schultheiß*, and sometimes the local pastor or teacher). These informants appear to have played a significant role in the sorts of symptoms the doctor "saw" and used to construct his diagnosis.

As we have seen, the major difference between Dr. Wuth's report and the villagers' account lay in the former's emphasis of Christine's sexuality to the exclusion of the crucial event of the fire. That Wuth may have been ignorant of the event is suggested by the fact that in mental medicine, "fright" was considered a common and accepted cause of insanity.[16] Moreover, medical officers were under some pressure by both the state and the asylum to write "complete"

commitment reports.[17] Not coincidentally, two of the most likely informants—
the husband and the *Schultheiß*—had, for different reasons, an interest in pre-
senting the facts so that they downplayed (or omitted) the fire and emphasized
Christine's sexual immorality. The husband, after all, had been battling his wife
for years about this matter. The medical report suspiciously presented exclusively what would have been the husband's side of the argument, focusing on
the wife's alleged promiscuity and "laziness," and omitting the husband's de-
fects, and the fact that it was he, not his wife, who was the poor householder
and worker. Such a self-serving account by a revengeful husband could be
easily assimilated to Dr. Wuth's model of genital pathology, and its frequency
and manic form in women (particularly in unchaste ones such as Christine).
The *Schultheiß* (along with other community members) also had an interest in
deemphasizing or keeping his mouth shut about the fire, since, as a participant
in Christine's "mistreatment," he was personally implicated in the episode that
triggered her mental disorder. If this was the case, it too would have contributed
to keeping the doctor focused on Christine's internal "fire" of desire, instead of
the external, actual one.[18]

   Dr. Wuth's (and later, indirectly, the asylum's) relationship to the events and
people within the Ruppertshofen community was ambiguous. As an outsider,
he used his expertise to redefine social events as genital pathology. Moreover,
as a member of a professional elite, Wuth's interests, tied to his class and civil
service position within the state, were in many ways at odds with much of the
community. For this physician in the 1840s, members of the impoverished lower
classes, such as Christine's husband, were themselves part of the problem—
economically, socially, and, potentially, politically. On the other hand, Wuth
served as an enforcer of community norms, ridding the village of a public disturbance. In this, he was, wittingly or not, an accomplice of his informants.

Man-Craziness: Personal and Social Narratives of Sex

As Christine's case illustrates, medical authorities and rural communities had
different ways of evaluating female sexual deviancy and mental disturbance;
yet, the incarceration of nymphomanics required the participation of both parties (and the state). Only a few "nymphomaniacs" had given birth to illegitimate children, or even had affairs. These women, however, shared in common
certain familial and social circumstances that made them potentially capable
and desirous of sex outside of marriage and courtship in the eyes of their communities; and this fact, we can assume, played an important role in their incarceration. Indeed, many of these women had become disturbed over men.
Their "madness," however, can be understood in historical terms distinct from

the mental and physiological categories of nineteenth-century medicine. This section therefore explores in more systematic fashion the social profile of "nymphomaniacs" and the sorts of social and familial conflicts that formed the context of female sexual deviancy and transgression. The cases are divided into two groups for purposes of analysis: women in severely troubled marriages; and single (mostly servant) women in search of marriage. The aim is to understand the women's troubles from their points of view. My objective is not the impossible one of getting "inside" their heads or of subjecting them to retroactive psychoanalysis. It is to piece together the historical field of meaning of lust and desire, men and sexuality, and thus to socially embed sexuality as a set of practices and statements within the world that produced it.

Marital Strife and the Language of Accusation

Sex in peasant society, as we have seen, was part of a social and economic transaction. The bestowal of a woman's virginity to her lover in courtship or her sexual fidelity and honor to her husband was to be reciprocated on the part of the man by the social and economic benefits of marriage. Within this norm, the husbands of nymphomaniacs left much to be desired. At best, they were not adequately performing their marital side of the bargain, either in fact or in the imaginations of their wives. At worst, they were outrightly abusive. Christina F.'s husband was a "semi-simpleton, a secret drinker, who . . . spends all the money he gets . . . on food and drink and gives his wife no share of it," whereas she was said to be "always extraordinarily hardworking, working more than a male farmhand . . . up in the fields very early and took care of her household in an exemplary way." The husband of Elisabeth G. was an "old and poor" boot-cleaner and the marriage had remained childless.[19] Margaretta R., the wife of a poor day laborer, complained of her "wretched" life and asserted that her husband maintained her "too miserly." She had left him several times and returned to her parents, even in the first years of the marriage. The husband, in turn, accused his wife of being too "greedy."[20] Ursula P.'s husband was said to be a "man of rough nature with little sense for domesticity, who often daily mistreated her . . . and drank." At the time of her second incarceration at Eberbach, when she was described as a nymphomaniac by the people who brought her to the asylum, the medical register noted that she was emaciated and "seems to have suffered [?] great poverty at home."[21]

Other husbands were not performing their sexual duties. Several of these marriages remained childless. Some wives accused their husbands of impotency and/or adultery. Others seem to have considered their husbands partially responsible for the death of a child. Finally, there is the case of Elisabeth N., the wife of a tenant farmer. She had a sick child whom, it appears, she thought had been bewitched by neighbors, and she was "mistrustful and upset at her husband and "housemates" as a result.[22]

Sex and sexual dishonor became an issue, then, where husbands were not properly fulfilling sex's exchange price, so to speak. In marital conflicts such as Christine F's, one sees the wife's sexuality pitted as a symbolic weapon against the husband's economic weapon. Her husband's "stinginess" corresponded to Christine's sexual promiscuity: they punished each other by withholding from one another their respective marital duties (economic support and chastity). The case of Maria M. shows how useful a tainted past reputation could be in these fights. Before her marriage to a tailor, Maria had worked at an inn in Frankfurt am Main and had carried on an affair with an "Italian." Later, in a childless marriage, she had "attacks" of jealousy in which she accused her husband of adultery. "She would often then leave home and go off on a trip." During the marriage, it was said that her husband twice had to fetch his wife back from Frankfurt.[23]

These women used sex—their own and their husband's—as a public language of accusation, demand, and punishment. We see women intentionally making a public spectacle of sex at the time of extreme marital tensions. Barbara N., the thirty-five-year-old wife of a peasant, became crazy over the deaths of several of her children, and for reasons not entirely clear, later blamed her husband for the tragedies. She had been disturbed for years since the birth of her second child, "in turn crying, laughing, singing . . . attacking [people] with a pitch-fork." Her madness worsened after the death of her fourth and "very much loved" son. She hunted for him in wells and in the Rhine river, pursued people on the street demanding the return of her child, and neglected her household. It was in this context that Barbara began accusing her husband of having affairs. Whether due to the husband's alleged infidelity or his mysterious role in the death of her baby, Barbara felt violent hatred toward her husband:

> She began to rave, scream, curse; goes at [the husband] in order to scratch [?] and hit him; she also pursued him with a weapon, and often threatened to cut his throat. She often calls him the greatest 'Hurenkerl,' accuses him of being with other women. . . .[24]

Given these feelings, it is no surprise that Barbara had lost all sexual desire for her husband. "She has shown the greatest loathing for sex [with her husband] since several years, and since then entirely refused to go to bed with [him]." Most significantly, it was also in this state of mind that "to the children on the street and to her relatives, she told immoral things which included describing the state of her husband's genitals."

The message of such behavior seems clear: publicly describing the genitals of one's husband was an act calculated to dishonor him by calling into question his performance in the sexual sphere. In order to accomplish this, the public's inclusion was essential as the arbiters of reputation in peasant society. Carola Lipp explains, with respect to factory workers in Württemberg, that "in contrast to the bourgeoisie, which in the eighteenth and nineteenth centuries had already developed a notion of 'inner honor' that referred to an . . . internalized moral law . . . the concept of honor among the . . . workers was still an external one."[25] The community determined honor and reputation, particularly through the gossip of women. As the "arbiters of collective norms," which policed and punished deviant conjugal relations such as adultery through such public shamings as the charivari, it was the "village collectivity" that traditionally exercised control over family affairs.[26] Barbara N., as other women in these cases, used this public language of blame and scandal to call attention to domestic disputes, and to accuse and punish her husband.

In the case of Elisabeth Magdelena H., once her husband, a landless laborer, began working out of town, she was said to have displayed both intense "jealousy" of him and "nymphomania," wrote her pastor. In other words, Elisabeth Magdelena was convinced of her husband's infidelity. The spectacle she made in response consisted of throwing her husband's clothes onto the street, running around the streets at night "undressed" making a "great racket," and hitting her husband on the head with a hoe.[27]

The peasant Wilhelmine B.'s domestic problems were seemingly related to her weak position vis-à-vis her husband's property, of which her stepdaughters stood to inherit a large part. Wilhelmine's future security thus depended on producing children of her own as heirs and future means of support. She gave birth to a girl in the first year of the marriage at the age of thirty-eight, and at the time was said to be a "moral, hard-working" wife who got along with her stepdaughters. But after five years of marriage without further pregnancies, and at the end of her childbearing years, Wilhelmine's behavior toward her family began to change. She became quiet, depressed, and "mistrustful" of her husband and stepdaughters; later, in her "paroxysms" she began "running around, drinking spirits, demonstrated lustful feelings, spoke in the most indecent ways, sang her lust in songs . . . stripped and ran around in the streets, accused her husband of not being able to have sex, called her stepdaughters whores, and even threatened them with murder."[28]

We do not know what the tailor's wife Maria M. did or said in her "jealousy attacks," but we do know from a government report that her speech and actions were of a public and "immoral" nature:

[Her] immoral behavior has become highly offensive to the public and . . . the medication for her troublesome nymphomania can not be applied, and so considering that morality, particularly among the youth, is very endangered, we have decided on . . . detention and treatment in the asylum. . . .[29]

Declaring a husband's impotency and unfaithfulness, describing his genitals, throwing his clothes out of the house—these were all acts that included
the public for the purposes of punishing a perceived domestic infracture. At the
very least, they were public acts of accusation that used scandal—the moral
and repressive force of community opinion—to proclaim domestic discord and
to call into question the rights of the husband to his wife's chastity, honor, and
loyalty. Like the tradition of charivari, which used in its punishments symbols
of "the world turned upside down" (such as the backward-facing donkey ride),
the acts of declaring one's husband impotent and publicly flouting one's
chastity and submissiveness in many ways reversed the moral and social order.

These women thus drew on a shared social language. Their communities,
however, considered them strange, dangerous, and mad. One of the reasons for
this was that, mentally distressed and isolated, the women simultaneously distorted that language and its rituals. The spectacles they created thus often lay
outside the acceptable village framework of communication. In the words of
the anthropologist Clifford Geertz, they got the cultural "structures of significa-
tion" wrong.[30] Barbara N.'s attempts to belittle her husband's character (her
public discussion of his genitals, for example) did not take place within any accepted social framework of complaint. Her "public" consisted of children, precisely those members of society who did not determine reputation, but who
were seemingly the only people willing to listen to a madwoman. In short, the
line between *creating* and *becoming* the scandal had become blurred in these
women. Through their acts, they became not only messengers, but also con-
duits of shame and dishonor.

So far, I have only discussed sexual deviancy as an act of hostility and rage
against an unsatisfactory husband, not as a matter of lust or promiscuity. Several of the aforementioned women were, in fact, not diagnosed as nymphomaniacs. The cases where women moved beyond symbolic gestures of dishonor to
promiscuity and even uncontrolled "nymphomania" were, however, not unrelated to the marital circumstances just discussed. The final case of Elisabeth W.
shows how a woman could pass over time from public accusations against the
husband, to promiscuity, and finally, to "nymphomania."

Always "moral, quiet, and hard-working," Elisabeth W. began acting
strangely after the death of her baby (four years into the marriage). Her utterances were "confused" and filled with "hatred and mistrust of her husband and
relatives, feelings of revenge, and jealousy of her husband due to his presumed
disloyalty." Because of her "tremendous garrulousness and a true loathing of
her husband," she caused a "crowd of people [to gather] in front of the house."
After medical treatment, she returned to working in the fields under her husband's "supervision." Then, one day, she attacked and tried to kill him. His cries
brought the neighbors, who pulled them apart, whereupon Elisabeth threatened to burn down the village and murder her neighbors' children. Her hus-

band demanded, and the medical official recommended, Elisabeth's commitment to the insane asylum, but, inexplicably, this did not occur until five years
later, after a second report detailed the threat she posed to her husband and
herself (having threatened to cut him or herself up), and to the community as a
whole. For as a "nymphomaniac," who has already given birth to two illegitimate children and "probably still finds occasion for extramarital, illicit contact," her potential for producing additional illegitmate children threatened to
further burden local poor funds. [31]

The story of Elisabeth's "nymphomania" began not in sexual desire, but in
the death of a baby. The feelings of hatred and revenge she felt toward her husband and family indicate that she blamed them for its death. Later, she expanded the list of coperpetrators to include the neighbors and the entire community, as seen in her threat to burn down the village and kill the neighbors'
children.

As in other cases, Elisabeth W. blamed the death of her baby on the intentional work of other people. The belief that domestic woes, such as the illness
and death of livestock, could be brought on by the witchcraft of ill-willed neighbors was still widespread in the nineteenth century. [32] But since Elisabeth and
her counterparts included their husbands among those responsible for bringing
on domestic tragedy, the evil occurrence was felt to emanate not simply from
outside, but from *within* the home. It was in the context of retribution that accusations of sexual infidelity first surfaced as a public issue.

In Elisabeth's accusations, her husband's infidelity—a violation of marital
obligations and symbolic of a wronged wife—seemingly functioned as a metaphor for the attack on the house. Though one cannot know exactly what was
going through her mind (or the minds of other women who made a similar
mental link), it is worth noting that in the role and function of sex in this society, the death of a child could be associated with the infidelity of a husband. If
marital sex served in the support and continuity of the household through the
children who would then inherit, work, and preserve the farm, then both the
death of a child and the infidelity of a husband could be seen as threats to
the house. And it perhaps required only one further mental step for the two
to become linked in the minds of distraught mothers. This was not a "rational"
or logical connection, but a way of associating in a fit of great emotion and
inner disturbance two things that felt like they belonged together. We do not
have any details about Elisabeth W.'s later promiscuity, but her case shows well
the domestic environment of extreme marital tensions in which it took place.

One can understand aspects of the mental disturbances of these women
without adopting the medical categories of either the sources or of present-day
psychiatry. Their traumas had an historical and cultural logic: these women
manipulated their "symbolic capital" of sexual honor to announce domestic
and other wrongs, punish their husbands, and make claims to certain spousal

rights, such as the husband's fidelity or economic support. At the same time, the women distorted that language and transgressed the boundaries of acceptable village discourse—in their speech and actions.[33] These themes are developed further in the following section on the "nymphomania" of single women.

Single Women and the Language of Desire

In 1846 a poor peasant woman, forty years old and single, was admitted to the Eberbach asylum. Nothing much was known about Catharina K., observed the commitment report, except that she was hard of hearing and, according to the *Schultheiß*, had once before been insane as a child of seven. She was often "lost in thought" and had inherited nothing due to her "idiocy." Lately, since the medical examination several months ago, the "signs of nymphomania" are unmistakable. Her "idée fixe" is that she is pregnant and wants to marry:

> Every male whom she sees she assails and seeks to embrace with a look of longing, and each time she asserts this is the father of her child [and] shamelessly lifts up her clothes in order to convince the people of her pregnancy.[34]

The asylum staff agreed with the initial diagnosis:

> The mental confusion is very great and appears clearly as nymphomania. She looks at every man with lust, approaches him with great desire and friendly smiles; she is expecting her groom [and] wedding finery. [Furthermore] she gives vague and unsatisfactory information about her former manner of living, [and] her mental development has remained behind.[35]

No amount of reasoning could convince Catharina that she was not pregnant. She complained incessantly of pain in her abdomen and breasts, and desperately pleaded for someone to help her give birth. But no one did. She protested, "For the last four and a half years I must carry around a strong child in my body and no one wants to remove it." The number of babies inside of her increased to three, and then to six. Later they died, their putrefaction fouling the air, preventing her from sleeping. Twenty years later she died in the asylum.[36]

Catharina's "nymphomania" was an obsession with marriage and birthing. Marriage in peasant society, as Schulte puts it, "offered a woman ultimately the only possibility of securing for herself and her children economic security, status, prestige, and a place in the village community."[37] Childbirth, producing children who ensured the continuity of the farm, was among the most important social functions of women.

While marriage was crucial to a normal adult existence, impoverishment and the restrictive marriage laws of the Vormärz made it increasingly impossible for large sections of the rural and urban poor. Like most other German states, Nassau required as a prerequisite for marriage *Bürgerrecht* (the rights of citizenship), which in turn depended on the possession of a secure occupation and a certain amount of property.[38] At the same time, the widespread poverty of Nassau's population ensured that many people would never succeed in fulfilling these requirements. Women were particularly impacted by these circumstances due to the female-male imbalance in Nassau's population.[39]

Catharina's experience typified that of dozens of female patients at Eberbach: single, poor, unable to marry and hence become independent, adult members of their society. The ages of these women ranged from nineteen to sixty-five. They had been servants, day laborers, beggars and vagabonds, and daughters of poor peasants or day laborers. Some, like Catharina K., had physical infirmities or had long been considered simpleminded or imbecilic; others had illegitimate children; still others had had unblemished reputations as upright and hard workers, and may even at one time have been engaged to marry.

The theme of marriage, its frustration and failure, runs as a leitmotif through these cases. It included women who came to be diagnosed as nymphomaniacs as well as those whose mental disturbances took other forms, such as depression or persecution fantasies. "Failed marriage plans" often figure in their case histories. Maria L.'s marriage was prevented because her fiancé was denied *Bürgerrecht* on the basis of his "meager circumstances."[40] Elisabeth D.'s marriage plans fell through when her master reneged on an inheritance he had promised her.[41] Anna S.'s progression from "melancholic" to "nymphomaniac" began after her fiancé suddenly left her to marry another girl.[42] Margaretta M. became insanely obsessed with a "middle-class" boy whom she met at the inn where she had worked as a servant and who had "drunk to her" (a sign of love).[43] Because of this obsession, she was forced to leave her job and was finally committed to the asylum.[44] The insanity of Agnes T., a thirty-two-year-old servant, was said to be related to "failed marriage plans." In the asylum, she complained of being "tormented by the poverty of her siblings." With her parents dead, her siblings were the only family from whom she could have expected help in amassing a dowry in order to marry.[45] Catharina V., a thirty-year-old day laborer, was described by her parents as pacing the room at night "speaking constantly of romances and marriage."[46]

Jewish women faced the additional problem of discriminatory laws. The disproportionate number of Jewish "nymphomaniacs" (nine out of ten female Jewish patients were diagnosed as such) was perhaps a product of stereotypes of Jews as immoral and oversexed. Still, no other social group faced more barriers to marriage than Jews, who not only required the requisite amount of wealth (a rarity for the generally poverty-stricken Jews of Nassau), but also the status of *Schutzjude,* which was limited to only those few able to pay *Schutzgeld* (protection money).[47] Thus we see Hannchen M., the twenty-three-year-old daughter of a poor Jewish butcher, express in her "raving" not only "marriage plans," but also the fact that she "does not want to be her parents' child."[48]

In short, the obsessive desire for men that seemed to characterize "nymphomaniacs" was not undifferentiated lust in search of an outlet; it was connected to the problem of attaining marriage. The doctors believed that Catharina K.'s indiscriminate pursuit of men, her dishonoring assertion of pregnancy, her "shameless" raising of her skirts in public, and her "mental confusion" were the results of a genital eruption that had consumed mind and body. Catherina's behavior, however, was focused on marriage: when she "assails and seeks to embrace . . . every man she sees," the idea in her mind was that she was "pregnant and wants to marry." Her alleged pregnancy, though a delusion, was a key to attaining that goal. In peasant society, a pregnant woman who had consented to premarital sex with the expectation of marriage but whose lover subsequently denied her this, could force marriage or monetary compensation if she could prove that the "engagement" had taken place. But to be successful, she needed a spotless reputation; the existence of a prior relationship ("engagement") had to be proven; and the relationship had to be a socially sanctioned one between two people of equal social and economic standing who had the means to support a family.[49]

In her fantasies, Catharina took bits and pieces of this tradition, recombining them into a wholly eccentric usage that invalidated the very claims it sought to make. Instead of a single, specific man, Catharina asserted that "every man she saw" was the father of her child. She seemed to think that multiplying her claims would make them more persuasive. She did this in the asylum with her increasing number of unborn babies, and also in the community with the profusion of fathers to her child. But, of course, the act of indiscriminately claiming a number of men as the father of her child made a mockery of the whole tradition she sought to use to her advantage, since its purpose and justification was the enforcement of sexual honor and the value of chastity, as well as the protection of the material interests of the propertied. A member of the community, the *Schultheiß* seems to have understood Catharina's confusion of its signs and symbols, for he considered her an "idiot," not man-crazy.

The late nineteenth century saw the appearance of a new diagnostic term for nymphomania: "hypersexuality." The historian Elizabeth Lunbeck has analyzed how this concept was used to control the sexuality of young, single, working-class women in turn-of-the-century America.[50] The women labeled hypersexual and subject to the repressive measures of psychiatry and the criminal justice system were the "'new women' of the working class,"[51]— the first generation of women living independent lives in cities, able to enjoy the pleasures of commercial entertainments and a new sexual autonomy in dating and premarital sex.

Despite some parallels, a vast distance separates Lunbeck's modern, urban working-class women experimenting with their sexuality from the peasant "nymphomaniacs" of this study. For the latter, sexuality was not conceptualized as a matter of personal autonomy and self-expression; this conceptualization required a notion of sexuality as inhering in the person, to be liberated or repressed, as well as a degree of financial and personal freedom that did not exist in the small towns and villages of Nassau. For these women, lust and desire were inseparable from and embedded in issues of property, social status, honor, and survival. The social logic of Catharina's "man-craziness" was that of the single, propertyless woman in a society where marriage was both necessary and beyond one's reach. Its cultural logic lay in the manner in which she expressed her troubles through a shared village language of rights, claims, honor, and shame. Nymphomaniacs like Catharina both used and, in their mental distress, distorted that language.

Women were obsessed with marriage because it was essential for attaining economic security and social status—in other words, the material and symbolic resources of the community. Demands for a man by poor man-crazy servant women were thus in part about access to those resources by the village lower class from those who monopolized them. Man-craziness thus, at one level, has to be understood within the context of the rural class tensions endemic to Vormärz Germany—the product of demographic, social, economic, and political changes that had led to a proletarization of the countryside. The interesting thing, though, about nymphomania was the distorted and usually indirect way in which these class tensions were played out in the community; namely, as illness rather than as direct, political action. Medicine, state, family, community, and sometimes the women themselves played a role in the process by which social problems were transformed into psychopathology.

The case of Elisabeth K., a village servant woman unable to marry, starkly illustrates this process. Hard of hearing, forty-six years old, poor, single, and without family, Elisabeth had become convinced that, as her former mistress put it, "evil people are responsible for the fact that she still has not gotten a husband."[52] Elisabeth's guardian, a villager housing her since her outbreak of insanity, described the symptoms at the onset of the mental disturbance:

> Elisabeth [K.] . . . served at Johann Philipp Ries in Esch . . . until February of this year. Already last year, [Ries] had often complained to me that he could no longer hold out with this person since she is no longer obedient. Rather she opposes his wife when she wants to oblige [Elisabeth] to work, and attacks [the mistress] with shovel, wood, and similiar things, so that [the mistress] must flee from her. [Elisabeth] also not infrequently calls her a whore . . . who prevents the gentlemen from coming to [Elisabeth].

Elisabeth's hostility soon embraced others in the village:

> I have had her in my house since she left her position. At night she talks with herself, grumbles about God and the world because [as she says] she has been prevented from marrying, and threatens to cut her throat. She runs after the people on the street with scythe, sickle, and whatever she can get hold of. . . .

The use of the vague "the people" (not unlike the generic "men" of the asylum staff) served to cover up any outer, social context that could have lent rationality to Elisabeth's rages. This was precisely the function of the many village testimonies in the case: to rid themselves of a disturbing and dangerous person, the villagers suppressed enough of the context of behavior to make Elisabeth appear wholly out of her mind and to cover up their own complicity in insanity and rage. Elisabeth's mistress was not just any employer, but connected by family to the power elite of the village. Of the eight people who testified to Elisabeth's dangerous outbursts and insanity, three had the last name Ries: the former mistress, the wife of a peasant, and the *Schultheiß* himself. The other testimonies came from Elisabeth's guardian, the local minister, a widowed seamstress, an eighteen-year-old nailmaker, and a baker who, at the relatively young age of twenty-three, possessed the financial means to marry. Thus, Elisabeth's accusations were largely directed at those who controlled the power and resources of the community, and her demands for a husband were in part claims to access those resources. In her rages and, perhaps, even in her assumption of a conspiracy against her, Elisabeth had put her finger on a larger, less evident truth about the relationship between marriage, power, and property in the community.

The medical view of Elisabeth was completely at odds with that of the villagers. The medical reports of her were very sympathetic, describing her as an "entirely harmless," "good-natured" woman who, though mentally confused, was still capable of working and did not belong in an insane asylum. Her "amorous fantasies, which she brings in connection with men of higher standing," were interpreted as "compensation . . . by the imagination . . . for the lack of a favorable situation." In the asylum, Elisabeth "willingly complies with everything . . . and strives with great attention to appear pleasing and active." Feeble-minded and hard of hearing since her youth, "through teasing, abuses, and other unsuitable treatment at home, she was, it seems, induced to violent acts."

In stark contrast, the village reports by the pastor and *Schultheiß* described Elisabeth as extremely dangerous, threatening to burn down the village, attacking people on the street, hitting the *Schultheiß*'s daughter, and speaking about "sexual relationships in the crudest and most unrestrained manner. . . ." Village testimonies were gathered in addition to plead the case for her incarceration against the initial medical recommendation. These testimonies strongly confirmed the views of the *Schultheiß* and pastor. The seamstress described how Elisabeth pursued her seventeen-year-old son into the house and cursed him; the eighteen-year-old nail-maker related how Elisabeth cursed him and went after him with a scythe; the former mistress told of Elisabeth's "immoral speech," her threats to cut the throats of "people" and burn down the village, and that "when she sees children on the street, without any cause she pursues them with curses and threats . . .", and so forth.

The discrepancy between the medical and village views was in part related to the fact that Elisabeth's rage was not directed at the doctors, but at those people she believed had prevented her from marrying. But, as Basting surmised, it was also the case that she was treated poorly in the village. Such details as the "children on the street," whom the mistress portrayed as victims of Elisabeth's wrath, indicate how the village testimony involved the suppression and transformation of events to deny its own responsibility in Elisabeth's insanity. Teasing and torment by children in the streets was one of the most common and predictable ways in which village culture reacted to a bizarre or mad individual. Understandably, the latter usually reacted with rage and cursing. But the testimonies against Elisabeth gave the impression of only unprovoked, irrational violence.

The topic of sexual desire was a convenient one in this village project of denial and suppression. From the evidence, the village did not view Elisabeth as a nymphomaniac: she was publicly talking about sex and offending people, but apparently she had not behaved promiscuously. However, one villager did bring up the topic of sexuality: the *Schultheiß*. In his report to the asylum, he commented on the causes of her insanity:

> [H]er mental confusion and danger [were in part caused by the fact that] since childhood the person has been hard of hearing and thus could not have the benefit of school-teaching, and in religious matters has remained entirely unversed [*unerfahren*]. Later on, in her darkness, thoughts of marriage from the stimulus of nature [*Reiz der Natur*] fixed themselves rigidly in her head.

Thus the *Schultheiß* turned what was essentially a fight for community resources into a matter of sexual desire and ignorance. Sexual desire here functioned as an ideology of rural power to deny or cover up its own power and the demands of the powerless. This is not unlike what occurred in the doctor-patient relationship. Only in this case, medicine played the role of sympathetic supporter against the hostilities and fears of the community.

These women were not born marginalized and man-crazy; they became so through a drawn-out social and psychological process that occurred within families, communities, and the women themselves. In most of the cases, that process has been lost to us because of the limitations of the sources. However, the case of Anna S. is different, allowing us to follow the events of one woman's life as she became mentally troubled and finally a "nymphomaniac." It suggests the interdependence of social marginalization and man-craziness, the position of powerlessness from which these women fought to defend their honor and fend off marginalization, and the circumstances, both internal and external, of final mental breakdown and outcast status.

At the time of the first medical report on her in 1847, Anna S. was twenty-seven years old and had been living in Niederlahnstein with her widowed mother since being forced to leave her servant job one year earlier in nearby (Bad) Ems. Though poor, Anna's upbringing had been "moral and pious," and she had always "behaved well."[53] The physician diagnosed melancholia and described her symptoms as follows:

> At first she manifested sadness, fear of people, [a] taciturn, fearful demeanor, and by degrees [she] articulated [her feelings]: she is an unhappy, vile creature not worthy of living, and wishes she were dead. She hides herself in a corner under the bed in the loft, or escapes to remote places where she stays away for days; then moans aloud and tears her hair.[54]

The first signs of Anna's illness began one year earlier, while she was working in Ems. "She had to leave her position as house servant because she no longer had the energy and attention to work." The report concluded that the cause of her melancholia was "purely somatic," lying in the "watery circulation of the blood . . . [and its] congestion to the brain and spinal cord."[55] The "purely somatic" diagnosis was not, it seems, unrelated to the limited amount and nature of information about the patient the doctor had at his disposal. With respect to her mental predispositions and inclinations, he noted that "the patient can not be brought to speak more than a few words, and her relatives are not at the cultural level to be able to sufficiently express themselves on this matter." In other words, the patient was not talking, and her relatives' opinions were not considered worth listening to.

The reasons for Anna's feelings of anxiety, depression, and self-loathing begin to come into focus when we learn from her 1879 autopsy report what had happened to her in Ems: She "had a relationship with a fellow who had already promised to marry her. However, just before the arranged wedding day, he jilted her and married another girl."[56] "Disappointment in love," as alienists liked to call such situations, does not adequately explain the extremity and nature of Anna's reactions. These were in direct proportion to the enormity of what was at stake for her in the marriage and its loss—"economic security, status, prestige, and . . . [a] place in the village community." Her poverty further decreased the chances of another marriage offer. Then there was the dishonoring way in which the relationship had ended. With her "moral and pious" upbringing, Anna appears to have dutifully followed the sexual codes of her society, granting her lover a "relationship" only with the clear understanding that marriage was to follow. By virtue of the jilting, she had squandered her sexual honor and thereby part of her symbolic capital for the future:

> The reputation of a woman seems to have been dependent on her ability to realize the price for "consented " sexuality, that is, the providing of social and economic security on the part of the man [through marriage]. The adherence to these "terms of exchange" was in the interest of women themselves, representing for her reputation an essential element of her capital, a precious commodity, which was to be turned into material capital at the highest possi-

ble price, and whose possession was the prerequisite for a "good" marriage and thereby material independence.[57]

Finally, compounding the tragedy of her failed marriage, Anna S. had lost her job, a loss of potentially devastating consequences for a servant girl from a very poor family. It forced her and her mother onto poor relief; and since the job loss was the result of incompetency, in the long run it would also negatively impact her reputation and thus her ability to find both work and another marriage offer.

The medical official recommended Anna's commitment to the asylum:

> I do not believe she can be cured in her present place of residence, for the melancholy sometimes increases to raving attacks and in this state she becomes dangerous to her surroundings. Also, she often runs off [during] intensifications of a purely melancholic condition, stays away a long time, and is without supervision. Her mother, as I have said, is poor and posseses neither the means to look after her nor to have her treated. . . . [58]

Committal, however, did not occur until two years later. The events triggering it were explained in a report by the medical officer writing to the district office of the government:

> Already two years ago, Anna [S.] was ripe for the asylum . . . but since the family is entirely without means [*ganz arm*] and the local poor relief office was not able to cover the costs, and, further, her condition noticeably improved, becoming more tolerable, so she was left with her mother . . . and there were no further occurrences and complaints . . . But for a few weeks now, the illness has been noticably increasing, and a true nymphomania [*Mannssucht*] is appearing. Evenings, she runs out of the house and gets herself the first best deckhand and indulges in love with him; further, she imprudently goes to the village and even [goes] unseemly uncovered to church with the boys, so that moral decency is very much offended.[59]

In the space of two years, then, Anna had gradually moved from a state of social limbo, after the loss of her fiancé and job, to complete social ostracism; from depression to sexual behavior that placed her outside of and against the norms of her society. Whereas her situation two years earlier had meant a loss of reputation, the behavior prior to commitment was so dishonoring that it could only have represented a kind of social suicide.

Anna's nymphomania and social marginalization developed symbiotically. In both her emotions and behavior, we initially see her integrated into the social order, scrupulously adhering to its sexual codes. However, the jilting revealed the uselessness of her efforts: she had failed at turning her good behavior—her honor—into real, material integration. Servant girls worked with the hope of amassing a dowry for marriage. With her hopes and plans dashed, Anna S. no longer had "the energy and attention" to work. In a very short time, then, she had lost the symbolic and material relations—as a marriageable woman with a good reputation, as a worker, and as, finally, a fiancée—that bound her to the community. Traumatized, she began acting in ways that further marginalized her. "Complaints" were lodged about certain "incidents." She was stigmatized as mentally ill, "ripe" for the asylum.

Anna's initial reactions to being wronged and dishonored were those of someone who, though in despair, still had a stake in the rules and judgments of her world. She was afraid and ashamed of herself, seeking to hide herself physically and the past (neither she nor her mother breathed a word of her failed marriage to the medical offical). Her offensive behavior continued to be seen as that of a "purely melancholy state." It was in the context of her outcast position as madwoman—someone shut out of the normal path of sexuality through marriage and therefore no longer possessing a stake in upholding the norms of sexual chastity—that she later became sexually promiscuous. But at the same time, like the aforementioned Catharina K., Anna continued to be internally bound by the rules she flouted and to pursue marriage and respectability. She now did so, however, by resorting to desperate and crazy measures that served only to marginalize her further. A second report at this time gives us a better sense of Anna's desperate and conflicted state of mind as outcast and village lunatic:

> A few weeks ago, [Anna S] . . . began again to suffer from a striking restlessness. At night she got out of one bed and into others; could not sleep, [was] anxious "because [as she says] guys are at her window, looking into her room, and making a scandal." During the day, she could not be made to stay at home; her conduct on the street gradually became such that the children ran after and teased her; and even in church, which she visits every morning, she is merely the laughingstock of the children. In her speech she is daily becoming unclearer, names specific people who will marry her, even though those people have never given her reason for such thoughts.[60]

In Anna S.'s world, boys who gathered at night in front of a girl's window did so as a form of courtship. Rainer Beck describes the nightly ritual:

> Individually or in groups the young men paid visits to [the girls] under the window to engage in the game that signified the encounter of the sexes—a game of skill in word exchanges, in challenge and retort, a test of behavior in the form of request and denial, and a competition for the allocation of success and respect within the collective village youth.

This "*Fenstern gehn*" could also "serve to mediate the boys entrance to the girl's room," where boys and girls courted by laying together in bed, but only engaging in sex when and if the couple had become engaged.[61]

The imagined boys at Anna's window expressed, it seems, both a wish and its danger and denial. No courting boys would in reality have stood at her window; only outsiders, transient "deckhands," who risked nothing to their reputation and future, would have anything to do with her. The appearance of courting boys at her window was precisely what she longed for. But in her fantasy, the boys outside came to make a scandal, to harm her reputation. No longer a "play" of "challenge and retort," the boys represented an ominous, threatening presence. In this way, the fantasy encapsulated a truth of Anna's life experiences: she had once been the girl at the window; she had played the risky game of "denial" and "seduction,"[62] and had lost. Men were dangerous; the betrayal of her lover had cost her her honor and begun the chain of events resulting in scandal and madness. The scandal made by the boys also expressed the knowledge and its denial of Anna's own scandalous behavior and its social repercussions, now returning in the fantasy as a projection onto the boys. It was not marginalization per se that made Anna mentally disturbed, but the contradiction between the internally "pious and moral" girl, and the external nature of events that drove her to ever more desperate and dishonoring measures to salvage her honor, while at the same time loosening the bonds—internal and external—that made renunciation of sex both necessary and possible in her society.[63]

Precisely in their desirability, men were a dangerous threat. Maria S., also a servant but raised *bürgerlich* by a joiner father, had not only had an affair but had gotten pregnant by a man (a *Kaufmannsdiener*) who subsequently refused to marry her. Her fantasies twelve years later at the time of her commitment to the asylum were summarized by the doctor as follows:

> According to [Maria S.], she is constantly gripped by nearby and far-off men—only men—through a magical power whose effect is trembling in her legs and anxious restlessness. The pressure [*Spannung*] is caused chiefly by distinguished secular and ecclesiastical gentlemen. She is religious, and [she believes] a close connection with God protects the honor of her sex against the threatening dangers from the pressure.[64]

Desire for men could not be admitted; it was therefore transformed and projected onto a male magical force. If this was the work of a punitive "super-ego," it was also the result of the very real danger to the self posed by men and sex in this and other women's lives of the time.

Strikingly, Anna S. did not take legal steps to demand either marriage or financial compensation for her lost honor as a result of her lover's betrayal. Schulte explains how poor, propertyless villagers were not able to defend their honor against better-off peasants through legal means, and thus were sometimes even driven to the radical and desperate step of arson—for revenge and the restitution of their honor.

> Property inequality produced . . . inequality in the possibilities of protecting and restoring one's honor. The more limited and the thinner the ground on which the individual reproduced himself, the less chance one had to obtain justice in a dispute; only the rich could allow themselves to go to court. Someone who had nothing, and was nothing, was treated as such.[65]

This situation probably explains Anna's inability or reluctance to take legal steps. Anna's impoverished background, her separation from a support network of family and acquaintances, and her precarious, provisional status in the town of Ems (not her hometown), would have put her in a weak position to assert her claims.

There was a connection between the inability or unwillingness to take legal action and Anna's mental illness. Rather than blame her ex-lover or any other external cause, she turned her anger against herself, convinced she was a "vile creature not worthy of living." In some ways, her later man-crazy behavior was merely an extension of this self-loathing, involving as it did the extremely self-destructive step of actually acting out what a "vile creature" does.

Anna S. shared with other single women who became mentally disturbed over the problem of marriage and/or sexual honor a position of powerlessness to "make her case." The reactions of these women varied. Having become pregnant while "working for a young master," Maria G. saw the devil and spoke of being damned.[66] The thirty-four-year-old servant Helene H.'s mental troubles were said to be connected with "the unfaithfulness of a lover." In her "insanity," she "views all old people as witches and sorcerers, and an old man in W. as the devil"; "she believes that [these] witches and evil people exert influence over her."[67] Maria K., fired from her job as a house servant by her master's wife, who suspected an affair between Maria K. and her husband, did try fiercely to defend her sexual honor in the manner available to her. Fearing she was pregnant, having finally admitted to allowing her master "a sexual favor," she now demanded a "capital" as repayment for the loss of her "virginity." The weakness of her position vis-à-vis her former employer and within the community as a whole can be seen in the mounting desperation with which she pursued her goal:

> If at the beginning she was reserved about her alleged moral lapse, so now, after the course of several weeks, she speaks all the more eagerly to everyone about this, and relates without being asked the smallest details. If she was earlier quiet, now she is a very talkative person who goes from house to house in the village, does not work . . . [and] speaks constantly of a capital which she asserts must be paid her due to her lost virginity [*Unschuld*].[68]

The servant woman Maria L. had been engaged to marry a farmhand, but the marriage had to be canceled when her fiancé was denied *Bürgerrecht* due to his poverty. However, her "mental disturbance was first noticed" not at the time the marriage permission was denied (1819), but two years later, "particularly," according to her brother, "since Michaelmas" (September 29)—the day her former lover married another woman.[69] After this event, Maria could no longer keep a job. At home, she violently blamed her mother for her failed engagement; spoke constantly of her planned marriage; said she wanted to kill herself and other people; threatened, in particular, to cut the throat of a certain servant woman; viewed herself as bewitched and damned; and was haunted by a ghost.[70]

Until her ex-fiancé's marriage, Maria L. apparently had continued to nurse hopes, however desperate, that the original decision against her marriage could be reversed—that things would finally work out. As in Anna S.'s case, mental disturbance surfaced at the point where expectations and hopes for a marriage appeared irrevocably lost. The feeding ground for mental disturbance, in other words, was not poverty per se or a generalized feeling of hopelessness among poor peasant women. On the contrary, it would appear that, perhaps because they were so poor and had such few opportunities in life, these women placed tremendous worth in thinking about and planning for the future in their imaginative lives. Mental breakdowns occurred when those sustaining hopes and fantasies collapsed.

Both in terms of symptoms and circumstance, the nature of "nyphomaniacs'" breakdowns, as we have seen, was related to (though not causally determined by) the social-economic crisis of the Vormärz and its specific affects on women, given the nature of village morality, social-familial relations, and the facts of biology (i.e., pregnancy and childbirth). Sexual honor and marriage were defining elements of women's lives in general and of the anguish and conflicts that pushed these women in particular over the edge to become outcast madwomen and nymphomaniacs. The married women in these cases had lived in deeply troubled marriages where, in their eyes, husbands were either violating or simply not fulfilling their marital duties. Single women, faced with an array of social and economic barriers, had been unable to marry and turn their sexual honor into material and social integration within the community. Given these circumstances, it does not seem surprising that mental breakdowns revolved around the problem of men and sexual identity, that rage and revenge were expressed through a language of sexual honor and scandal, that fantasies and longings focused obsessively on getting a man, and that, finally, mentally confused and socially ostracized, a desperate search for honor and respectability could be pursued with the most dishonoring promiscuity. In this social and nonclinical sense, perhaps one can go so far as to speak of a gender- and class-specific form of going mad. Though partly overlapping with nymphomania, man-craziness had a life of its own outside the confines of medicine and can be understood in terms of the social tensions and cultural framework of village life in Vormärz Germany.

Gilbert Heerdt's anthropological study of sexuality and madness in New Guinea provides an interesting counterpoint and comparison to the issues in Nassau.[71] The condition of New Guinea women disturbed by "wild man," a recognizable form of madness in the culture, took the form of hypersexuality in ways that closely resemble many of the Eberbach cases. "Wild man" included behavior that was "sexually shocking and seductive," gossiping, failure to "perform normal routines and work," and speaking about "sexual adventures."[72] Those afflicted with "wild man" were mostly married women whose husbands, apparently, were abusive and adulterous.[73] Whereas madness in women was sexualized, the symptoms of "wild man" in men revolved around hyperaggressivity and violence. These polarized forms of madness reflected, according to Heerdt, the polarized sex roles in the culture: women were socialized to be subordinate, dependent, and sexually repressed, and viewed as "pollution-bearing agent[s]"; men were viewed as dominant and socialized "for aggression and violence in the context of warfare." In this sense, "wild man" madness, Heerdt argues, represented New Guinea gender norms in exaggerated and normally forbidden forms. At the same time, for women it functioned as "an escape mechanism, a safety valve," that allowed the expression of repressed sexuality and anger.[74]

European peasant conceptions of sex roles do not appear to have been as polarized, and man-craziness did not have the same quasi-official status as an identifiable illness. Despite these and other differences related to their very different contexts, there are some striking parrallels between man-craziness and wild man: in both cases women were subordinate in the society and family, and that subordination was closely tied to norms of female sexual chastity. Further, female hypersexuality in both cases was associated with abusive marital relationships (although not exclusively in the Eberbach sources) and rage. Is this then a question of a single cross-cultural phenomenon with merely different cultural expressions? To answer in the affirmative one would have to assume sexuality to be an innate force, whose repression inevitably finds an outlet (a "safety valve") through sexualized forms of madness. And yet this study (along with others) has shown that this essentialist conception of sexuality is itself an historical construct, one that underpinned nineteenth-century medical conceptions of nymphomania and enabled medicine to redefine man-craziness and other female sexual transgressions as clinical entities. There were alternative, competing models and experiences of sexuality in the Eberbach sources, even as the medical model of nymphomania worked to stifle and transform the patients' views. What man-crazy German peasants and hypersexual "wild man" women shared in common was less the experience of sexual repression per se than the fact that both lived in societies that constructed female subordination in sexualized terms, which thus provided troubled women with a set of sexualized female idioms to express social and personal distress.

III

Delinquency
and Criminality

7

Masturbatory Insanity
and Delinquency

As argued in chapter 4, masturbatory insanity was closely linked to male identity and contemporary notions of masculinity. An additional factor contributing to the obsessive focus of medical practitioners on masturbation was the usefulness of the concept of masturbatory illness to the professional interests and aspirations of medicine and of alienists in particular, a group who embraced the notion of masturbatory illness with special fervor.[1] According to Gilbert, the masturbation diagnosis partly derived from a gap between the "prestige and skill level" of the medical profession. This disjuncture drove doctors "to explain diseases of which they had inadequate knowledge in terms of the moral feelings of their patients."[2] The issue for psychiatry, this chapter argues, was not so much a gap between prestige and knowledge as the use of a new type of knowledge to enhance the prestige of mental medicine. For it is surely not coincidental that the frenzy over masturbatory insanity coincided with the period in which a nascent psychiatry was struggling to establish itself as a legitimate medical specialty. The notion of masturbatory illness was also, as Foucault has pointed out, connected with the power relationships of nineteenth-century institutions, such as the school, the army, and the insane asylum.

The following case study of Johann A., a single, thirty-five-year-old farm laborer and former soldier, shows the role played by the institutions of the army and the insane asylum in masturbatory insanity. It also suggests how masturbation could play a crucial role in the expansion and legitimation of psychiatric expertise through the insertion of a discourse of sexual pathology into areas of behavior long viewed and treated as disciplinary or criminal matters. It did this by providing the scientific basis for the diagnosis of illness in ambiguous cases, where distinctions between delinquency and illness were unclear. The use of the masturbation diagnosis for disciplining male delinquency varied, both institutionally and culturally, by social class. The second part of the chapter explores the different ways that male masturbatory insanity was coded in, and experienced by, lower- and middle-class men.

The Case of Johann A.

Guilty of misbehaving in the military, begging, drinking, and not working, Johann A. became the object of a series of disciplinary measures and medical observations that eventually culminated in his committal to the insane asylum. In the course of Johann's evolution from disciplinary problem to certified lunatic, various experts and local officals generated a body of explanations and proposals that is strikingly indecisive and contradictory. Shunted in and out of institutions, retained for further observation; and described as a lazy simulator (of insanity), ripe for the workhouse, mentally deficient, and insane, it was at first not clear whether Johann was a criminal, a moron, a lunatic, or merely lazy. The concept of masturbatory illness ultimately unlocked the case.

Johann was first called to the attention of the authorities in 1842 by the *Schultheiß* of his town, Münster. "Feebleminded," "parentless and propertyless," Johann was deemed incapable of working and likely to cause a disaster: "he has already sharpened a knife and wants to cut his throat." The report concluded with a request from the district authorities for instructions on how to proceed.[3]

The medical officer Dr. Thilenius, who was subsequently ordered to deliver an opinion on the case, sent his assistant, Dr. Streitter, who reported his findings:

> I visited him immediately after receiving the requisition, but after a one-time examination, I could not give an opinion, especially because I heard different judgments on [Johann's] mental state by various people. He has a healthy physical constitution, was always healthy in his youth, and [was] supposed to have shown not inconsiderable mental capabilities at school. He later served six years in the Nassau military to the satisfaction of his superiors. After he was released, [Johann] served for 2 1/4 years in Frankfurt, and then was released as ill. *I could not find out what illness he suffered from* [at that time]. During his present stay in Münster, he manifests an especially great laziness: he either does not do the work given him, or incompletely, or incorrectly; speaks little, and, as a rule, answers questions directed at him with, "I don't know" or "it's none of your business." This is how he answered me as well. As a rule, he goes from one inn to the next, extorts drink and food, and then lays himself down in the nearest barn or stall to rest. Also, he is supposed to have thought

of cutting his throat. [I am] not able to find a hereditary predisposition to insanity in his family. Although his behavior, speech, and expression give reason to believe that he suffers from feeblemindedness [*Geistesschwäche*], all of this could be simulated in order to be able to indulge his laziness. I would thus consider it expedient to observe him for a while in the local jail; then, if his feeblemindedness turns out to be true, to send him to the insane asylum in order to prevent him from doing harm to himself and others" (emphasis mine).[4]

Typical of the Eberbach cases, the initial notification on Johann's mental state—the event beginning the incarceration process—originated not from a doctor greedily searching out mental cases, but from a local official concerned with problems of public order and security. The *Schultheiß* did not use the term "feebleminded" in a clinical sense based on a theory of mind. He was interested purely in Johann's behavior, which he judged in terms of the man's willingness and capacity to perform daily tasks and preserve his existence. Johann was a problem because his social position (poor and orphaned) and his behavior placed him at the margins of the community, potentially dependent on public poor funds and committing criminal acts.

Once notified of Johann's behavior, the authorities called into motion the medical apparatus, not the police. By the time of Johann's comittal, medicine had become central to state strategy in its policies toward social deviancy, a fact, at the institutional level, made possible by both Nassau's newly created medical system and the existence of the Eberbach asylum. The authorities' readiness to perceive the problem of Johann A. in medical terms is striking. Objectively, the evidence could have supported either disciplinary or medical measures. That the medical view prevailed, apparently in large part on the basis of the term "feebleminded," is even more striking, given that the *Schultheiß* himself had been thinking in terms of disciplinary measures. In a second report, the *Schultheiß* recommended that Johann be put "under supervision in a place where he is made to work," even though he is "mentally ill."[5] Still relatively new, the medical strategy of employing a disease model of insanity and seeking to free the insane from their criminal status had not yet prevailed at the local level. For Münster's *Schultheiß* and many other ordinary Nassauer, the asylum was a disciplinary, not a medical, institution.

The state may have favored a medical strategy for dealing with Johann, but the doctor called in to examine him could not himself decide whether the matter was medical. If the *Schultheiß*'s rather hazy use of "feebleminded" sufficed in the area of public security, it remained for Dr. Streitter to find the scientific basis on which deviancy could be established as illness. This proved to be difficult. Proceeding from the assumption of the interconnectedness of body and mind, Streitter searched for a possible somatic cause—physical illness, inborn idiocy, or heredity—of mental illness. However, the data came out negative: strong body, had always been healthy, displayed not inconsiderable mental capabilities in school, and had no hereditary propensity to insanity in his family. Regarding Johann's illness in the military—the last somatic possibility—Streitter's inquiries had not yet yielded the pertinent information.

Unable to find the cause of Johann's symptoms in organic dysfunction, Streitter turned to the murkier area of behavior and speech. But lacking a somatic cause, Streitter was left with a purely normative basis for interpreting Johann's behavior, largely dependent on public, lay opinion, itself divided. He noted that Johann was not working, which now took on overtones of laziness instead of incapacity, and that the latter had taken to visiting inns ("prowling about"). There were also the new factors of Johann's lack of speech and "expression," which the *Schultheiß* had not mentioned. Analysis of such factors was necessary for a determination of the inner workings of the mind and whether it was deranged. Here as well, however, it was not clear whether Johann's taciturnity could be read as mental dysfunction or as speech consciously controlled with a specific purpose, related to work behavior not by way of mental incapacity but via delinquency. For given the absence of overtly (raving) insane behavior, and Johann's demonstrated mental capabilities, together with the lack of a somatic basis and the divided views about him, the question necessarily arose as to whether he was simply pretending or was truly ill. How was one to distinguish between laziness and idiocy?

Though Dr. Streitter did not yet have the answer, the articulation of such a question was itself significant. The *Schultheiß* had *equated* Johann's behavior with feeblemindedness (and later, insanity), under the apparent presumption that no one in their right mind could act so contrary to their own social and economic interests. Streitter's notion of simulation, however, raised the issue that Johann may have *wanted* to appear ill, consciously constructing the image of idiocy in order to indulge his delinquent habits. This was a common refrain in the files of criminals and delinquents who underwent examinations for possible insanity. It was a term particularly suited to and reflective of contemporary liberal conceptions of the individual as an inherently (when healthy) rational being, who attains freedom through the exercise of a free will grounded in reason. Mental illness thus represented the "loss of freedom"—a mind bereft of control over will and desire—and thus the inability to act in one's own best interests. The concept of simulation embodied this view of mental illness in its language (and strategy) of deciphering the signs of free will (simulation) or its absence (mental illness). In the second half of the century, when the mind was reconceived in biologically deterministic terms, criminality itself became a form of pathology.[6] Here, it was a question of categorizing and distinguishing between criminality (delinquency) and illness.

That a poor laborer would freely and consciously *want* to appear as an idiot, something that the *Schultheiß* seemed not able to conceive of, derived from contemporary images of the immoral and delinquent lower orders. Such people, it was believed, needed to be kept in check and inculcated with the moral values of industry and discipline. This bourgeois notion of lower-class delinquency acted in Johann's case as a check against the medicalization of his condition. For the idea of immorality normatively inhering in a person by virtue of his belonging to a specific group (the lower classes) provided the conceptual space for the coexistence within him of free will (i.e., mental health) and deviancy. This mapping of class onto the grid of medical categories seems to have been at the heart of Streitter's indecisiveness.

Johann was released when no decision was taken on Streitter's recommendation for further medical observation in the local jail. One week later, the *Schultheiß* again wrote to the district authorities, complaining of Johann's behavior and recommending his incarceration: "the people are fed up with [Johann's begging], and they don't give him anything anymore"; he also now went around "suspiciously" dressed in torn clothes, having lost his "good clothes." Johann, he opined, should be incarcerated in order that he "no longer can go around like this, in the event that he can easily cause a misfortune" (*Ungluck*). Even more clearly than in his first report, the *Schultheiß* portrayed Johann as a dangerous, marginal figure who had progressively taken on the attributes of the criminal underclass. Despite Johann's unacceptable behavior, the fact that "the people" had given him food and alms indicates that he had hitherto retained some connection to the community. His appearance ultimately cast him out (at least in the *Schultheiß*'s eyes), making him a "suspicious," potentially dangerous figure.

Clothes symbolically located the person in a social space: "good clothes" meant, at the very least, the ability and right to participate in the ceremonial (religious and civic) activites of the town. The shedding of these clothes for those of a poor beggar signified in perhaps the most concrete terms not only Johann's changed economic status, which had already taken place, but also the symbolic stripping of his social being. Not coincidentally, this loss of social identity coincided with the *Schultheiß*'s shifting adjectives—from "feebleminded" to "insane." The substitution of insane for "feebleminded" seemingly referred to the aggravated threat posed by the symbolic death of Johann's social self. For the lunatic was a danger because, no longer guided by social norms and regulations, his/her behavior became unpredictable and uncontrollable. Likewise, through the self-immolation of his social being, Johann placed himself outside of his community and its rules and customs. He thus moved conceptually from "feeblemindedness" to madness.

For medicine, on the other hand, the loss at issue in insanity was "reason." A proper medical diagnosis required (in addition to the factor of abnormal behavior) the discovery of a malfunctioning of the body or the mind. The illness might manifest itself in social deviancy, but its essence was essentially a private bodily/mental process—hence Streitter's examination of first Johann's body and then his speech and expression.

The medical men continued to be stymied. Streitter failed to come up with a judgment one way or the other. As a result, Johann was transferred to the civil prison in Höchst, "where then the possible existence of insanity can best be ascertained"—in other words, where the more experienced and higher-ranking *Medizinalrath* Dr. Thilenius could take over the case.[7] It was while Johann was under observation in the Höchst prison that a fresh piece of evidence came to light that clarified the case once and for all: masturbation. This was the piece of somatic evidence—the illness he had suffered from in the military—that had earlier prevented Streitter from arriving at a diagnosis.

Together with Johann's former military record, the evidence of masturbation had arrived in a medical report from Frankfurt am Main. Its author, garrison physician Dr. Pfefferkorn, had treated Johann six months earlier for "feeblemindedness" in the Frankfurt military hospital. The latter had been transferred to the hospital as a result of "unmanageable and obstinate behavior," for which he repeatedly had been punished. The behavior consisted of dirtying his room, neglecting his personal belongings, neglecting his uniform, behaving coarsely to his superiors, drunkenness, refusing to obey orders, and squandering his personal belongings. Disorderliness, disobedience, drunkenness—these were disciplinary problems, and had been treated as such for months. But despite ever-harsher punishments, nothing seemed to get through to the delinquent recruit: "neither persuasion nor punishment did any good," and the delicts actually began to occur "more frequently." The officer in charge, *Hauptmann* Busch, finally transferred Johann to the military hospital, with the remark: "[I] can't make him out"; he "seems to be feebleminded."[8]

Dr. Pfefferkorn found Johann to be "on the whole rational"; but his "unmistakable feeblemindedness" called for "closer observation." We know in part what that observation consisted of from the evidence it yielded: "frequently stained shirts and linen." The diagnosis was now clear. "[Johann A.] had succumbed to the vice of onanism, and this was the cause of his feeblemindedness." Pfefferkorn proceeded to "fully cure" his patient by tying up his hands at night, administering cold douches over his head, and giving him medication. At the end of this treatment, not surprisingly, Johann requested a discharge from the army. Since "his malady could easily return if he succumbed again to onanism," his request was granted. Dr. Pfefferkorn concluded that because Johann A. was again exhibiting signs of "mental confusion" that he had, despite his resolve, "again become addicted to the vice of onanism," and if careful and strict measures were not taken, "idiocy" would develop over time.

With Pfefferkorn's report in hand, Dr. Thilenius wrote to the district authorities several days later that, after "closer observation" of the patient, he was now "convinced of the genuine existence of insanity, manifesting itself in a weakened mind and mental dullness" (*Verstandesschwäche und Stumpfsinn*). The attached "testimony" (Pfefferkorn's report) "confirms this assumption, and indicates a very important cause—onanism." Johann's previous behavior in the military also supported this diagnosis. Thilenius concluded by recommending Johann's incarceration in the insane asylum, since he could not be properly cared for and guarded, let alone cured, in his present circumstances, and might even become dangerous.[9]

Three weeks later, by order of the *Landesregierung*, Johann A. was committed to the Eberbach asylum. Masturbation had been the critical factor in deciding the case in favor of mental illness. Indeed, it was the *only* proof offered in Thilenius's opinion. He had written of being convinced of insanity after "closer observation," but had not provided a single piece of empirical evidence. The order and language he used to present the facts of the case implied that the "testimony" of Pfefferkorn merely "confirmed" (with the cause masturbation) a diagnosis previously arrived at independently on the basis of his own "observation." In fact, we can assume it worked precisely the opposite way: knowledge of Johann's history of masturbation, gleaned from Pfefferkorn's report, promptly allowed Thilenius to read illness into previously ambiguous and confusing signs, ones that had baffled Dr. Streitter who had not been privy to the garrison reports. At the same time, there was a certain "confirmation," though not exactly in the way Thilenius implied. The masturbation information confirmed illness by endowing an already held, but medically unprovable, belief with the gloss of scientific explanation. Thilenius's readiness to accept Pfefferkorn's diagnosis derived in large part from the way that Johann's symptoms perfectly matched the medical model of masturbatory illness. In his "laziness," his avoidance of work in favor of the good life (drinking and sleeping), and his "feeblemindedness," Johann embodied the classic male masturbator. In this sense, Pfefferkorn's report confirmed what Thilenius may have suspected from the beginning.

For the second time in the space of six months, Johann A. had gotten himself in trouble with the authorities, who finally, exasperated, came to suspect mental illness. For the second time, doctors were able to confirm this as a medical fact with the diagnosis of masturbatory insanity. There was, however, a difference: the first doctor had found the "evidence"; the second one based his judgment on the fact that another physician six months earlier had found the evidence. This was not the last time Johann's case was to be diagnosed on the basis of Pfefferkorn's (now practically famous) stains. From the day of Johann's admission to Eberbach, Pfefferkorn's diagnosis determined his treatment. Soon after his arrival at Eberbach, Basting wrote that "onanism is supposedly . . . the cause of [Johann's] idiocy, however the existence of this sin has not yet been established; closer observation is thus indicated."[10] That the confirmation subsequently failed to materialize did not dissuade the asylum from its course of treatment.[11]

There were probably two related reasons why, lacking direct proof, the asylum embraced the masturbation hypothesis. First, they lacked another, more convincing explanation for his "symptoms." Basting noted that, based on his appearance, appetite, and "all physical functions," Johann's "physical state seems in the best of condition."[12] But Johann's healthy appearance "contrasted extraordinarily" with his mental weakness: he was now described as "an extremely dumb and degenerate person . . . He is a perfect image of idiocy." Windt phrased it as a "lack of attention, intelligence . . . [and] desires . . . rather great indolence and indifference." These symptoms matched the textbook image of the masturbator, and thus, once again, given the lack of any other cause, seemed to clinch the case for masturbation.

The relationship between symptoms and diagnosis was, however, not merely a matter of matching the appropriate diagnosis (masturbation) to a set of "objective" signs: in temporal terms, diagnosis did not unambiguously follow the prior and independent assessment of symptoms. Rather, the symptoms could only be seen after a diagnosis was at hand. Thilenius saw "true mental deficiency" only after he was in possession of Pfefferkorn's masturbation "testimony." Likewise, the asylum read the classic masturbatory symptoms of idiocy into behavior that was at best ambiguous. Despite his "idiocy," according to Basting, Johann "still sometimes rises and answers questions slowly but fairly clearly and rationally; but, as a rule, he does not answer at all, and looks around shyly and is always embarrassed." Windt noted that he "either did not answer questions at all or [did so] monosyllabically and evasively. His staring expression gives proof of dull brooding [and] lack of intelligence. . . ." With the exception of shyness and embarrassment, the now-convincing signs of idiocy were the very same ones that Dr. Streitter earlier saw as possible simulation or delinquency.[13] In this way, once suspected, masturbation took on a momentum of its own, lending not only scientific credence to their diagnoses but enabling the various doctors to decode as illness signs that otherwise had no clear meaning or that led in the direction of indiscipline and delinquency.

Institutions and Lower-Class Masturbators

Masturbatory insanity proved to be a highly effective tool for the expansion of medical expertise into the areas of social deviancy and delinquency. In this respect, it was the ideal disease: having pathologized a (presumably) common act, the likelihood of discovering it—through observation, the telltale stains, or patient confession—was high. In any case, direct proof was not even necessary, given the secretive and supposedly shameful nature of the act. It was presumed that patients naturally hid their behavior. In such cases, one had at one's disposal an all-encompassing set of symptoms—various states of mind, attitudes, and physical appearance—from which to draw out the truth. Moreover, as an act that was repeatable and hard to monitor, and given theories that allowed for a direct and sometimes instantaneous relationship between act and disease effects, secret masturbation could be used to explain otherwise inexplicable relapses or to rationalize the inefficacy of medical treatment. Such was the case with Carl W., a twenty-four-year-old student of philology, whose doctor, after treating him with no success for what he had diagnosed as abdominally based hypochondria, turned to onanism as the suspected cause.[14]

In Johann A.'s case, institutions were central to the making of a masturbator. The setting of masturbation observation was not the barns and stalls of Münster, but the garrison hospital, a space of confinement, where the expert's "gaze," searching the most intimate details of body and mind, was able to penetrate lower-class taciturnity ("it's none of your business"). In many middle-class cases, families vigilantly monitored and reported to physicians any signs of onanism. Institutional confinement (normally the insane asylum) was, by contrast, the space par excellence for the discovery of lower-class onanism. It rarely came to light in the village context; and generally only after doctors had plied family members with questions about semen stains or suspicious hand positions.

The case of Christian S., a thirty-year-old, unmarried son of well-off peasants, provides a sense of how this process could work. The examining physician described Christian's symptoms as disobedience, avoidance of work, and excessive lying in bed. On the question of whether the "nerve-dynamic has suffered from excesses in love, onanism, nightly pollutions," the doctor noted:

> Showed no particular liking for the female sex. The father does not know if [Christian] has taken to onanism, yet [*doch*] he clearly notices for some time that [Christian] brings his hands in the vicinity of his genitals. However, of excessive spilling of semen [*Samengießungen*] nothing yet noticed.

In the above particular sentence construction, the word "doch" (yet), a qualifying term that reverses a negative statement, indicates that the father had not voluntarily offered the information on the position of his son's hands; he did so only after the doctor's questions forced reflection on the matter. If in this medical examination, the father had "not yet" noticed "semen spilling," by the time of his son's commitment he was able to "indicate [to the asylum staff] that [Christian had] frequently had semen stains in his underwear."[15]

Generally, masturbation questions yielded no results: the families simply had not been watching out. Though the act itself may have been proscribed as sin (as per church doctrine), and there are indications from patient statements that it could be interpreted in medical terms, there is no sense from the Eberbach files that masturbation was viewed as a disease entity in village culture. Even less is there a sense that masturbation generated the kind of anxiety and obsessive at-

tention that it did among the middle classes. It was apparently not closely monitored, and it did not occur to most families that there could be, as medicine suspected, a connection between this act and their relatives' mental symptoms. The
family of the dyer Ludwig J., for example, had long been struck by his indifference
to the female sex, "without, however, suspecting the real cause": masturbation
since age twelve, which the patient had "confessed" to the doctor.[16] Typical of
lower-class families, the peasant family of Johann V. had "not noticed" if he masturbated.[17] In only one case did a lower-class family member indicate onanism as
a sign of insanity, and this case involved a wife observing her husband masturbate "the entire night" after he had been released from the insane asylum and
was still under strict medical observation.[18] Lower-class patients became masturbation cases through the intervention of doctors, either from patient confessions or, more frequently, from a variety of observational techniques in the insane
asylum. There were many reasons why families and communities considered
these patients mad; masturbation, however, was not (explicitly) among them.[19]

Patients kept their views and feelings about masturbation to themselves.
They answered the medical interrogations curtly—either confirming, denying,
or waffling on the issue. No doubt, this reticence reflected the more general distrust of medicine and asylum that is apparent in numerous lower-class cases. It
also probably reflected the feeling that, as Johann A. had put it, "it's none of your
business." Case notes usually described reactions of embarassment to questions
about masturbation, which physicians interpreted as an affirmation that it had
occurred. In only one case did a lower-class patient feel a need to justify his actions to the doctors, and he did so by using the language of medicine to make a
case for the *benefits* of masturbation, arguing that he could only get healthy
through the "proper flow of seminal fluids"; indeed, that his illness was the result
of "repressed sperm-evacuations."[20] In fact, this patient's medical logic proceeded impeccably from the same humoral theories now used by educated doctors to reach the very opposite conclusion—that masturbation caused illness.[21]

If lower-class patients displayed a "wrong-headed" or lackadaisical attitude
toward the "vice," the asylum acted promptly and vigorously to disabuse them
of their views. The joiner Phillip B. "received factual instruction regarding the
harmful effects of onanism."[22] About the patient August H., the seventeen-
year-old son of a tailor, an asylum report explained:

> Onanism is the occasioning cause of [his] physical disorder and insanity. He
> claims he no longer does it; however, this assertion is very much in doubt.
> Ideas of all sorts already seem to have made some impression on the [pa-
> tient's] mind. Particularly frightening to him are the examples of people
> ruined by onanism.[23]

The medical log noted of the thatcher Joseph K., after he had spent several
months in the asylum: "Committed bestiality . . . He regrets very much this
act and feels ashamed of it."[24]

Families, Experts, and Middle-Class Masturbators

Punishment and "education" were required to awaken a terror of masturbation in lower-class patients. It was a different story with middle-class patients. An 1824 commitment report of a twenty-one-year-old court clerk (*Scribent*) described how the "thought of having himself destroyed his body from that sin [masturbation]" led him to try to "put an end to his life with poison."[25] Unlike their (preinstitutionalized) lower-class counterparts, middle-class patients had been surrounded—in the family, school, work, and medical consultations—by a series of authority figures and self-appointed masturbation experts educated and vigilant in the signs and gravity of "the sin." The medical candidate Joseph H. was first caught masturbating at school (a *Gymnasium*); his teacher threatened to expel him if he did not stop it. Years later, at age twenty-five, after having failed his medical exams and become emotionally disturbed, his mother and brother-in-law assured the examining doctor that Joseph still masturbates "when he finds the opportunity."[26] The civil servant (*Recepturaccessist*)[27] Gustav V. first came under suspicion of being an onanist by a charge made by his former employer, who had arrived at this idea on the basis of Gustav's "external appearance and the occasional distortions of his facial features."[28]

One also sees this monitoring of onanism in a family consisting of both craftsmen and more elevated members of the bourgeoisie proper. The patient himself (Phillip S.) was a journeyman joiner, and one of his brothers was a master joiner. But two of his other brothers were military officers, and a brother-in-law was an *Amt* secretary.[29] This family needed no direct prompting from a medical authority to suspect and investigate the possibility of masturbation after Phillip's first "attack of insanity." His captain brother explained: "one observed him sharply, inspected his underwear and linen, but discovered no sign of it." In a letter to the asylum, the brother also noted having found among Phillip's papers pictures of naked women with their genitals showing, adding: "I mention this because he [Phillip] led me to suspect that secret sins had occurred."[30]

This spying and reporting on, discussing, and analyzing of masturbation—what Foucault calls the "incitement to discourse" about sexuality—involved a fundamental ambivalence. As Foucault puts it: "Is it not with the aim of inciting people to speak of sex that it is made to mirror . . . something akin to a secret whose discovery is imperative, a thing abusively reduced to silence, and at the same time difficult and necessary, dangerous and precious to divulge?"[31]

The case of Adolph H., the previously mentioned twenty-year-old law student, shows how this ambivalence played itself out in the relationship between family, patient, and doctor in the discovery of masturbation. A brother-in-law in Weilburg, whom I will refer to as B., initially vehemently denied the doctor's suspicion of masturbation. Later, however, this same brother-in-law sought out the doctor "in order . . . to notify me [the physician] that [Adolph] is an onanist, that [Adolph] had confessed this to him [B.], and that [the latter] had himself communicated this information to his relatives, adding that in the future one should notify the doctor immediately."[32]. At about the same time, Adolph's brother in Nassau received a letter from a friend of the family, Georg, in Heidelberg (where, presumably, Adolph had been studying) informing him:

> I know, but you do not, that [Adolph's] entire illness is the result of onanism, and his future doctor must be informed of this, otherwise he can not adjust his treatment accordingly. Don't let [Adolph] know that you know about his guilt. For otherwise, he could perhaps become totally raving. In general, it is a characteristic of this type of sick person that they love secrecy and privacy.[33]

Apparently this friend had received his insights from another doctor—the "most capable doctor in Heidelberg" (Karl Pfeufer)—whom he had recently consulted about Adolph's condition.

This case was not a simple matter of monitoring and discovery, of making known the unknown. Rather, the masturbation problem entailed at once knowing and not knowing, vigilance and denial, speech and silence. The initial indignation aroused in B. by the doctor's presumption was a mark of the shame and silence surrounding masturbation. But not knowing meant the repression of knowledge, not ignorance or indifference. The intensity of B.'s subsequent confession to the doctor, the anxious, exaggeratedly conscientious way he sought out the latter, was equal to, and the psychological complement of, the intensity of the initial denial; both reactions reflected the shame and danger of masturbation. On the one hand, silence, on the other, the anxious need to speak the truth. This polarity underlies as well the letter from the friend Georg to the brother. The remark "You do not know, but I do" contains the same heavy (verging on aggressive) confessional tone of B.'s encounter with the doctor. Georg then made a plea for informing the relevant doctor—for speaking the truth. At the same time, nothing of this should be uttered to Adolph, as he would not be able to take it. The idea that the masturbator himself (his potential response) was to be made responsible for the regime of silence and the denial of knowledge —"[the onanist] loves secrecy and privacy"—was a neat way of protecting the family from their own squeamishness by projecting the shame onto the patient.

On two separate occasions, the suspicion or knowledge of masturbation originated with physicians via the communication of a male family member or close intimate acting as a mediator between the family and the doctor. Initially rejecting the very idea, Adolph H.'s family, once having come to terms with and proven the truth of Adolph's masturbation, in turn became the purveyors of the knowledge to his future doctors. Something of the serious responsibility and burden weighing on the possessors of masturbation knowledge comes through in both B.'s and Georg's statements. For such knowledge bore the duty of speech/confession against the desire for silence. The family-doctor relationship in the matter of onanism bore all the markings of such ambivalence: on the one hand, the sense of medical intrusiveness and the desire to hide a private, shameful matter; on the other hand, speech—the confession of patient to relatives and the confession, in turn, of relatives to doctor—was required to provide the expert with the tools to effect a cure.

This speaking about and monitoring of onanism continued unabated in the asylum, where Adolph H. was again forced to "confess" the act and plied with ever more "detailed" questions about, for example, the "extent" of his masturbation, and when it first began. Adolph agreed with the asylum about the cause of his illness (masturbation), but he refused to "give more precise information" about how much he had done it.[34] The asylum noted that at school, Adolph had been one of its best pupils; but "hallucinations," brought on by onanism, had prevented him from taking his examinations, and he was forced to drop out. His genitals were examined and, despite the "self-abuse," they seemed healthy, but he had a "weakly constitution."[35] Once again, it was a question of the mental and physical ruin of manhood from the "vice." It was good news to the asylum that Adolph "hopes and tries to master his passion." Treatment, however, involved strengthening and envigorating the body, while ridding it of its confusions.

Masturbatory insanity provided a new way of seeing the person, one that included a set of symptoms so all-encompassing that it opened the doors to the pathologizing of a wide array of behavior, much of which lay in the realm of indiscipline and disobedience. Masturbatory insanity, in other words, became a tool of almost unlimited potential to force men into shape—mentally, physically, financially, and socially. These men posed problems for their families and communities: they were behaving in inappropriate and disturbing ways, such that action was required—either of a medical or disciplinary sort. But how were the authorities to decide what sort of action to take? Most of these men did not outwardly appear mad: they were not raving, hallucinating, or displaying any of the other obvious signs of madness that doctors used to diagnose insanity. Yet their behavior seemed strange, often irrational, and was certainly unacceptable. Here, in this grey zone of illness and indiscipline, is where "masturbatory insanity" was so useful. It provided a coherent, scientifically based explanation for otherwise mystifying cases of social deviancy. In so doing, it pointed the way to a solution: medical cure in the asylum. In this way, the "illness" was a boon both to families and communities, seeking to rid themselves of unwanted members, and to the nascent field of psychiatry.

8

Jews and the
Criminalization of Madness

Baron: And is it not true, their countenance has something that prejudices one against them? It seems to me as if one could read in their eyes their maliciousness, unscrupulousness, selfishness of character, their deceit and perjury. (G.E. Lessing, 1749)[1]

He has not yet shown his true character . . . through [his] mask of dissimulation he wants to escape punishment of his crime. The roguish Jew-face, the groveling flattery, the purposeful silence and withdrawal are not suited for weakening this suspicion. (Eberbach medical register, 1829–1830)[2]

Distinctions between delinquency and illness were ill-defined and problematic, as we have seen in the case of the masturbator Johann A. And it was precisely in this vague grey zone between the two that psychiatry was able to insert itself in defining a new mental pathology. The problem of deciphering the difference between delinquency/criminality and madness was further complicated and given a unique twist in the cases of Jewish patients, whose Jewishness (in the eyes of the asylum) was by definition a kind of criminality and immorality. Jewishness, in other words, represented a category of interpretation distinct from illness, one which, in turn, had become highly politicized in the debates about Jewish emancipation since the eighteenth century. Therefore, when race was used to interpret patient behavior, it constituted a form of thinking outside of the medical domain in the strictest sense. In this way, it was potentially at odds with the medical process, and could, as I will show in two case studies, function to prevent the asylum staff from seeing and treating patients as ill.

This chapter thus examines the limits of the medicalization of deviancy—the points where, in contrast to the "illnesses" discussed heretofore (male masturbation, nymphomania, and religious madness), medicine pulled back, seeking explanations for the person in a framework outside of the terms of medicine. That extramedical framework drew from long-standing stereotypes of Jews as immoral and criminal; but it also had a more immediate source in a contemporary trope that united Jewishness and criminality in a social type: the *jüdischer Gauner* (Jewish crook). Such images of Jews had in turn become part of the political arsenal of those opposing Jewish emancipation on the grounds of an incorrigible Jewish "character."

My argument here runs counter to the few historical works on Jews and insanity, which, consistent with the medicalization thesis, have focused exclusively on the conflation of Jewishness and illness in medical theories. In part, this approach derives from their focus on the second half of the nineteenth century, where the conflation was indeed overwhelming, psychiatry and medicine (as well as other human sciences) having become saturated with racial and degeneration theories. Jan Goldstein has traced the emergence of a discourse on Jewish propensity to mental illness in France, from the disciplines of medical statistics, anthropology, and demography in the 1860s, to the "Jewish nervousness" treated by Jean-Martin Charcot and the Paris Salpêtrière school at the turn of the century.[3]

Sander Gilman makes much more sweeping and less convincing claims about the historical identification of Jews with illness, arguing for a conflation of Jews with illness that stretches back to the Middle Ages.[4] "Medieval thought had long associated the Jews with disease." Jews, like lepers, were "marked . . . with inherent signs of their difference . . . [they] were also associated with the transmission of illness . . . [allegedly causing] the plague by poisoning wells."[5] As the ultimate "outsiders," according to Gilman, Jews were always more likely to be seen as ill, but in the nineteenth century the medicalization of Jews took on added steam in reaction to Jewish emancipation as a means to maintain them in their inferior, excluded status. The notion of a Jewish propensity to mental illness served as a neat justification to keep Jews as outsiders, just as psychiatry in general served to maintain the second-class status of other marginal groups:

> In the course of the nineteenth and early twentieth centuries a number of . . . justifications of the myth of the mental illness of the Jews emerged. European biology served . . . to reify accepted attitudes toward all marginal groups, especially the Jews . . . Jews, like women, possessed a basic biological predisposition to specific forms of mental illness. Thus, like women, who were also making specific political demands on the privileged group . . .

Jews could be dismissed as unworthy of becoming part of the privileged group because of their aberration.[6]

Edward Shorter has approached the topic with a quantitative study of admissions records of a late nineteenth-century Viennese nervous clinic.[7] Shorter seeks to explain the reasons for the disproportionate number of Jewish patients in the clinic and their overrepresentation among those patients diagnosed with manic-depressive disorders. While the focus is on precisely the sort of data consistent with arguments about medicalization, Shorter approaches the material from a completely different theoretical position. He rejects the notion that mental illness in history is to be seen as a social construct—of controlling deviants through labeling them mad—an assumption that provides the conceptual starting point for much of the work on medicalization, including the two studies previously discussed. Rather, his argument largely derives from the older Whiggish approach that sees insanity as a real disease entity, whose forms may be influenced by culture, but which is at base a biological (and thereby transhistorical) fact. Shorter therefore uses medical data from other periods and places to support the curious thesis that the diagnostic patterns in nineteenth-century Viennese Jews had at least in part "a very real biological basis," namely, defective genes that predispose them to certain types of nervous disorders. This is an argument, in other words, that rejects the concept of medicalization only to embrace something approaching the terms and assumptions about Jewish illness of its nineteenth-century sources.

There are two striking things about Jewish madness that emerged in this study's qualitative analysis of the daily encounters between Jewish inmates and their gentile keepers, both of which challenge many of the assumptions and categories of the secondary literature on medicalization. First, attempts by asylum (and prison) authorities to define what it was that they saw in Jewish patients had an extraordinary fluidity, indecisiveness, and shifting quality. There was more than one way of interpreting Jewish deviancy (as illness or as Jewishness), and categories of perception differed according to the particular patient under observation; they also could shift over time in the observation of individual patients. Second, Jewishness and illness were not conflated in medical practice; they were quite distinct categories in the early nineteenth century. Indeed, it was precisely those Jews who were most stereotypically "Jewish," those Jews who felt the full brunt of anti-Semitism in the asylum, who were least likely to be seen and treated as ill. Those Jews who were treated as ill were so, not because they were Jews, but despite this fact. In other words, the more a person was a Jew, the less he or she was a patient.

Extramedical factors such as class and gender, we have seen, figured constantly in medical evaluations of patients. Unique to Jewish patients is the explicitness of this fact, which makes the operation of extramedical (anti-Semitic) thinking easily distinguishable from moments of "pure" medical interpretation. Characteristics of patients were explicitly called Jewish, and the Jews themselves were the only patients whose nonmedical identity had an explicit appellation: "the Jew. . . ." In contrast, peasant or Catholic patients were not called "the peasant . . ." or "the Catholic. . . ." Jews were also generally treated more harshly than other patients. An 1821 asylum report to the government, for example, stated that "Punishment measures are only rarely used due to the especially manageable patient population. Exceptions are some lunatics from the line of Judas [*aus dem Stammen Juda*], against whom one must always proceed with the greatest severity."[8]

The Jewish cases therefore provide an especially good opportunity to analyze the interaction between two different, and in some ways competing, modes of thought in the treatment and interpretation of patients. They allow access to the social dynamics of anti-Semitism as it operated in daily practice. I have therefore deliberately chosen to examine in depth two cases where anti-Semitism became a dominant theme, taking particularly vicious forms, in order to probe the boundaries and limits of contemporary medicine. As we shall see, the limits lay where Jews were *most* marginal, deviant, and "outsider"—as criminals, defecators, and religious fanatics. "Jewishness" in the asylum was a social identity, which the asylum itself helped to (re)produce through, ironically, the very institutional mechanisms set up to cure illness.

The very small number of Jewish patients at Eberbach makes any quantitative analysis of the sources problematic and limited. Still, it is worth noting that Jews did have a slightly higher rate of incarceration than non-Jews, a fact that could be interpreted to support the notion that the former were more likely to be medicalized. Out of the 459 Eberbach cases, sixteen, or 2.87 percent, were those of Jews, while in Nassau, on average from 1821–1843, Jews formed only 1.66 percent of the population. The Jewish rate of incarceration was therefore 3:1,000, as compared to the slightly lower rate of 1:1,000 among non-Jewish patients (Catholics and Protestants).[9]

Poverty, and all the problems associated with it (the inability to marry, fear for one's survival, alcoholism, social marginalization, etc.), was the leading cause of mental disturbance and incarceration among Eberbach's patients. Of all the social groups in Nassau, Jews were the poorest and in every way the most disadvantaged. Despite the influence of Enlightenment ideas, and a short period of liberalization under Napoleon, Jews in Nassau lived under the old legal restrictions, discriminations, and "special" (noncitizen) status embodied in the concept of the *Schutzjude* (tolerated Jew). Nassau's 1806 law regarding Jews established a series of restrictions for acquiring *Schutz*, whose purpose was "to limit the number of Jews in the territory and to make the establishment of poor Jews in Nassau entirely impossible."[10] The right to found a family and earn a living was reserved only for certain categories of Jews who qualified for and possessed the financial means to purchase the required *Schutzbrief* from the government. Moreover, Jews were denied all civic rights in the community and barred from certain trades and professions.

The role played by poverty and legal discrimination in the events leading to incarceration can be seen in an examination of the commitment reports of Eberbach's Jewish patients, almost all of which tell stories of economic and social hardship, including the inability to marry, the loss of a trade, a failed love affair with a Christian, and complete pauperization. The institutionalization of virtually all of these patients was paid for out of local poor funds.

There was not an across-the-board higher incarceration rate for all Jews. The percentage of female Jewish patients was more than twice as high as that of their male counterparts. Out of a total of 177 female files, 5.6 percent were Jewish females, whereas, out of 284 male files, Jewish males constituted 2.1 percent of the total. Interestingly, this gender-based overrepresentation was the reverse among gentile patients, whose males outnumbered females on average by a ratio of 2:1. Again, the numbers involved are very small and therefore could be misleading. Still, it is worth speculating on their meaning.

Nassau's official statistics do not allow one to correlate these figures with total population numbers by gender. However, given the restrictive laws on Jews' rights of residence and economic activity, the overrepresentation of female Jewish patients may have reflected in part their higher proportion of the Jewish population as a whole, with male family members often forced to emigrate or find work intermittently outside of Nassau. Of the many other possible factors, two others deserve mention. The admission policy of Eberbach favored "dangerous" and out-of-control lunatics. Drinking among gentile males was among the leading causes of dangerous behavior (or the perception of its possibility) leading to incarceration, whereas it was never a factor in the cases of Jewish males. Goldstein, citing the work of a French doctor (whose views represented those of the Paris faculty to which he belonged) in the second half of the century, states that "alcoholism was virtually unknown among the Jews; yet it was an epidemiological axiom of the day that alcoholism accounted for one-third of all cases of insanity."[11]

But it was not just alcoholism that may have been absent from Jewish communities. There was also probably a much tighter rein on violent behavior, and certainly in relation to non-Jews. Given their extremely precarious legal position in Nassau, as elsewhere in the diaspora, in which Jews were at best "tolerated," not citizens, and subject to persecution and expulsion, it would stand to reason that Jews had developed coping strategies that ruled out the privileges of anger and violence.[12] Since males of working age were crucial to the support of the family for both gentiles and Jews, the step towards incarceration of such a family member was not taken lightly; it normally occurred only when the person had become either dangerous or completely unproductive, and the two often figured together. If it is true that there was a much lower violence level among Jewish males, this could account for the refusal of families and communities to commit their Jewish male members, even when such people displayed deviant or crazy behavior.

Finally, the examination of two male Jewish patients, and the way interpretations of "Jewishness" interfered with the medical process, suggest that the lower numbers of male patients may have had to do with a propensity on the part of the authorities and medical profession to deal with male Jewish deviants as something other than insane, namely, as criminal.

Whatever its reasons, the overrepresentation of Jews in Eberbach was not related to the conflation of Jewishness and illness in the thinking of doctors and officials. One is in fact struck by the silence of both the contemporary psychiatric literature and Eberbach's commitment reports on the subject of anything linking Jews, as a people, with mental illness. Despite the fact that Jews were referred to at this time as a "nation," they do not appear in contemporary psychiatric textbooks discussing the role of national characteristics in the form and etiology of insanity.[13] Likewise, the commitment reports, mandated by law and written by Nassau's medical officials, scrupulously avoided mention of Jewish patients' "Jewishness" in their diagnoses. When, for example, the cause of illness was deemed hereditary, this was discussed solely in terms of prior illness in the patient's family; never, as it was later in the century, in terms of a Jewish hereditary predisposition to illness (e.g., racial inbreeding) or any other racial categories. The standard questions about the patient's upbringing and education, seemingly a ready-made venue for remarks on the role of Jewish "national characteristics" in the formation of disease, was never discussed in these terms. When mention of a patient's Jewishness occurred, it was only to designate the person's religion—standard practice in all such commitment reports.

References to Jewishness were avoided because in the early nineteenth century "Jewishness" was seemingly not yet a valid and accepted category of science and medicine. The grounds for a racial medicine were being laid in this period with the rise of physiognomy, phrenology, and anthropology, but racial categories were only to be incorporated into mainstream scientific discourse when they found their biological underpinnings in the sciences of the second half of the century.[14] By contrast, in the early nineteenth century, the concept of a Jewish race generally referred to "national" and religious characteristics, not to biology. Such characteristics could be construed as inborn and immutable (the argument of those opposing the emancipation of the Jews), or as the products of environment and hence subject to reform.[15] But in neither case did the concept of race fit easily with the terms and treatment measures of contemporary psychiatry. For racial statements were of a different order than the

medical terms of bodily and mental processes through which insanity was diagnosed and treated in the early nineteenth century.

One of the tenets of contemporary psychiatry was the individual nature of
disease and its development over time. A variety of both "somatic" and "psychic" factors—social, environmental, hereditary, physical, and psychological—
needed to be carefully considered in each case in order to determine the causes,
nature, and treatment plan of the mental disturbance.[16] On this basis, an individualized treatment program was to be put into effect—hence the need for a
thorough medical opinion before admission to the asylum, requiring the doctors to consider all possible factors of the disease; hence, as well, Eberbach's
policy of isolating the patient upon admission for further observation.[17] The
reading of "Jewishness," on the other hand, collapsed individual distinctions
into the shared characteristics of a race or "nation." Symptoms read normally
as the culmination and unfolding of an individual's physical and mental past
were read instead as a static repetition of the characteristics ascribed to the
group, to be explained not in terms of an individual's past but in terms of the
person's membership in a group.

Thus, far from being conflated, Jewishness and illness represented two fairly
distinct interpretative categories. In an Eberbach release report, for example,
Windt commented that the patient's "allusions and bad jokes have their origin
more from the peculiarity of the Jewish race than from madness or mental
bondage."[18] The woman in question was released, despite the staff's acknowl-
edgment of her continued manifestations of deviancy. Implicit in her release
was the belief that such behavior had an ingrained, immutable character,
owing to its racial origins, and thus fell outside of the medical domain.

Despite their lack of clinical value, references to patients' "Jewishness" appear repeatedly in asylum reports (and in the prison reports where one patient
had previously been confined). By contrast, as we have seen, Nassau's medical
officials avoided such comments altogether in their commitment reports. The
possibility that the Eberbach staff was simply more anti-Semitic is belied by at
least two factors: the overtness with which extremely anti-Semitic views were
voiced in asylum reports to the government, indicating that the authors assumed widespread support for such attitudes; and the fact that the attitudes of
the Eberbach staff toward Jewish patients (explained below) varied according to
the patient, with the "Jewishness" of a patient sometimes playing no role at all
in his or her treatment.

The explanation lies rather in the differing nature and context of medical
observation and writing in the commitment reports and in the asylum notes.
The former's limited purpose (determining eligibility for incarceration) contrasted with the multipurpose role of the asylum—as a disciplining, pedagogical, and medical institution. This fact seems to have encouraged and legiti-
mized, perhaps even necessitated, a variety of ways beyond the medical of

grasping the indvidual. There was perhaps also the additional element in the asylum of close, continuous, and often dangerous contact between staff and patients. If it is true that the psychological context of stereotyping is anxiety,[19] then the constant fear and danger surrounding work in an insane asylum would have made staff members particularly susceptible to such psychological mechanisms. Finally, as I will suggest later, the reading of Jews as "Jews" in the asylum was related to the fit between the *specific nature* of Jewish stereotypes and the natural activities of asylum and prison.

The logic of anti-Semitism appearing in an institution associated in part with discipline and criminality proceeded from the way in which Jewishness itself was grasped in the asylum. In one sense, statements by the staff about "Jewish" characteristics seem to have derived from an emerging science of race. Consistent with the belief in the correpondence between inner person and outer features, both physiognomy and phrenology sought to discover inner personal characteristics through reading outer physical features. Despite the fact that Franz Joseph Gall, the founder of phrenology, had explicitly denied the existence of "national" skulls, phrenologists soon were applying his ideas to just that, the search for archetypal racial or national skulls. Similarly, Johann Caspar Lavatar, the father of physiognomy, had not applied the reading of facial features to racial types.[20] While phrenology's materialism generally met with unreceptive ears in Germany, it did experience a "brief vogue" in the 1840s.[21] Not surprisingly, it was at this time that the Eberbach staff frequently commented on the shape of patients' skulls, although never in relationship to racial types. Even earlier, physiognomy and the notion of the reading of personality from outer features figured in the staff's thinking; it can be seen in comments on the facial features and bodily structures of their patients, noting in the case of several Jewish patients that their faces either did or did not "betray the Jew."[22]

And yet what that quality of "Jewishness" betrayed was a character type that had nothing to do with illness. Jewishness was imagined in the language not of pathology but of criminality and badness. Characteristics referred to explicitly as Jewish included scornfulness, filthiness, craftiness, roguishness, maliciousness, curiosity, mistrust, and a scornful, mocking humor. Behind many of these qualities lay the central theme of deception—the notion, appearing repeatedly in Jewish files, that the patient harbored hidden, ulterior motives. The doctors read deception in the patients' eyes ("his eyes betray the roguish Jew"), in their face and speech ("Jewish scorn and malicious pleasure are emitted from his face and speech") and in their general appearance ("all over").

Deception on the part of patients was by no means rare at Eberbach. Alone, the large number of inmates who either sought or succeeded in escaping from the institution attests to the wiles and cunning of the inmate population in general. Deception seems to have been built into the asylum system as a survival technique. The constant monitoring of behavior and thoughts required a variety of strategies to avoid detection and painful treatment measures or punishments. It was, for example, often noted how patients talked out loud to themselves only when they thought they were not being observed. Despite this, terms of deception almost never appear in the files of Eberbach's gentile patients;[23] where they do appear with frequency is in the prison reports of inmates later transferred to Eberbach. Illness or crazy behavior typically evoked great distrust of the prisoner's motives. As described in the works of forensic specialists of the day, one needed to be on guard for the prisoner who feigned illness in order to escape punishment.[24] Hence, instances of apparent mental disturbance in prisons often required lengthy and, indeed, cunning medical observation.

The Jew as "Jew" thus shared characteristics with the simulating prisoner. One can see at work here at the very least the persistence of very old anti-Jewish stereotypes of the deceitful, conniving "Wucher" (usurer) Jew—the betrayer of Christ and the practitioner of a double standard of morality that allegedly sanctioned dishonest dealings with non-Jews.[25] As we have seen, such ideas, which had played an important role in the centuries-old persecution and ghettoization of Jews, continued to be institutionalized in the Nassau state and were closely associated with anti-Jewish opinion in the debate about the emancipation of Jews.

Naming and recognizing Jews in this context were politically charged acts. Central to the anti-emancipationist position was the attempt to preserve Jewish difference through demarcating and fixing Jewish identity with such mechanisms as special names. Emancipationists supported the adoption by Jews of Christian names in order to eradicate Jewish differences and thereby spur the assimilation of Jews into German society; by contrast, the anti-emancipationist Prussian King Friedrich Wilhelm III (1797–1840) barred the adoption of Christian names precisely because it would serve to blur distinctions between Jews and non-Jews and thereby symbolically allow the former out of the ghetto.[26]

The staff's stereotypes of Jewish criminality and its obsession with issues of transparency and difference, which I will discuss later, place the asylum squarely within the ranks of anti-Jewish opinion. But anti-Semitism in the asylum was complicated by the fact that the staff did not see or treat all Jews alike. Some Jewish patients, particularly female ones, were treated as ill and underwent the same medical procedures and evaluations as the gentile patients.[27] In applying moral treatment to these patients, the staff implicitly worked with the liberal principles of emancipationist opinion: the equality and reformability of individuals through reason and education. In other cases, anti-Semitism seriously impeded medical practice. Individual physician-observers held these contradictory positions simultaneously. In short, not set positions on the nature of Jews and illness but rather an improvisatory choice between alternative readings operated in the asylum. Anti-Semitism was thus only a latent possibility; it needed a trigger. Criminality, more than anything else, set this trigger off.

The notion of the Jew as criminal deceiver took on obsessive proportions in the case of Abraham J., a prison inmate and penniless Jew transferred to Eberbach in 1829.[28] Locating and identifying the (criminal) Jew behind a "mask" of goodness became the pressing concern of the asylum, dominating the thinking of the staff and ultimately driving Abraham to suicide. For no matter how hard he tried, Abraham was never able to dispel the distrust and sense of danger that surrounded him to the day of his death. "All the personnel were advised that he is suspicious," stated an attendant in the suicide investigation. "The Jew [Abraham J.] was known as dangerous to his surroundings," claimed another.[29]

In fact, danger was assumed from the moment of Abraham's arrival at Eberbach, even before anything was known about him other than that he had been serving a twenty-year prison sentence for repeated theft. Lindpaintner, apparently through some cultural sixth sense about Jewish criminal lunatics, had translated such information supplied on the transport papers into the notion that Abraham was "very dangerous," and the belief stuck. Later, apparent proof of potential violence did arrive in a report sent by the Hessian prison of Marienberg, where Abraham had been serving his latest sentence. The report began with a description of Abraham's "temperament"—restless, dissatisfied, quarrelsome, wicked, and vengeful—and the fact that he had wounded two prisoners (in unexplained circumstances).[30] "Also in his calmest behavior, one can easily deduce from the all-too-great mobility or, rather, from the entirely involuntary movement of his facial muscles what is occurring within him [*im Innern*] and which passions are predominating in him." The above was designated as Abraham's "temperament" (*Gemuthsart*). From time to time, his "irrational behavior" (presumably such as the wounding of the inmates) directly followed a state of madness, in which Abraham expressed the "idée fixe that he was appointed by higher inspiration to act in such a way and not otherwise, and that he must carry out this or that in order to complete that to which he was called."

Abraham's madness was for years believed to be simulated. However, close and secretive observation of him showed, on the basis of the repetition of the outbreaks at similiar but increasingly shorter intervals, his utterances of the same idée fixe in each attack, his lack of sensitivity to pain (such as his swollen hands due to his having to wear handcuffs for months), his seeming imperviousness to high dosages of nausea-inducing medicine, and his lack of hope at attaining his goal, that Abraham was suffering from "temporary insanity."

The wicked, evil criminal of this report, however, bore no resemblance to Abraham the asylum inmate. This Abraham behaved in a way that could only have been considered ideal: he was hardworking, quiet, obedient, scrupulously followed the house rules, and desperately sought to be pleasing and liked. Such behavior in other patients was praised, rewarded, and seen as signs of health. In the Jew Abraham, the opposite occurred. His behavior provoked intense suspicion, becoming itself the driving force behind a belief in his dangerous nature. For it was not change, but the discrepancy between who Abraham "really" was beneath his "mask," and who he appeared to be on the surface, that was at issue for the asylum. Given the terms of his character as defined in the prison report, Abraham's present personae could only be seen as deception. And it therefore became the task of the asylum to uncover that hidden inner quality, whether defined as character, insanity, or sanity (the terms changed over time). The asylum's strategy would be to monitor and wait for, even to coax from the patient, his "real" character.

The pursuit of Abraham's inner self behind his "mask" had been the task and central dilemma of the prison authorities as well. Divining his "real" identity had been "empirical" to the extent that it looked to observable signs. The "involuntary movement of the facial muscles," for example, showed Abraham's "passion" within. The legal question of soundness of mind and responsibility (*Zurechnungsfähigkeit*)—that is, of simulation versus insanity—the prison doctor had resolved through empirical observation, by ingeniously shifting the focus of observation largely away from the overt insanity to the points surrounding it (the periodicity of the non-insane periods) and to areas where Abraham was considered not able or aware enough to control his reactions—namely, the physical realm of pain.

For the asylum, equally concerned with unmasking the "inner" and hidden, and equally dedicated to observation, the dilemma posed by Abraham was not that of ignorance or an unknown, yet undiscovered quality, but that of the lack of a match between what one already "knew" about the person and how he appeared. Their strategy thus seems to have been one of waiting, even of coaxing from the patient his "real character."

The first phase of Abraham's hospitalization consisted of a few weeks in which his insanity was directly established in a medical examination, where he voiced the belief he was an "executioner angel" and other "irrational" thoughts. The second phase, which lasted nearly the entire three years of his incarceration, began with his "recanting" those ideas as "lies" and the beginning of his exemplary behavior: "quiet," "works hard," "acts rationally," "obedient." It is here where Abraham began to provoke the suspicion that he was hiding something about himself. The distrust drove Abraham to ever more frantic attempts at being "pleasing" and good, which only intensified suspicions: "He seeks in all manner to show himself as pleasing, is obsequious, flattering to the attendants, and, as it appears to me, he has not yet shown his true character."[31] Several weeks later: "He is being sharply observed, it seems as if one ought not trust him; he is obsequious and meek." Abraham continued to be "sharply observed," and still, nothing "definite from his behavior can be determined"; "can not be accused of any complaints." Later in that year a temporary resolution to the doubts and confusions occurred: "Abraham seems to be a good-natured Jew, who has been very taciturn [*verschlossen*] [but] otherwise calm." The "good" Jew of this passage implies that the former, suspicion-inducing and disagreeable behavior was that of the "bad" Jew. The passage also reveals a shift in tactics on Abraham's part: completely unsuccessful in his attempts at ingratiation through sociability, and sensing, no doubt, that he was evoking the opposite reaction from what was intended, he had withdrawn into himself and decided to keep quiet, while also continuing to behave as a model patient.

Suspicion now shifted to the question of whether the patient's deceit lay not in covering up his sanity, but in "hiding his insanity." To the attendant, it was noted, he was more trusting and "makes known his insanity." In the next entry, the adjective "dangerous" was used for the first time, followed by the sentence: "[He] can not be fathomed."[32] This is what had been bothering the staff for over a year and would continue to do so until shortly before the patient's suicide. It was the discrepancy between what was assumed to be within Abraham and how he behaved on the outside—that inner quality that the asylum watched for, in a sense demanded of Abraham, and which was constantly belied by his outer behavior.

Abraham and members of his family also appear in several contemporary police manuals, compilations of descriptions of criminals for purposes of apprehension and prosecution. The information from these sources allows one to flesh out Abraham's identity in greater detail and to historicize more precisely the perception of him by the asylum staff. According to a manual compiled by the criminal magistrate Schwenken in 1820, Abraham was thirty-eight years old, the eldest son of an "arch-pickpocket" (*Erz-Torfdrucker*),[33] and married to a vagabond. His six siblings were all crooks (*Gauner*) who had been or were in prison, and an uncle had been beaten to death by peasants after stealing at a market. Abraham was a "consummate pickpocket" (*vollendeter Torfdrucker*), who went by several different names and had repeatedly been under investigation for his crimes. Before 1800 he lived with his father in Eckederoth—"a haunt for every scoundrel."[34] Subsequently, until 1815, when he was last caught and imprisoned in Gießen, his life, according to the book, consisted of wandering over large areas of Germany committing petty crimes, followed by imprisonment and expulsion.[35]

Abraham was part of the marginal underclass of vagabonds, beggars, and petty criminals who roamed the cities and countryside of Germany and Europe, a group whose numbers had exploded since the late eighteenth century and who thus had become the object of a voluminous literature and an array of

state policing and disciplining measures. Jews especially suffered from the demographic and economic shifts of this period, which swelled the numbers of
poverty-stricken Jews, who, lacking *Schutz* and posing a burden to Jewish communities, were forced onto the roads in search of a means of survival.[36]
Among this rising tide of destitution were Jews like Abraham and his family,
who found their way into bands of professional thieves. Such bands had undergone extensive changes since the Middle Ages, when organized robber bands
that included both Jews and non-Jews were first formed. By the early nineteenth century, Jewish thieves generally worked in small, independent, all-
Jewish robber bands consisting of entire families, that had evolved a distinctive
subculture—in language, religious observance, dress, and lifestyle.[37] If the earlier participation of Jews in German robber bands had already "amazed" people, because it contradicted so thoroughly the popular image of "Jews as passively bearing their suffering," the emergence of independent Jewish bands of
thieves, which were considered the superiors of their gentile counterparts in
"tactics, method, and skill," turned amazement into a kind of hysteria that re-
vived and fed upon all the old myths and fears about Jews.[38]

The Jewish vagabond/beggar/professional criminal—doubly marginal,
combining both religious and social danger—figured in police manuals and
criminal justice literature as the "Jewish crook" (*jüdischer Gauner*), a code term
for a type of criminal that could apply to non-Jews as well.[39] Schwenken described the Jewish *Gauner* in the following terms: "under the mask of a traveling
salesman, a Jewish teacher seeking a position, a helpless beggar, is hidden the
most cunning scoundrel . . . robber, or murderer." "It happens daily that the
most dangerous scoundrels . . . are picked up as suspicious but released
again or sent to the place which they have claimed is theirs on their [false]
transport papers," without anyone suspecting the hidden truth of their criminality.[40] The model, in other words, was of dangerous criminality masked by an
assumed identity—a falsely benign exterior.[41]

The image of the Jewish *Gauner* drew on a certain reality: Jewish robber
bands did use elaborate disguises to avoid detection as Jews and thieves, disguises that could include wigs, the shaving of beards, use of gentile speech, and
the assumption of such alias occupations as peddler and circus performer, to
provide cover for their itinerant lifestyle.[42] But the term Jewish *Gauner* was
more than mere description; it had become a kind of trope that referred to an
entire underclass—beggars and thieves alike, two groups which were in reality
quite distinct—that threatened property in the most insidious way by its ability
to take on the appearance of normalcy and legality. The term seems to have
drawn its emotional force not only from the rising tide of pauperization, but
from the process of Jewish emancipation, which threatened to blur age-old social distinctions between Jews and gentiles.[43] It formed part of that broader dis-

cursive field concerned with the problem of locating and fixing (or eradicating) the differences between Jews and gentiles.

It is unlikely that any of the Eberbach staff had direct access to Schwenken's or any other police manual.[44] The Jewish *Gauner*, however, was a familiar figure of the period, and it played a role in structuring the social dynamics of patient-hood in Abraham's case. In the asylum case notes, references to Abraham's Jewishness appear *not* in those passages describing his recognizable moments of insanity—a "pure," readable event—but where the staff addressed the issue of the disparity between inner motivation and outer appearance. Such a reference appears, for example, at a point where the asylum had abandoned its hypothesis of hidden insanity in favor of a new possibility: "dissimulation," i.e., hidden sanity (there was no escaping the terms of deceit, whether of hiding insanity or sanity). "Through this mask [of faked insanity] he wants to escape punishment of his crime. The roguish Jew-face, the groveling flattery, the purposeful silence and withdrawal are not suited for weakening this suspicion."[45] By contrast, there was no reference to Abraham's Jewishness nine months later, when he suffered a "great upset": "[he] openly pronounced himself to be the Emperor Joseph Ludwig XVI, Christ, and other high personages. He is convinced that he has lived twelve times and believes in the transmigration of souls. He feels himself called to carry out great acts and requires therefore the greatest and strictest surveillance." The dangerous Jew returned, however, one week later. The staff noted that Abraham "has taken on again his old character [*Natur*], quiet, hardworking, hides his insanity. Is a roguish, dangerous Jew."[46]

If the two types of interpretation—medical and racial, madman and Jew—come together in the previous passage, it is not through a conflation. The insane Jew does not hide his insanity; the deceiver Jew (that part of Abraham that is his "character") hides the insanity. Yet while the two categories—Jew and madman—were epistemologically distinct, in practice they were wholly confused with one another. The case notes imply two fully intertwined discrepancies that were never consciously separated in the minds of the staff: that between (hidden) insanity and (external) rationality, on the one hand, and that between an evil-intentioned, Jewish character and the obedient, "fully legal" behavior, on the other.

Central to the confusion was the way in which the terms of Jewishness and the Jewish *Gauner*—of danger, duplicity, and wariness—closely paralleled those of insanity and were therefore easily available for substitution. It seems that *both* asylum and patient engaged in this scrambling of signs, and it structured both Abraham's treatment and his responses.

In a sense, the asylum authorities were right when they connected Abraham's behavior with his Jewishness. Abraham had a strategy for dealing with the asylum, and it is captured in the observation that he sought "in all ways to appear accommodating [*gefällig*]."[47] In other words, he sought to alleviate the suspicion and fear surrounding him. If insanity made him dangerous, then he would "recant" and "hide" it. If it was a question of an evil-intentioned, violent "character," he would seek to be as "pleasing" as possible—to "flatter"; when this, in turn, became a source of suspicion, he pulled back and kept to himself. And always, he was acutely sensitive to the asylum rules, scrupulously conforming to them. This was not the behavior of a criminal simulating insanity to "escape punishment"; nor was it precisely that of a madman simulating sanity. It seems, rather, the strategy of a Jew warding off hostility by demonstrating that he was a "good Jew."

Abraham's fantasies suggest the central place of Jewish identity in his experience of the asylum (and prison), and how such a framework was used to assimilate, transform, and derive meaning from it. Many of his fantasies revolved around religious themes and images, such as the messiah, Christ, the calling, inspirations, transmigration of souls, the executioner angel. Abraham's ideas were summed up in his autopsy report as follows: "[He] believed in the transmigration of souls, identified himself at times with the Turkish emperor, at times with the messiah, and, in this capacity, handed out offices and wealth. He related with the greatest calmness how he had lived twelve times, and would not tolerate contradiction [of his ideas]."[48]

Many patients thought of themselves in messianic terms relating to the figure of Christ. The identification with Christ, the savior and martyr of the suffering and oppressed, was a powerful way to articulate one's own afflictions as lunatic and inmate, and to provide oneself with a way, if only in fantasy, out of one's predicament. As a Jew, however, Abraham's identification with Christ had a double and ambiguous meaning, of both martyrdom and apostasy—the "renunciation of a religious faith."[49] In a double sense, Abraham had been engaged for years in renunciation: hiding and disavowing his beliefs because they made him appear mad (subjecting him to surveillance and punishment), and because the beliefs themselves were heretical. The ideas he "recanted" were messianic: he was "called" to carry out great acts as a "messiah." Did Abraham see himself as Jesus Christ or as a Jewish messiah? The aspect of Jewish mysticism in Abraham's beliefs indicates that the latter may have been the case. His belief in the transmigration of souls connects him to the Jewish mystical traditions of the Kabbalah. The notion of reincarnation was in turn linked to messianism through the figure of Sabbatai Zevi, the seventeenth-century self-described Jewish messiah who, imprisoned by the Turks, had been given the choice of conversion to Islam or execution; he chose apostasy.[50]

Of all modern-day Jewish messiahs, Abraham was most likely to have known of Sabbatai Zevi. Unlike other messianic movements in Jewish history, all of which "were destroyed by historical disappointment and left no trace in Jewish consciousness," the legend and ideas of Zevi continued to live for generations in a "heretical movement within Judaism which in Central and Eastern Europe continued to proliferate down to the beginnings of the age of Emancipation in the first part of the nineteenth century."[51] Zevi's conversion had been a ruse to save his life; hereafter he "led a double life as Muslim and Jew." His followers (originally the Dönmeh in Salonika) incorporated apostasy into their faith, living as Muslims on the outside while internally retaining their faith in a mystical form of Judaism that included a belief in reincarnation. They were thus "regarded with mistrust and disdain by the Turks because of their double lives despite their often declared loyalty. . . ."[52]

In the late eighteenth century, the center of a Sabbataian splinter group, the Frankists, was located in Offenbach, not far from where Abraham grew up. The Frankists, notably, were not "Muslims"; instead, they had substituted a *Catholic* "facade."[53] Given Abraham's vagabond lifestyle and the geography of his wanderings, he is likely to have had contact with Frankist ideas. The town of Laubuseschbach, where he spent at least part of his childhood, was not far from Offenbach (about thirty-five miles away), where at the time Jacob Frank himself lived and preached. Later, Abraham traversed the area around Offenbach.[54]

The legend of Sabbatai Zevi's apostasy, as handed down by the Frankists, may have structured Abraham's identity and strategy as Jewish prisoner and insane asylum inmate. Under constant surveillance and punishment for "crazy" ideas and behavior, some form of deception on the part of all patients was a necessary survival tool in the asylum. For Abraham, not just inmate but also criminal Jew, the double life required of the patient took on special meaning and urgency: not simply the signs of sanity and goodness but, in addition, one's goodness as Jew had to be carefully cultivated and represented to those in charge. Under the interrogating eye of the staff, Abraham outwardly recanted, while hiding his true thoughts and beliefs. But he was not able to maintain the internal tension between the various identities he sought to juggle. Instead, he incorporated those identities and allegiances into the self, actually (in fantasy) becoming Christ/the Messiah, as well as the persecutor Turkish emperor/asylum authority, both doomed martyr and the "executioner angel"; the two joined in his final act of suicide.

Abraham's extreme accommodation was a centuries-old survival strategy of Jewish communities under the constant threat of persecution and expulsion. Jacob Katz links "the precarious situation of Jews among non-Jews,"—where, lacking residence and citizens' rights, and despised, whole Jewish communities could be held "collectively responsible" for an individual's infractions—to the very strict ethical standards of conduct in dealings with non-Jews enforced by the Jewish authorities. It was prescribed that individuals were to "refrain from deeds that might endanger the physical well-being of [their] fellow Jews."[55] For Abraham, a member of the "rabble"[56] underclass, constantly in trouble with the law, arrested, interrogated, and expelled, who was suspect in both the gentile and Jewish communities, accommodation did not include abstinence from crime, but required all the more the cultivation of survival skills, such as an acute sensitivity to one's surroundings, flattery, and the affectation of humility in relations with the authorities. It also required the repression of outward expressions of anger and aggression.

To the extent that the expectation of, and search for, a hidden and dangerous Jewish character forced a response of "Jewish" duplicity from Abraham, the asylum can be seen as an institution that, under the mantle of eradicating insanity, produced "Jewishness." This "Jewishness" (by which I mean not the patient's reactions alone but a gentile-Jew social dynamic between doctor and patient) was not simply an anachronism of the outside world—of social attitudes and prejudices continuing to exist where they no longer properly belonged in the medical setting. Rather, the asylum produced "Jewishness" by its own natural activities: the interpretation and curing of insanity. These included the problem of discovering and assessing the patient's inner state and character, the association of madness with danger, the environment of expectancy and fear, the array of institutional procedures in place to deal with any outbreak of raving or violent behavior, and, finally, the pedagogical and disciplinary nature of the asylum. For the patients, they included the use of strategies such as duplicity and accommodation to cope with this situation.

In the minds of both Abraham and the asylum, Jewishness seemingly came to stand for and be intertwined with the issue of insanity. The patient's practice of hiding his insanity and the doctors' search to discover the hidden illness—built into the asylum's doctor-patient relationship—could shift just as easily into a struggle over Jewishness and back again to one over insanity, or occur simultaneously.

Mordachai J., another penniless Jew, sixty years old and married with four children, had been serving a prison sentence for poaching, when he developed a severe case of incontinence.[57] Rather than seeing his uncontrollable defecation as symptomatic of illness, a host of penal and medical authorities could view it as nothing but a sign of Jewish depravity and deception, thus dealing with it as a disciplinary matter in penal institutions, with punishments so severe that they required special authorization from the *Landesregierung*. In Mordachai's case, "Jewishness" actively prevented officials and doctors from seeing the man as ill.

After a year of beatings and starvation (accompanied by transfers from prison to the correctional house and back again) failed to stop the behavior, the authorities concluded that Mordachai suffered from "feeblemindedness" and finally sent him to the asylum in 1829. Here as well his scatological behavior continued unabated: "He smears everything with his excrement"; "He answers all questions rationally, and only due to his love of filth is he to be recognized as a lunatic."[58] Lindpaintner was already requesting that Mordachai be released less than two weeks after his incarceration: "[Mordachai is] incontinent in the highest degree, work-shy, but not idiotic, not insane, not raving, and not wrong-headed." Like the other institutions, the asylum could not abide Mordachai's "filth," and he was finally sent home for good.

The problem of Mordachai for the authorities—prison, correctional house, and asylum—was not just eradicating the "filth," but also categorizing and identifying the person who produced it. Was the man criminal or sick? The answer revolved around the question of motive—on whether or not incontinence was voluntary. Was Mordachai intentionally defecating in order to force his release or otherwise manipulate the authorities, or could his behavior be ascribed to an illness (mental or physical) that would absolve him of responsibility? The prison wrestled with this question for some time. Mordachai's "behavior," explained the prison, "was sometimes such that *one tried to see him as crazy*" (emphasis mine). But criminality better fit the facts: "it was only that he knows how to dissimulate and wanted to force his release [with his excrement]."[59] In his capacity as physician for Eberbach's correctional house, Windt found nothing physically wrong with the inmate, and came to a similiar conclusion: Mordachai was an evil dissimulator.

The suspicion that a prisoner would intentionally feign illness in order to get himself released was common. What is striking in this case is the willingness and ability of almost everyone in contact with Mordachai—medical, prison and governmental authorities, as well as prison inmates and guards—to view him as perfectly healthy despite the horrendously aberrant behavior and his own utterances that he could not control himself. There is no question that scatological behavior could be, and was, seen in illness terms at this time. On a gentile patient who, prior to hospitalization, had sat for days in his own excrement, Basting commented: "This bestial filthiness is regarded as the first sign of insanity, for it would be impossible for a rational person to be able to voluntarily hold out in such a condition."[60]

During the period when Mordachai was an inmate in the correctional house, Windt wrote a revealing report that makes explicit the link between Mordachai's Jewishness and Windt's inability to view him as ill:

> The Jew [Mordachai], whom I have often observed due to his striking behavior, offers no symptoms of real insanity, but rather a cunning character supported by Jewish immoralities and national attributes to the point of repulsiveness. According to his own confession to me, he intended to force his release through simulating madness and bestial dirtiness; in this, he demonstrates an unusual pragmatism and perseverance. There is no question of involuntary evacuation of the bowels from physical illness. [Mordachai] has a well-fed body, a healthy appearance not free of scoundrelly features, and never complains about disturbed [bodily] functions. As a previous vagrant, he has no liking for an industrious mode of life. He will spare no victim in

order to be able to indulge his old inclinations . . . I advise thus that he be taught respect through corporal punishment by means of lashings [on the buttocks] and intimidations with repeated tangible threats.[61]

We have seen that the staff was perfectly capable of considering Jews as ill and treating them as patients. Defecation and "filthiness" in Jewish patients, however, seems to have triggered the most intense and savage anti-Semitism, which otherwise could lay dormant. To the *Landesregierung* the asylum described a female Jewish patient, who openly masturbated and smeared her clothes with excrement, as "an ugly, black, dirty Jewess, abundantly endowed with all incivilities and moral depravities, who combines in herself all of the repulsive characteristics of the lowest class of this worthless people [i.e., Jews]."[62]

Windt offered two types of explanations to account for Mordachai's behavior, both of which were related to his Jewishness: filthiness is an inherently Jewish character trait ("supported by Jewish immoralities and national attributes"), and thus Mordachai in particular *likes* living in his excrement ("He will spare no victim in order to be able to indulge his old inclinations"). In addition, Mordachai—the "cunning," "perserving," and "pragmatic" Jew—is intentionally deceiving and manipulating the authorities with his feces to gain his release. In neither case was it a question of treating the defecation as a medical problem. Rather, it was seen as a form of defiance, a subversion of order and authority. This was a disciplinary matter. Mordachai would be beaten into "respect."

Feces became the medium of a brutal and extremely unequal power struggle between Jewish inmate and penal/medical authorities. It pitted on one side Mordachai's defecations, interpreted as willful acts of disobedience, against various sets of authorities whose job it was to break that will. In the battle to force Mordachai's submission, his excrement took on enormous symbolic proportions, far beyond the issue of cleanliness. On the part of the authorities, it involved not just brutal punishments, but also a fetishistic and bureaucratic reckoning of the feces. In order to determine the severity of Mordachai's punishment, for example, they weighed the frequency of defecations against the amount of wool he spun.[63]

In one of the numerous interrogations following his "bad conduct," Mordachai asserted, "I work from morning to night, and it is not so that I dirty myself"; to which Lindpaintner, the interrogator, replied: "How can [you] lie like that?" Mordachai: "I'd like to be employed chopping wood." Lindpaintner: "Before, you also did not work at the wood position." Mordachai, exasperated: "Give me back my freedom!"[64] The issue was not feces (or work) per se but a battle of wills between him and the authorities. This took place largely in incessant and petty interrogations like the interchange just quoted, where the asylum tried to bully Mordachai into an admission of "truth," and where reprimands usually came in the form of entrapping questions, against which Mordachai's avoidances, excuses, and lies were no match.

The timing and circumstances of Mordachai's bouts of incontinence suggest their link to rage, resistance, and the power dynamics of institutional life. His incontinence began when he was in prison. In the asylum, the first occurrence, two days after admission, followed immediately after an incident in which the staff intentionally humiliated him; returned to his cell, he "dirt[ied] himself," smeared the feces about, and ripped up his blanket. During his six months in the correctional house, Mordachai literally shat on its order: when forced to work, he defecated; when made to pray (in Christian services), he relieved himself in the prayer hall.[65] In a situation of utter powerlessness and dependency, at the mercy of authorities who not only monopolized all means of violence but were prepared to use them, and where the spoken word as defense was meaningless, Mordachai responded with a part of the body the authorities could never control.

Mordachai ended up outsmarting the authorities, for he ultimately did "get his way." His offensiveness was finally greater than the offense, and he was released. But his excremental acts cannot be equated with conscious, planned rebellion. The fact remains that the person he shat on was himself. Precisely his lack of (conscious) control over his bodily functions is what makes the case so tragic and brutal. When Basting asked Mordachai why he dirtied himself, the latter replied, "I know well what I do, but not why I do it." He had been locked in a "cage," had been starved and beaten—still, he continued to "dirty himself." Basting ruled out dissimulation "because [Mordachai] acts too naturally, he is very afraid of being punished, and is happy when one is satisfied with him." Despite these observations, Basting, like the other authorities, remained wedded to perceiving his patient as delinquent. Mordachai was "not dissimulating" and "really suffers from hallucinations." Basting, however, did not recommend medical treatment in the asylum. Instead, "strict surveillance will accustom [Mordachai] to order and morality."[66]

The viciousness of anti-Semitism and the extent to which it disrupted the "normal" doctor-patient relationship in the cases of Abraham and Mordachai were atypical. Their significance, however, lies precisely in their extremity. They allow us to glimpse something of the limits of medicine and the medicalization process. Anti-Semitism and its nonmedical representation of the person was a latent possibility that surfaced when Jews became suspect—as criminals, defecators, or religious fanatics. In these cases, it was not a question of medicine used to keep the marginal "outside." To the contrary, the more marginal and socially dangerous the person, the further medicine retreated or reverted to a nonmedical explanatory framework.

We know very little about the everyday social dynamics of anti-Semitism in nineteenth-century Germany. Debates about the nature of anti-Semitism tend to assume a distinct and coherent set of attitudes on the part of contemporaries—whether of the traditional, religious or the modern, racial variety. In this context, there are two striking things about the Eberbach sources. First, both anti-Semitism and its opposite (attitudes associated with emancipationist opinion) coexisted within individual medical practitioners. For the psychiatric equivalent of pro-emancipation was the application of moral treatment to Jewish patients. In attempting to cure Jews by this method, alienists implicitly worked with the very same set of liberal principles that underpinned political arguments for Jewish emancipation—principles of the essential equality of individuals and their reformability through reason and education.

Second, "Jewishness" in the asylum was a constantly shifting, unstable, and improvised category as practitioners (re)negotiated their relationships with, and evaluations of, individual patients over time. This aspect of Jewish-gentile relations perhaps reflected the still largely traditional nature of early nineteenth-century anti-Semitism (i.e., its casual and individualized aspects). It certainly had something to do with the fact that, unlike their counterparts after 1850, medical practitioners were not yet working within a paradigm of racial science and biological determinism. Even the use of physiognymy and phrenology in the asylum was not yet applied to race. Yet Elizabeth Lunbeck's study of an early twentieth-century American asylum indicates that even in the era of racial science, asylum practice toward Jews did not necessarily follow along expected ideological lines.[67]

The history of the institutional dynamics of race is simply too unknown and unstudied to hazard any generalizations at all on the subject. The Eberbach sources, however, do suggest that "Jewishness" was as much a social relationship as a category of thought, and that "racial" discourses implicated inmates in complex and disturbing ways. The sources also suggest that the asylum itself—a modern institution, founded upon enlightened ideas and utilizing new scientific techniques—served to reproduce age-old anti-Semitic stereotypes and Jewish-gentile relations, just as it contributed to demarcating and fixing differences based on class and gender. Little is known about the interactions between cultural discourses about Jews and institutional practices; they deserve further research in ongoing attempts to unravel the continuities and changes in the history of anti-Semitism.

Conclusion

Almost unknown before the 1970s, multiple personality disorder (M.P.D.) has become an epidemic in the last twenty years. One estimate puts the incidence of new cases between 1985 and 1995 at forty thousand. The patients are over-whelmingly "white, female, and North American."[1] *The New Yorker* tells of one such case: Elizabeth Carlson, a suburban housewife, who began psychiatric treatment in 1989 for depression. Within a year she had discovered more than two dozen personalities inhabiting her mind and had recovered horrifying memories of childhood sexual molestation at the hands of a satanic ritual cult. The psychiatrist, Diane Humenansky, had supplied her patient with a M.P.D. illness script— books, videotapes, and leading questions— which Carlson faithfully internalized and made her own. It was a dangerous script. Before long, Carlson's condition was deteriorating: she no longer left her bedroom and her marriage was falling apart; she became suicidal, and felt she was going crazy.[2]

M.P.D. is not a disease entity. Not the tools of the psychiatrist, but those of the historian, social psychologist, and sociologist are best suited to explain its epidemiology and symptomatology. The illness script Humenansky and other psychiatrists made believable to their patients drew from a number of political, social, and cultural currents: the child-protection movement of the 1970's, the later recovered-memory movement, and the involvement of an unlikely alliance of feminists and Christian fundamentalists. M.P.D. became a psychiatric growth industry, which promoted the illness from new institutional bases: a professional organization (I.S.S.M.P.&D.: International Society for the Study of Multiple Personality and Dissociation), annual conferences, specialized units within hospitals, and publications. Finally, the media spread the word through magazine, talk show, and news coverage (one program featuring a "star [M.P.D.] patient who switched personalities [on cue] for the camera").[3]

On the other hand, it is not accurate to make M.P.D. alone responsible for mental disorder in these women and the medicalization of otherwise purely social problems. Like Carlson, most of these women had long been troubled in mind and "already spent [on average] seven years in the mental—health system" before undergoing M.P.D. therapy.[4] Neither disease entity nor solely social constuct, M.P.D. is perhaps best understood in terms of the symbiotic relationship of patient and doctor, as the latter offers up (and imposes) a narrative of meaning that, for historical, institutional, and psychological reasons, is accepted by both participants.

Under severe attack, M.P.D. is rapidly waning, and will soon go the way of nymphomania, religious madness, masturbatory insanity, and other mental illnesses that have lost believability and social resonance. The aim of this book has been to examine that historical moment when, like M.P.D. in the 1980's, such illnesses displayed themselves in seeming transparency to a medical profession and a society that had reason to believe. In Vormärz Germany, anthropological psychiatry, separate spheres ideology, religious politics, and the social question helped to provide the conceptual and political space for belief in the existence of nymphomania, masturbatory insanity, and religious madness, and the widespread occurrence of the latter two illnesses. Simultaneously, the emergence of the asylum worked to turn the depressed, disturbed, lazy, superstitious, and sexually deviant into medical cases that were diagnosed accordingly. Finally, the "media"— popularized medical tracts, pedagogical works, journals, and novels—educated a middle-class reading public in the dangers and symptoms of mental illnesses.

The typical male, middle-class patient suffering from depression and low self-esteem found entirely plausible the idea that masturbation had ruined him. Much like M.P.D., doctor and patient shared in these cases a common illness script, which could speak to the patient's individual problems while drawing from broader social concerns about masculinity and gender relations. Nineteenth-century class differences, however, complicate the picture. In the mostly lower-class cases of nymphomania and religious madness, forms of collaboration between communities/families and medicine/asylum did indeed occur. Both practical concerns (safety and the economic viability of families) and shared attitudes (about female chastity, Christianity, and humoral medicine, for example) engendered this collaboration. On the other hand, in Nassau's largely preindustrial communities, psychiatric thinking was hardly a habit of mind. Among medical practitioners themselves, the field was only beginning to be recognized. Confusion and indecision was not infrequently the order of the day among medical officials charged with passing judgment on the mental state of prospective asylum inmates.

Current scholarly interest in the social history of psychiatry stems largely from the enormous influence this profession has achieved in the twentieth century—not merely the numbers (and new kinds) of patients in treatment, but the fact that psychiatry furnishes many of the categories we use to understand our minds and to demarcate the "normal" from the "abnormal" in human behavior. Expanding beyond mental illnesses and the asylum into "the realms of everyday concerns," psychiatry in the beginning of this century became part of the "cultural mainstream, where it has remained."[5] How we define mental illness and its relationship to psychiatry and society is therefore not peripheral to our understanding of modern culture as a whole. If, as this book argues, it is a mistake to dismiss mental disturbance as mere social construct, it is equally problematic to deny the normalizing functions of psychiatry and the historical contingency of its categories.

The class divide of this book throws in sharp relief those lines of mutual interaction whereby anxiety and trauma were turned into clinical entities. These illnesses, at psychiatry's inception in the last century, embodied the social norms and values of a middle class—the bearers of individualism, religious rationalism, separate spheres ideology, and political liberalism. Faced with a psychiatrically illiterate and, in Nassau, largely poor, peasant population, the challenge of curing madness involved instructing this population in new understandings of the self—in matters ranging from religion and conscience to sexual desire and social identity.

This was the disciplinary side to psychiatry, which silenced alternative interpretations of experience and turned social problems into matters of individual, psychic dysfunction. Psychiatry, in this sense, acted as a kind of cultural colonizer of peasant communities. A social disciplining approach, however, provides only a limited, incomplete view of the "madness" analyzed in this study. In fact, this book demonstrates the loose fit between, on the one hand, the clinical illnesses of nymphomania and religious madness, and, on the other, the sorts of mentally traumatized and disturbed people that those communities generated in the Vormärz. We need histories of this two-sided madness, works that would allow us to begin to theorize the interactions (over time and in comparative perspective) between institutional practices and psychiatric categories, on the one hand, and socioeconomic structures and culture, on the other.

The innovation of the asylum, according to Foucault, was its new kind of surveillance, a "system of rewards and punishments" aimed at returning the madman to reason and consciousness by instilling the sense of self-responsibility. Procedures generating alienation (learning to "objectify" the self for an "Other"), guilt, and fear were thus cornerstones of moral treatment. The asylum, accordingly, did not liberate madness from indifference and abuse; it silenced and "mastered" it, turning it into mental illness and shaping it along the lines of bourgeois values.[6] Foucault's history may be simplistic and overly polemical, but its conceptual underpinnings—the critique of modernity and the linkage of power and knowledge in institutional settings—remain powerful and challenging.[7]

The social construction of mental illness in Foucault, however, remains an abstraction: there are, for one, no patients in his account.[8] There are also no communities and families, national politics, economies, class and gender relations, social structures, and so forth. Johann M., the peasant poisoner (discussed in chapter 3), landed in the asylum not because he offended bourgeois norms, but because he went mad when confronted with a pending legal conviction. He did so because of the particular way in which guilt and conscience operated in his psyche. In this case, induced fear and guilt, practices of the penal system, were not the cure for, but the causes of madness. In other words, madness occured and was articulated at the intersection of institutional practices and structures of thought, both of which can and should be historicized.

There is an abundance of ethnographic research demonstrating the great cultural variability of symptoms, experiences, and meanings attributed to madness, illness, and more generally, bodily and mental phenomena.[9] To take one pertinent example, non-Western societies diverge significantly from the modern West in the ubiquity of "trance and possession states" in the former societies and their almost total disappearance (with the exception of "traditionally oriented subgroups") in the latter.[10] The incorporation of an anthropological approach to madness is, with few exceptions, one of the great neglected areas of the history of psychiatry; it provides, in my mind, the most promising avenue for historicizing madness. Many recent studies in cultural and social history focus on the mutual influences of "popular" and "elite" cultures. This book has intentionally highlighted class distinctions—the differences and tensions between bourgeois and peasant, high and low, cultures. This approach has the benefit of allowing one to tease out of the sources different cultures of madness. My conclusions, at the least, suggest the need for further explorations of the historical links between class, culture, and madness. But for this to happen, we need to overcome the narrow confines of the debate between essentialists and social constructionists. It is hoped that this book makes a contribution to that goal.

Until recently, scholars have mostly worked with models of history that assume a strict separation of private and public spheres, by turns neglecting the former and subordinating it to the latter in historical explanation. Practitioners of both *Alltagsgeschichte* and women's history are challenging those assumptions, showing the interconnections and mutual influences of private and public spheres. In so doing, these studies have brought about important new understandings of such quintessentially "public" activities as politics, work, and the labour movement.[11] They have also begun to historicize the private sphere, showing how sexuality, the body, and gender relations are not "natural," transhistorical entities, but historically constructed, variable, and linked to wider developments in the economy, politics, and social relations.

The history of madness appears to present an ideal focus for the investigation of the ways in which private and public spheres interacted and shaped each other: it involved the intensely private aspect of mental trauma, on the one hand, and, on the other, an array of medical and state authorities and social forces that acted upon, reinterpreted, and shaped the nature of that trauma. Yet, with few exceptions, histories of psychiatry have privileged either the private or the public aspect of madness to the exclusion of the other side of the equation. "Whig" histories of psychiatry, as well as psychohistories that work with a similar essentialism, assume a naturalized, private domain of mental illness that transcends the varying historical categories and measures that have named and treated it; Foucault and many revisionist historians, by contrast, privilege the public and socially constructed nature of madness at the expense of the private domain of human experience and suffering.

This study suggests the complex ways in which the "private" realm of feeling and fantasy structured and was structured by the wider world of state and society. As such, the experiences of poor asylum inmates tells us something of significance, beyond the history of madness, about broader social and political developments of the Vomärz. It indicates, for one, the gendered and culturally mediated ways in which rural and small-town people underwent the economic and demographic shifts that resulted in the catastrophe of mass pauperism in the 1830s and 1840s. It also suggests the complex ways in which sexuality was constituted by and, in turn, helped to construct social experience.

Desperate poverty, marital strains, and restrictive marriage laws affected women in unique ways tied to their reproductive lives, their socially subordinate positions, and the high premium placed on sexually defined notions of female honor. If, as a result of legal restrictions and the growing inequality of wealth in villages, poor people had difficulty marrying, this fact bore particularly hard on women, for whom there were no attractive alternatives—socially, economically, or sexually—outside of marriage. In these circumstances, men were precious commodities and finding a husband a prerequisite for any poor, single woman seeking a degree of economic security, independence, and social status in the community. Precisely the centrality of chastity to female honor could, however, lead married women seeking to punish delinquent or abusive husbands to adopt for this purpose a sexually charged set of public idioms.

These were the sorts of situations in which "man-crazy" behavior occurred. Attention to it not only helps to illuminate a hitherto ignored gendered byproduct of the developments of the Vormärz; the nymphomania cases suggest how social and economic problems were themselves formulated by and experienced through languages of sex and gender. The ferocious Elisabeth K., who laid claim to a husband against the elite of her village, may have become mentally unhinged over her battles, but those battles, and the way they played themselves out as illness, tell us something of value about the larger questions of power, gender, sexuality, and class relations in rural Nassau of the Vormärz.

If trance and possession states have largely disappeared in the West, so has the religious interpretation of madness. The modern, secular experience of mental illness was the product of an historical development, of which we know very little. The religious madness diagnosis employed by early psychiatry formed, this book argues, one important moment of this history. It both aimed at and was predicated upon a new, liberal conception of the self: divorced from the divine, individualized, and located in a self-contained, responsible subject. It was thus pivotal to an underlying cultural shift affected by the rise of psychiatric expertise, namely, the constitution of the social, psychological, and epistemological basis of the modern mental patient.

Religious politics and state-building were central to this endeavor as they provided the broader conceptual and policy framework for medical action against certain types of religious and supernatural beliefs. The religious madness diagnosis was not specific to Germany, but here it took on particular meaning within the politically charged debates between rationalists and the proponents of neoorthodoxy, and alongside state-building efforts in new, religiously diverse territories such as Nassau. These factors shaped the broader conceptual field in which it made sense to equate peasant superstition and neoorthodox fanaticism with mental illness, and to link the eradication of both to the cause of liberalism and the rationalization of the state. Religious madness thus had something to do with the political and administrative work of forming *Staatsbürger.* If the diagnosis made outsiders of hitherto merely odd, eccentric, or troubled individuals, it also, more importantly, contributed to marginalizing significant elements of peasant culture as a whole, as rural communities were integrated into new institutional and social structures of this "bourgeois" century.

Before the 1840s, the religious policies of the Nassau state seemed, on the surface, to be proceeding smoothly without encountering massive resistance. But by focusing on the local level and the experiences of the "little people," this study shows how problematic and contested the process could be. New conceptions of God, truth, identity, and conscience could and did encounter tremendous resistance; they could be assimilated by the patients in ways that transformed those conceptions; they could even cause madness itself, as in the case of Johann M.[12]

This study has focused on the very early years of the modern insane asylum, an era in which institutional care remained limited and psychiatry was a novel field of expertise that lacked many of the characteristics of a modern profession. All of this would dramatically change in the course of the nineteenth century. The decades after midcentury saw an enormous expansion of the asylum system. In Prussia, for example, between 1880 and 1910, asylum admissions increased 429%, while the population as a whole grew at a rate of 48%.[13] The overwhelming majority of these patients came, as earlier, from the lower classes. Meanwhile, the field of psychiatry, acquiring the elements of a modern profession (university chairs, professional journals and organizations, etc.), secured and expanded its institutional base, professional legitimacy, and social standing.[14]

These later developments make the issues discussed in this study all the more relevant and important. Those issues, in the broadest sense, have to do with the social constitution of mental illness. The book has sought to explore the complexities of the relationship between psychiatric labels (official illnesses), the thing they name ("real" people, gestures, and words), and the historical contexts in which this occurs. It has purposefully maintained the tension between "real" and ascribed madness in order to probe the boundaries and interactions between the two in the "making" of mental patients. It has shown the interplay between social conditions, cultural milieu, and the symptoms and experiences of mental trauma in the Vormärz. At the same time, it has explored a number of issues relating to the nature of psychiatric knowledge and practice: the coding of symptoms by gender, "race," and class; the formation of symptoms within institutional life; the fluid and indefinite distinctions between delinquency, criminality, and mental illness; the pragmatic exigencies that often superseded theory in the actions of medical professionals; and, not least, the joining together in the Vormärz asylum of a liberal ethos with many of the authoritarian and disciplinary practices of the former poor- and workhouses of the absolutist states.

Abbreviations

AEWK	Allgemeine Encyklopädie der Wissenschaften und Künste
AZfP	Allgemeine Zeitschrift für Psychiatrie
AMP	Annales Médico-Psychologiques
AfK	Archiv für Kulturgeschichte
AfmE	Archiv für medizinische Erfahrung
AfmrK	Archiv für mittelrheinische Kirchengeschichte
AfS	Archiv für Sozialgeschichte
BfP	Blätter für Psychiatrie
CEH	Central European History
CBlGP	Correspondenzblatt der deutschen Gesellschaft für Psychiatrie und gerichtliche Psychologie
DVj	Deutsche Vierteljahresschrift
DSM	Dictionaire des Sciences Médicales
DaL	Diözesanarchiv Limburg
DHS	Dix-Huitième Siècle
EWmW	Encyclopädisches Wörterbuch der medicinischen Wissenschaften
EP	L' Evolution Psychiatrique
FS	Feminist Studies
HStAW	Hessian State Archive, Wiesbaden
HZ	Historische Zeitschrift
HT	History and Theory
IRSH	International Review of Social History
JKV	Jahrbuch der Kirchengeschichtlichen Vereinigung in Hessen und Nassau
JCH	Journal of Contemporary History
JG	Journal Geschichte
JHBS	Journal of the History of Behavioral Sciences

JHI	Journal of the History of Ideas
JHMAS	Journal of the History of Medicine and Allied Sciences
JMS	Journal of Mental Science
JMH	Journal of Modern History
JSH	Journal of Social History
MfS	Magazin für philosophische, medicinische und gerichtliche Seelenkunde
MH	Medical History
NMfS	Neues Magazin für philosophische, medizinische und gerichtliche Seelenkunde
NA	Nassauische Annalen
NCC	Nineteenth-Century Contexts
SR	Social Research
YP	Yearbook of Psychoanalysis
SSI	Social Science Information
ZUL	Zedler's Großes vollständiges Universal-Lexikon
ZfA	Zeitschrift für die Anthropologie

Notes

Introduction

1. Hessian State Archive, Wiesbaden (HStAW), 430/1, no. 195; Dr. Windt release report, May 1839; and medical log.

2. In the industrialized county of Lancashire, England, John Walton found, however, that a disproportionate number of pauper admissions came from large cities ("Lunacy," *JSH* [1979]).

3. Ester, "'Ruhe—Ordnung—Fleiß,'" *AfK* (1989); Herzog, "Heilung, Erziehung, Sicherung," in Kocka (ed.), *Bürgertum* (1988).

4. They are located in the HStAW. There is no evidence (and I have checked in several ways) that the extant files are in any way atypical of the files as a whole.

5. Two medical dissertations provide information on various institutional aspects of Eberbach: Hötger, "Sozialstruktur" (1977); Niedergassel, "Behandlung" (1977).

6. On this issue in anthropology, see Geertz, "Thick Description" (1973).

7. On *Alltagsgeschichte*, see Lüdtke (ed.), *The History of Everyday Life* (1989), especially the introduction; Eley, "Labor History," *JMH* (1989).

8. Examples include Dwyer, *Homes for the Mad* (1987); Digby, *Madness, Morality and Medicine* (1985); Tomes, *A Generous Confidence* (1984).

9. The term "bourgeoisie" in this work refers to those middle-class groups whose social positions lay outside of the old corporatist order: entrepreneurs, bankers, state bureaucrats, clergymen, and those in education and the free professions. Despite important differences among these groups (e.g., those between the *Wirtschafts-* and *Bildungsbürgertum*), they shared enough in common (relative to the rural, lower classes) to be grouped together for purposes of this study, focused as it is not on the "bourgeoisie" per se, but on the class divide between middle and lower class. On the problem of defining the German bourgeoisie, see Kocka, "The European Pattern," in *Bourgeois Society* (1993).

10. For an excellent discussion of these issues in women's history, see Canning, "Feminist History," *Signs* (1994).

11. Michael MacDonald's work on madness in early modern England is an exception. He discusses broad methodological issues in "Anthropological Perspectives," *Information Sources* (1983). See also Kaufmann, "'Hartnäckiger Eigensinn,'" *JG* (1990).

12. The two standard histories of psychiatry (now very dated) that exemplify this position were both written by psychiatrists: Zilboorg, *Medical Psychology* (1941); Alexander and Selesnick, *History of Psychiatry* (1966).

13. The most important works in this genre include Michel Foucault, *Madness and Civilization* (1979); Goldstein, *Console and Classify* (1987); Castel, *The Regulation of Madness* (1988); Rothman, *The Discovery of the Asylum* (1971); Scull, *Museums of Madness* (1979) and, most recently, *The Most Solitary of Afflictions* (1993).

14. Bynum, *Holy Feast and Holy Fast* (1987), 205–207.

15. Obeyesekere, *Medusa's Hair* (1981). I have also found useful the anthropological studies of Kleinman, *Social Origins* (1986); Carstairs and Kapur, *The Great Universe of Kota* (1969); Heerdt, "Madness and Sexuality," *SR* (1986).

16. The influence here is the semiotic approach to culture of the anthropologist Clifford Geertz. See his *The Interpretation of Cultures* and his influential essay "Native's," in *Local Knowledge* (1983).

17. The term comes from functionalist theories, such as those of Talcott Parsons. See the discussion of how social thinkers have conceptualized action and agency in Giddens, *Social Theory*, (1979), chapter 2 and *passim*.

18. Ibid., 57.

19. The term refers to the complex of social, cultural, and political developments theorized by Jürgen Habermas, *Structural Transformation* (1989).

20. The recent literature and debates about the German bourgeoisie are reviewed by Sperber, "Bürger," *JMH* (1997).

21. Kaufmann, *Aufklärung* (1995).

22. I discuss this point at greater length in chapter 5.

23. See the works cited in note 8.

24. Jan Goldstein, *Console*, chapter 5.

25. A history of nymphomania has yet to be written. See Giedke, *Liebeskrankheit* (1983) for a useful overview of the history of medical theories.

26. See, for example, Breit, *"Leichtfertigkeit"* (1991). For Nassau, see Eisenbach, *Zuchthäuser* (1994).

27. Scott, *Gender* (1988), 43. See also Riley, *"Am I That Name?"* (1988).

Chapter 1

1. See Dörner, *Madmen* (1981), for a comparative analysis of the lunacy reforms in England, France, and Germany.

2. Jetter, *Typologie* (1971), 119. On Langermann, see Kirchoff (ed.), *Irrenärzte* (1921), 42–51.

3. Strictly speaking, the *Union* of 1817, which combined in one Evangelical church both Lutherans and Reformed Protestants, abolished the distinction between the two faiths.

4. The exact breakdown for the year 1842 is as follows: 213,039 Evangelical

(Protestant); 181,831 Catholic; 6,593 Jewish; 160 Mennonite. Vogel, *Beschreibung* (1843), 429.

5. Jäger, "Strukturwandel," in *Revolution* (1990); Treichel, *Primat* (1991).

6. Eisenbach, *Zuchthäuser* (1994).

7. Sanitätskommission report of May 30, 1805, cited in Hötger, "Sozialstruktur," 33.

8. The twenty-three new admissions were presumably some of those patients who had been earmarked for incarceration in the 1811 census (see discussion below).

9. 1844 is the last year for which statistics on total number of patients in Eberbach are available. Eberbach statistics, 1815–1844, HStAW, 211/394 (1–3).

10. Hötger, "Sozialstruktur," 41–46. Hötger does not connect the results of the 1811 census to the arguments against the erection of an asylum for the treatment of insanity, even though the census directly preceded in time these arguments and appears to be the single most powerful piece of evidence for such opinions.

11. Ibid., 59.

12. HStAW, 210/423a, Staatsministerium report, 1827. Eberbach also appeared in Morel's survey of European asylums ("Pathologie Mentale," *AMP* [1846]).

13. The enormous expansion of asylum populations occurred after 1850. For Germany, see Blasius, *'Einfache Seelenstörung'* (1994), 77–79. For England, see Scull, *Solitary*, chap. 7.

14. Access to health care for rural and poor people came not from expensive university-trained physicians, but from barber-surgeons, bathmasters, and a wide variety of "quacks." Finkenrath, *Sozialismus* (1930), 11–13. On the situation in Germany as a whole in the eighteenth century, see Fischer, *Gesundheitswesens* (1965), 52 and *passim*; Huerkamp, *Aufstieg* (1985), 26–27, 34–36.

15. Kropat, "Gesundheitsdienst," in *Herzogtum Nassau*, 247–51; Finkenrath, *Sozialismus*.

16. I estimate the average length to be about four pages.

17. Beginning in 1818, candidates for medical civil-service positions were required to pass a state exam, but due to the paucity of university-educated doctors in Nassau, the possession of a medical degree was no longer required. As a result of the mounting number of applications, a medical diploma became mandatory for a short period in 1839–1840. February 2, 1839 report on the testing of medical candidates, HStAW, 210/3554–II. Medical psychology was not among the fields in which candidates were examined (HStAW, 210/3556,a).

18. Still in its infancy as a specialized field, psychic medicine at German universities was, with few exceptions, taught (if at all) not by specialists, but by physicians and philosophers and incorporated into courses ranging from anthropology to forensic medicine. Trenckmann, *Leib* (1988), 53–54.

19. Wettengel, *Revolution* (1989), 68–69.

20. *Typologie*, 111–12.

21. See, for example, Roller, *Irrenanstalt* (1831), 28 ff.

22. Jetter, *Typologie*, 112, 16–62.

23. No. 54.

24. Jetter mistakenly refers to Lindpaintner as a "doctor." (*Typologie*, 112). Some official documents list Windt's name as Ferdinand Wilhelm Windt; others as Wilhelm Ferdinand Windt.

25. Lindpaintner, *Nachrichten;* idem, "Rechenschaft," *AZfP* (1847): 70–73; Basting, "menschenliebende Wärter," *AZfP* (1845), a prize-winning essay; idem, "pennsylvanische Strafsystem," *AZfP* (1847); idem, "Oldenburgische Irrenanstalt," *CBlGP* (1866).

26. Kreuter, *Deutschsprachige Neurologen und Psychiater* (1996), 870.

27. Consequently, this researcher has found it impossible to compile even the basic facts of Windt's medical training. Windt's obscurity was seemingly the result of his failure to publish, not his lack of knowledge. Together with Lindpaintner, he undertook several extensive trips on the European continent to visit and learn from leading psychiatric institutions. F. W. Emmermann, "Philipp Heinrich Lindpaintner," *Neuer Nekrolog* (1850), 583–85.

28. Emmermann, "Lindpaintner," 576.

29. HStAW, 210/4322; DaL, Eltville Z8, no. 17/1848.

30. "Basting," Kreuter (ed.), *Deutschsprachige,* 76; *Die Matrikel der Georg-August-Universität in Göttingen, 1734–1837* (Hildesheim and Leipzig, 1937), 703; HStAW, 210/6379.

31. Both Dirk Blasius, *verwaltete Wahnsinn* (1980), chapter 2, and Doris Kaufmann, *Aufklärung,* chapter 2, demonstrate the resistance of a medical model of insanity within government itself, particularly on the part of the provincial *Stände.*

32. No. 156, 14 January, 1832.

33. This issue is discussed further below.

34. This comes through in the reports of Lindpaintner, Windt, and Basting; it is also reflected in the tours of leading German and European asylums, which all three men undertook more than once over the years.

35. Lindpaintner to Nassau government, 1823, HStAW, 211/394 (1).

36. See, for example, Roller, *Irrenanstalt,* 28.

37. Verwey, *Psychiatry* (1985), 1. On German Romantic medicine, see Wiesing, *Kunst oder Wissenschaft* (1995). On the "harmonic vision of reality" in the vitalism of late Enlightenment cultural and natural sciences, see Reill, "Anti-Mechanism," *Francia* (1989); idem, "Science," *HT* (1994).

38. Verwey, *Psychiatry,* 8.

39. Ibid., 9–22.

40. Ibid., 22, 25.

41. See chapter 2 for further discussion of the religious aspects of anthropological psychiatry.

42. Lindpaintner to Nassau government, 1820, HStAW, 211/394 (1).

43. No. 14, 15 March 1818. This translation is based in part on the one provided in Kraepelin, *Psychiatry* (1962), 69. Lindpaintner also rejected an extreme psychicist position (Lindpaintner to Nassau government, 1833, HStAW 211/394 [2]).

44. These terms were apparently taken from Heinroth's influential textbook, *Textbook* (1818; trans., 1975).

45. Dörner, *Madmen,* 217.

46. Lindpaintner to Nassau government, 1820, HStAW, 211/394 (1).

47. The costs of the construction and administration of the institution came directly from the state treasury.

48. Foreign patients (mostly from other areas of Germany) were charged at double the rate of Nassau natives. These patients were desirable for the asylum both because they increased its prestige and reputation and because their high payments could be used to cover the costs of the indigent, native patients.

49. Beginning with the new house regulations of 1820, patients earned small wages for much of their work. Lindpaintner to Nassau government, 1821–1822, HStAW, 211/394 [1].

50. Lindpaintner to Nassau government, 1829, HStAW, 211/394 (1).

51. Akin to "Chinese water torture," the patient's head was drenched with cold buckets of water poured from a distant height, presumably to increase the water's force and painful effect.

52. Lindpaintner to Nassau government, 1820, HStAW, 211/394 (1).

53. Its purpose was "to divert the patient from his aberrant course, to lead him back . . . to the world of reality . . . to direct his attention toward the attainment of a definite goal and to awaken and identify his self-consciousness." Kraepelin, *Psychiatry*, 89.

54. Ibid., 87.

55. Lindpaintner to Nassau government, 1823, HStAW, 211/394 (1).

56. The use of mechanical restraints was, however, common practice in the West as well.

57. *Dörner, Madmen*, 216–17. Dörner's discussion of Germany is based almost solely on developments in Prussia. Elsewhere in the book, he does qualify somewhat his characterization of German psychiatry (257).

58. Ibid., 91–95, 274.

59. The term *Sonderweg* refers to the view that Germany's modernization diverged from the norms of Western democratic states, an interpretation that has been the subject of heated debate within German historiography.

60. HStAW, 430/1, no. 530. On early modern disciplinary and welfare institutions, see Spierenburg, "Sociogenesis," in *Carceral Institutions* (1984).

61. Lindpaintner, "Nachrichten," 32.

62. Lindpaintner to Nassau government, 1822, HStAW, 211/394 (1).

63. HStAW, 211/394, Lindpaintner to Nassau government. See especially the reports for the years 1827, 1829–30, 1833, 1842, 1844.

64. HStAW, 430/1, no. 960. August G. had been a low-level civil servant and took great pride and effort in writing his detailed chronicles of asylum life, some of which are preserved in his file. They combine exacting, pedantic detail with the wildest flights of fancy.

65. 211/394, Lindpaintner to Nassau government, January, 1828.

66. Habermas, *Structural*. On voluntary associations, see Nipperdey, "Verein," in *Gesellschaft* (1976). On casinos, see also Gall, *Bürgertum* (1989), 196 and *passim*.

67. This is Goffman's term for institutions of total control: insane asylum, prison, army. *Asylums* (1961).

68. Hull, *Sexuality* (1996), 209–10.

69. Schüler, "Wirtschaft," *NA* (1980), 134.

70. Lerner, *Wirtschafts- und Sozialgeschichte* (1965), 18.

71. Fuchs, "Zur Entwicklung," *NA* (1982), 64–65.

72. Nassau's population increased from 286,206 in 1816 to 465,636 in 1865. Blum, *Staatliche* (1987), 26–27.

73. Schüler, "Sozialstruktur" in *Herzogtum Nassau* (1981), 111.

74. Nassau was one of the main areas of German ceramic production from ca. 1500–1850. I thank Ken Barkin for this information.

75. Winfried Schüler, "Sozialstruktur," 110.

76. Schüler, "Revolution," in *Herzogtum Nassau*, 25.

77. Häbel, "Land- und Forstwirtschaft," in *Herzogtum Nassau*, 174–75.

78. Kropat, "Herzogtum Nassau," in *Das Werden* (1986), 532.

79. In terms of admissions, the sole exception to this pattern was the revolutionary year of 1848, in which the ratio was reversed, with twenty-two female and eleven male admissions.

80. A more precise breakdown by occupation of lower-class patients is difficult (and partly misleading), given that many of them scraped together livelihoods from several occupations.

81. Estimates put the German *Wirtschafts-* and *Bildungsbürgertum* at 5 percent of the population in the Vormärz. See Kocka, "The European Pattern," 4.

82. See Kaufmann's discussion of this issue in "`Irre und Wahnsinnige,'" in *Verbrechen* (1990), 198–202.

Chapter 2

1. Spengler, "Predigerkrankheit," *AZfP* (1849).

2. "Nachtrag," *AZfP* (1849), 259–61.

3. Ideler, *Versuch*, vol. 1, p. 123, claimed to have treated "several hundred cases" of "Teufelswahn" alone. In 1810, the British physician William Black reported "religion and Methodism" to be among the chief causes of insanity in the Bethelem asylum. (Porter, *Mind-Forg'd*, 33.) For other European asylums, see Fuchs, "Statistik der Irrenhäuser und des Irrseyns," *NMfS* (1833), table 8, p. 113. For the United States, see Hill, "Religion" (1991), 104.

4. Kaufmann, *Aufklärung*.

5. The exceptions are almost all studies focused on a particular case of religious possession in Savoy (annexed by France in 1860) in the late 1850s and 1860s. The most recent and insightful of these studies is Harris, "Possession," *JMH* (1997). For Germany, see the analysis of religion and madness in the case of a Württemberg peasant woman in Kaufmann, *Aufklärung*, 78–89.

6. These include two sophisticated and useful works: Saurer, "Religiöse Praxis," in *Dynamik* (1992); and, for a slightly earlier period, Schär, *Seelennöte* (1985). More simplistic and problematic are Hill, "Religion"; Feldmann, "'religiöse Melancholie'" (1973).

7. *Versuch*, vol. 1, pp. 2. 8–9.

8. Ibid., 28.

9. The term was coined by the English pastor Robert Burton, *Anatomy of Melancholy* (1621), who, however, saw it *not* as an illness, but as the work of the devil. The secularization of the term and its association with illness began in the late seventeenth century. MacDonald, "Religion" (1982).

10. Bucknill and Tuke, *Manual* (1858), 98; Biermann, "Aerztlich-psychologisches Gutachten über einen Zustand von Wahnsinn durch religiöse Schwärmerei . . ." *AfmE* (1831); Hoffbauer, *Untersuchungen* (1807).

11. Bird, "Melancholie" *ZfA* (1823), 229. Bird's question was a rephrasing of that of the English physician George M. Burrows.

12. Ibid., 231.

13. Verwey, *Psychiatry*, 15.

14. These tropes were not in themselves diagnostic categories. There were those writers who made no diagnostic distinction between the varieties of behavior of religious madness. There were others, such as Blumröder, "Trübsinn," *BfP* (1837),

who proposed a dualistic conceptual framework that, to a degree, overlapped with the tropes of the mystic and religious melancholic.

15. The nature of these religious currents and their place within Vormärz politics and society will be discussed later.

16. MacDonald, *Mystical*; idem, "Religion."

17. Scholder, "Grundzüge," in *Aufklärung* (1976); Rosenberg, *Denkströmungen* (1972); Hölscher, "Religion," *HZ* (1990).

18. *Grundriß*, vol. 2, p. 461.

19. See the cases cited in Blumröder and Bird.

20. Idem, *Versuch*, 183–84. Ideler also related—in Latin—the sexual scandals of one sixteenth-century nunnery (185).

21. For the eighteenth-century *Schwärmerstreit* in particular, see Kaufmann, *Aufklärung*, chapter 1; Elias, *History* (1978).

22. Chapter 4 explores the same issue for male masturbation. See also Hull, "'Sexualität,'" in *Bürgerinnen* (1988).

23. Even Ideler, the great spokesman against "passion," admitted that "frustration of the sexual drive" had its potential pathological effects in a "superstitious person." *Versuch*, 132–33.

24. Ibid., 29.

25. *Grundriß*, vol.2, p. 467.

26. Hoffbauer, *Untersuchungen*, vol. 2, 312–17.

27. Grohmann, "Aberglauben," *ZfA* (1825), 217.

28. HStAW Abt. 430/1, no. 162, report by Drs. Thilenius and Kleinschmidt, 26 June, 1835.

29. On the history of the self, particularly of the modern, bourgeois individual, see Elias, *History*; Taylor, *Sources* (1989).

30. Heinroth, *Geschichte* (1830), 514–15.

31. Kaufmann, *Aufklärung*; Schings, *Melancholie* (1977).

32. For an excellent overview of Vormärz theology and religious currents, from which this section heavily draws, see Nipperdey, *Germany* (1996), 356–98.

33. Sheehan, *German* (1978); Rosenberg, *Denkströmungen*, 18–50.

34. Nipperdey, *Germany*, 375–76; Mooser, *Frommes Volk* (1989).

35. Mooser, "Erweckung und Gesellschaft. Zur Einführung," in *Frommes Volk*, 12.

36. On the issues at stake in the clashes between religious dissenters and ultramontanists, see Paletschek, *Frauen* (1990); Herzog, *Intimacy* (1996).

37. Nipperdey, *Germany*, 362. For ultramontanism in Nassau, see Schüler, "katholische Partei," *AfmrK* (1982); Schwedt, "katholische Kirche," in *Herzogtum Nassau*, 275–82.

38. Nipperdey, *Germany*, 462–66. For recent debates on the periodization and interpretation of the Catholic revival, see Anderson, "Piety and Politics," *JMH* (1991), 685 ff.

39. Ibid., 691–92.

40. Anonymous review of two works in the debate, *MfS* 3 (1830), 242. The quote derives from the reviewer, not the administrative report.

41. This discussion was carried on in pamphlets and in a number of newspapers and specialized journals, including the *Allgemeine Kirchenzeitung* (vol. 2, 1826). Hudtwalcker, *Ueber* (1827). In the 1830s, Hudtwalcker became police chief of Hamburg, in which capacity he carried on the neopietist crusade in the form of a crack-

down on drunkenness among city nightwatchmen. See Evans, *Death* (1987), 102. A more significant and widely discussed event of religious madness was the "Swedish preaching illness" of 1841–1842. See the discussion by Ideler, *Versuch*, 222–49.

42. Rotteck, "Aberglaube," 89–90.

43. Dörner, *Madmen*, 270, 338 note 257.

44. Blumröder, "Trübsinn," 14.

45. Bird, "Melancholie," 231.

46. Burrows, *Inquiry* (1820) had been recently translated into German. Bird's article was a response to this work.

47. Ideler, *Grundriß*, vol. 1, 362.

48. Dörner, *Madmen*, 250 ff.

49. Ibid., 361.

50. Bird, "Melancholie," 232 ff.

51. Ibid, 235, 237.

52. Ibid., 235.

53. Ibid., 231.

54. *Versuch*, 132–33.

55. Ibid., 179–81.

56. "Melancholie," 240.

57. Blumröder, "Trübsinn," 17.

58. On this belief in early modern Württemberg, see Sabean, *Power* (1984).

59. Biermann, "Aerztlich," 116, 110.

60. Ibid., 116.

61. Ibid., 125–26.

62. Biermann, "Aerztlich," 115–16; Ideler, *Versuch*.

63. On the sociology of professionalization, see Freidson, *Profession* (1970). On the professionalization of German medicine, see Huerkamp, *Aufstieg* (1985). See Broman, "Rethinking," *JMH* (1995), 849 ff., for a cogent critique of this position.

64. Fischer, *Geschichte* vol. 2, 408–13.

65. Schieder, "Kirche," *AfS* (1974). A good deal of the Awakening's missionary work was focused on helping the poor, sick, and needy. On the missionary organizations in Nassau, see Steitz, *Geschichte* (1977), 370 ff.

66. *Console*, chapter 3.

67. Morel, "Pathologie," 208. Jacobi, "Irrenanstalten," *EWmW* (1839), 153, claimed that the "necessity for religious edification in insane asylums" is no longer in doubt and praised the beneficial effects of "regular, appropriate religious services."

68. Heinroth, *Textbook*, vol. 1, 27.

69. On Romantic medicine in general, see Cunningham, *Romanticism* (1990); Richards, *Mental* (1992), 289 ff.

70. Ideler, *Versuch*, 18–19, 9–10.

71. Ulrich, "Bemerkungen," *ZfA* (1823).

72. Ibid., 400–402.

73. Loetz, *Kranken* (1993).

74. Yet in positioning themselves as advocates of natural science, physicians trod a fine line, for they also needed to disavow the former's radical, atheistic implications in the form of materialism. The Coblenz report (p. 401) makes this very clear.

Chapter 3

1. Evans (ed), *Rethinking* (1987), chapter 4; Labouvie, *Verbotene* (1992). The issue of popular superstition in Germany has been extensively examined in the literature on the *Volksaufklärung*. An extensive bibliography can be found in Knudsen, "On Enlightenment," in *Enlightenment* (1994). For French peasants, see Devlin, *Superstitious* (1987).

2. No. 141, medical commitment report, 20 May, 1832. See also Hoffmann, *Rheinhessische* (1980).

3. No. 95, report of medical official Döring, January 1823.

4. Steitz, *Geschichte*, 351 ff. See also the interesting memoirs of the Nassau pietist preacher Friedrich Brunn, *Mitteilungen* (1893), which describes his successful missionary efforts to "awaken" his parish (Runkel) and surrounding communities. Nassau was also a center of religious dissent. Paletschek, *Frauen*, 79, 240, 281.

5. 1855 article published in the *Allgemeine Zeitschrift für Psychiatrie*, quoted in Bucknill, *Manual*, 332.

6. MacDonald, *Mystical* (1981).

7. No. 96.

8. No. 162.

9. No. 77, medical commitment report, Dr. Held, 9 July, 1830.

10. No. 199.

11. No. 1186, report of medical official Haas, April 1847.

12. No. 122, medical report of Dr. Coels, February 1828.

13. For an extended analysis of these issues, see chapter 6.

14. The pietist preacher Friedrich Brunn complained bitterly in his memoirs (a not unbiased source) about what he perceived to be the pervasiveness of religious rationalism in Nassau. Brunn, *Mitteilungen*, 4–30.

15. For a short overview of this issue in the late medieval and early modern periods, see Scribner, "Elements of Popular Belief," in Brady et al. (eds.), *Handbook* (1994), 238–42. There is a large anthropological literature on syncretism—the coexistence in colonial and postcolonial societies of Christianity and native traditions. See, for example, MacCormack, *Religion* (1991), 180, 407–33.

16. No. 81, undated report of [????] Bender.

17. No. 95, "Geschehen," Montabaur, 29 January, 1823.

18. See, for example, no. 885.

19. No. 199. For an excellent account of one case in the second half of the century, see Blackbourn, *Marpingen* (1993).

20. No. 883, Dr. Peez to Lindpaintner, 24 July, 1827; report of Dr. Huthsteiner, 24 September, 1828; Anna S. to son ("Mein theure Guido"), undated letter; husband to Lindpaintner, undated letter.

21. Feldman, "'religiöse Melancholie'."

22. No. 59, Alois F. to unnamed priest, Niederlahnstein, August 1825.

23. Before the 1830s, the university of Freiburg was an important center of religious rationalism.

24. No. 59, undated sermon.

25. Sperber, *Popular* (1984); Blessing, *Staat*; Phayer, *Religion* (1970).

26. Sperber's and Blessing's equation of the external behavior contravening church laws (e.g., illegitimacy and diminished church attendance) with "irreli-

giosity" is highly suspect, especially because it is based solely on the biased reports of clergymen. The Eberbach sources, atypical as they are, certainly do not support this equation.

27. No. 55, Windt release report, November 1828.

28. Medical commitment report, Wiesbaden, July 1828.

29. No. 437, *Justizrath* Magdeburg to Lindpaintner, 1819.

30. No. 162, Medical Gutachten, Dillenburg, June 1835.

31. For a brilliant anthropological analysis of this type of thinking, see Douglas, *Purity* (1966).

32. Schulte, *Dorf* (1989).

33. Duden, *Geschichte* (1987).

34. No. 162, Medical Gutachten, pp. 56–57.

35. Ideler, *Versuch,* 27.

36. Ibid., 27–28. Here Ideler was speaking also of the larger problem of distinguishing between "passions" and "insanity."

37. A classic example can be found in Hoffbauer, *Untersuchungen,* vol. 1, 302 ff.; vol. 3., 376 ff.

38. No. 885, Dr. Frangel to *Justizrath* von Sachs, November 1824; Windt release report, August 1825.

39. Forty years, interrupted only by two short releases.

40. Windt release report, August 1825.

41. Dr. Frangel to Amt Idstein, October 1824.

42. Dr. Frangel to *Justizrath* von Sachs, November 1824.

43. Schatz, *Geschichte* (1983), 68, and *passim.*

44. Jäger, "Strukturwandel"; Schatz, *Geschichte,* 22 ff.

45. Both Catholic and Protestant teachers were employed in elementary schools of confessionally mixed communities; in one-classroom schools Catholic and Protestant teachers alternated at defined intervals. The four *Pedagogien,* preparatory schools for the *Gymnasium,* each represented one of the Christian confessions—Lutheran, Reformed, and Catholic—with the exception of the confessionally mixed Wiesbaden *Padagogen.* The *Landesgymnasium* and *Lehrseminar* were both confessionally mixed. Wolf-Heino Struck, "Die nassauische Simultanschule," *Herzogtum Nassau,* p. 257; Jäger, "Strukturwandel," 191–92; Schatz, *Geschichte,* 42 ff.; Firnhaber, *Simultanvolksschule,* vol. 1 (1881). Confessional parity also existed in the Eberbach staff: Lindpaintner and Basting were Catholics; Windt was Protestant. The sources do not reveal whether this religious parity was intentional, but it does fit with general state policy.

46. No. 80, Windt admissions report, March 1829; Windt autopsy report, October, 1830. Mathias D.'s other admission was a transfer from the correctional house.

47. July, 1827.

48. No. 959, medical log, 21 September, 1833.

49. No. 437, medical log, 2 June 1821.

50. No. 72, Windt autopsy, June 1829.

51. The Nassau ducal house was Protestant. No. 304, report of Camp parish priest Schröder to Amt Braubach, 16 December, 1844; patient letter, n.d.

52. No. 530, medical log, 12 January, 1833.

53. HStAW 211/394 (1), Lindpaintner to Nassau government, 1822.

54. No. 959, medical log, 6 October, 1838.

55. No. 959, medical log, 14 February 1835.

56. No. 437.

57. There were of course always a number of factors that determined releases, some of which, like the willingness of families and communities to take in the patient, lay outside the control of the asylum.

58. No. 959, medical log, 20 December 1824; 10 January, 1835.

59. No. 437, medical log, 24 March, 1824.

60. No. 218, Lindpaintner report 1 April, 1840. See Saurer, "Religiöse Praxis," for the medical discourse on pietist reading material.

61. Dr. Seicker (?), 24 June, 1839.

62. Protocol 29 March, 1840.

63. No. 195, Windt release May 1839 and medical log.

64. No. 137, medical log, 3 March, 1827.

65. No. 959, medical log, 1 May 1834.

66. No. 437, undated patient letters.

67. No. 202, medical log, 14 May, 1831; 7 May, 1832.

68. No. 474, medical log, 1831–1834.

69. No. 156.

70. No. 63, medical log, March 1821.

71. Both the patient and the asylum located her problem in the abdomen, but the asylum defined it as a somatic illness, not devil possession. Still, the asylum was perfectly happy to allow the patient to reinterpret treatment in supernatural terms if it worked to make her feel well again (which it did). The log speaks, for example, of the beneficial effect of cold showers as "driving out the evil spirit from her body." No. 132, log, 16 February, 1833.

72. Kittsteiner, *Entstehung* (1991), 304 ff.

73. For example, while she was in labor, the obstetrician (*Geburtshelfer*) heard her cry out several times: "I can no longer live in this world, I must be burned. I have brought the entire household misfortune." Again, after the birth and even before the infanticide, she felt herself damned, because "she has allowed her housekeeping to fall into disorder." No. 162, commitment report, 26 June, 1835.

74. No. 202, Dr. Vogler commitment report, 14 September, 1826.

75. No. 95, medical log, 25, November, 1825 (". . . doch nie über sich selbst ins klare kommt").

76. "Noch nicht mit sich im Klaren." No. 95, medical log, 25 November, 1826; 13 January, 1827.

77. ". . . acts without deliberation [*Uberlegung*], merely following her drives." Medical log, 2 June, 1827.

78. "Aus sich selbst thut." Medical log, 29 January, 1829.

79. Jacobi, "Irrenanstalten," 151.

80. No. 95, medical log, 13 January, 1827.

81. Sigmund Freud, "Mourning and Melancholia," *Standard Edition* (1957), 247.

82. Kittsteiner, *Entstehung*; Foucault, *Discipline* (1979).

83. Kittsteiner, "Grace," *SSI* (1984).

84. Kittsteiner, *Entstehung*, 311.

85. Ibid., 310.

86. Ibid., 354.

87. Ibid., 310, 337.

88. Such as the case of Lucia T. (above), the "possessed" woman who murdered her baby.

89. No. 360, Dr. Reuter medical report, 22 July, 1845.

90. No. 530, Windt release report, 14 March, 1833; Basting, log, April, 1843.

91. Dr. Kleinschmidt medical report, 29 March, 1843.

92. Blasius, *Kriminalität* (1978), 46–58; Häbel, "Land- und Forstwirtschaft," 173–85.

93. Windt release report, 18 April, 1845.

94. No. 530, medical log, 19 January, 1833.

95. No. 255, report of Dr. Haas, Wiesbaden 14 December, 1841.

96. Medical log, 28 December, 1841.

97. Medical log, 4 January, 1842. Despite his faulty conscience, Johann M. was transferred back to prison to serve out his sentence just days after this entry; once again, he had misjudged his position vis-à-vis the authorities.

98. See, for example, no. 250.

99. No. 250, report of the *Criminalgericht*, Wiesbaden to Eberbach Director, 2 July, 1842.

100. No. 707, medical commitment report, Dr. Kanth, 16 February, 1847.

101. Basting report, 7 August, 1847.

102. No. 39, medical commitment report, Dr. Geiger, 23 July, 1825; Windt release report, 2 June, 1826. See also the female cases analyzed in chapters 5–6.

103. Sabean, *Power*, 170–71.

104. On experiences of the self and its embeddedness in early modern village culture, see also Sabean, "Production," *CEH* (1996).

105. No. 54. He had earlier in life helped out in his father's pig trade and had most recently worked for years in a leather "factory"—a workshop of seven employees.

106. Medical log, 4 December, 1824.

107. Protocol, 3 December, 1824.

108. By contrast, his friend, whom Johann saw daily at work, felt no guilt about the murders and often tried to persuade the latter to forget the whole thing.

109. Adam, "Nassauische," *JKV* (1949), provides many of the primary documents, including hymns and sermons.

110. Ibid., 73, 83, 151.

111. Jäger, "Strukturwandel."

112. On the issue of disciplining peasant religiosity and the resistance encountered, compare Scharfe, "Subversive," in *Kultur* (1983); Korff, "Zwischen," ibid.

Chapter 4

1. Poovey, *Uneven* (1988); Russett, *Sexual* (1989); Honegger, *Ordnung* (1991).

2. For an overview of feminist interpretations of hysteria, see Mark Micale, *Approaching Hysteria* (Princeton, 1995), 66 f. Elaine Showalter, *The Female Malady* (New York, 1985), provides an engaging treatment of gender and madness that covers the sweep of nineteenth-century history in Britain, and it does not focus solely on hysteria. Her narrow, primarily literary source base has, however, been rightly criticized, and her thesis on the feminization of nineteenth-century madness remains controversial. See the discussion and citations in Micale, *Approaching*, 75–77.

3. Until the 1990s, the historical literature on nymphomania was limited to two essays on Bienville's eighteenth-century treatise: Rousseau, "Nymphomania," in *Sexuality* (1982); Goulemot, "Prêtons," *DHS* (1980); and an article surveying some

of the literature in the sixteenth through the eighteenth century: Diethelm "Surexcitation," *EP* (1966). The first and, hitherto, only two feminist studies are Ann Goldberg, "A Social Analysis of Insanity in Nineteenth-Century Germany: Sexuality, Delinquency, and Anti-Semitism in the Records of the Eberbach Asylum," (PhD diss., UCLA, 1992), chapters 2 and 3; and Groneman, "Nymphomania," *Signs* (1994). For a study of the application of a more recent psychiatric version of nymphomania—hypersexuality—to working-class women at the end of the nineteenth century, see Lunbeck, "New Generation," *FS* (1987).

4. The earliest histories of hysteria were polemical pieces written by disciples of Charcot and Bernheim in defense of their respective schools of thought. Veith's standard history of hysteria (*Hysteria*, 1965) is written from a Freudian perspective. Micale, *Approaching*, 33–107, reviews the historiography.

5. However, as explained below, the terms used in German popular culture—"Mannstollheit" and "mannssüchtig" (man-craziness)—had different origins and meaning from the technical medical term nymphomania.

6. "Nymphomania" or "sexual excitement," indicating an early stage of the "illness," can be found in 30 percent of the 177 surviving female files.

7. The hysteria diagnosis was, however, also applied to lower-class asylum inmates. Risse, "Hysteria," *MH* (1988).

8. Scott, *Gender*, 28–50.

9. Nymphomania derived from the Greek terms for the nature goddesses (nymphs) of ancient myth and the word for madness (mania). On ancient mythology and iconocraphy, see Maaskant-Kleibrink, "Nymphomania," in *Sexual* (1987). I base the dating of the first medical use of the term on several bibliographies, including that of the Surgeon General's Office: "Nymphomania," *Index-Catalogue of the Library of Surgeon General's Office* 9 (1888): 1051–52. Over the centuries the medical terms for hysteria, lovesickness, uterine fury, erotomania, and nymphomania were so entangled, overlapping, and variously classified (even in the same period) that any concise summary of the history of the nymphomania concept is impossible. The following provides some of the facts as I have pieced them together from disparate sources. The second-century Greek physician Soranus, whose enormously influential *Gynecology* held sway over gynecological medicine into the sixteenth century, used the term satyriasis to refer to both female and male sexual pathology that was characterized by an "irresistable desire for sexual intercourse" (148). Likewise, Jacques Ferrand, *A Treatise on Lovesickness* (1623), did not use the term nymphomania, but spoke of "satyriasis in women," which he differentiated from uterine fury only by the fact that in the latter disease there is "no pain in the genitals" (263). By the eighteenth century, the terms nymphomania and uterine fury appear to have been used interchangeably. At the same time, a process of disassociating nymphomania, hysteria, and erotomania (increasingly seen as a sexual or love obsession with a single love object) was gradually underway (Giedke, *Liebeskrankheit*). In the first half of the nineteenth century, nymphomania was undergoing a transition within medicine, and it appears that the *term* (not the idea) was in the process of gradually being excluded from mainstream medical discourse. The asylum alienist Peter Willers Jessen (1793–1875) claimed in his important article "Nymphomanie," *Encylopädisches* (1841), that the "higher and highest levels of nymphomania . . . only seldom occur" (361). He supported this claim with the example of the "Silesian insane asylum," where no such case had been seen in the last twenty years, and by the fact that "other mad-doctors [*Irrenärzte*] have never ob-

served such a case." For this reason, recent writers "generally only parenthetically specify it as a variety of mania, which needs no special description because, aside from the different causes, in general it does not differ from mania." Accordingly, Esquirol, *Mental Maladies* (1845), 335, subsumed nymphomania under the rubric of "Erotic Monomania." This contrasts with the treatment of nymphomania one generation earlier by Esquirol's mentor, Pinel, *Nosographie* (1813), 287–88, in whose nosography of mental illnesses nymphomania forms a distinct category (under the broader heading "Névroses de la Génération"). Maximilian Jacobi, *Hauptformen* vol. I (1844), the leading German psychiatrist of the somaticist school, also did not classify nymphomania separately. On the other hand, the *Encyclopädisches Wörterbuch* included a long article on nymphomania; and a glance at the Surgeon General's bibliography shows the term to be in active medical use into the 1880s.

10. Jessen, "Nymphomanie," reviews the different theories of its etiology.

11. Ibid., 369.

12. Bienville, *Nymphomanie*.

13. No. 151, medical log, 18, October, 1834; 7, February, 1835.

14. No. 128, 23, August, 1820.

15. The anonymous anti-masturbation brochure, first published in London, was written by (historians assume) a quack peddling a "masturbation medicine." Written by an established doctor, Tissot's treatise, *Onanism* (1772), provided the first "scientifically" based medical argument against masturbation. It "spread like wildfire." By 1785 it had been translated into several languages and was in its fourth edition in Germany. Spitz, "Authority," *YP* (1953), 116–17; Hare, "Masturbatory Insanity" *JMS* (1962).

16. MacDonald, "Frightful," *JHI* (1967).

17. Quoted in Villaume, "Unzuchtsünden," in *Allgemeinen* (1787), 21.

18. MacDonald, "Frightful," 429.

19. Barker-Benfield, *Horrors* (1976), 178–184; Cominos, "Late Victorian," *IRSH* (1963). Some of the literature is reviewed in Stengers, *Histoire* (1984). Steven Marcus, *Other* (1964), provides a Freudian interpretation. Thomas Laqueur, "Social Evil" in *Fragments* (1989), does not explicitly link masturbation anxiety to the bourgeoisie, but has suggested its connection with the anxieties generated by an "asocial" market economy.

20. Foucault, *Sexuality* (1980), 123–25; and the works by Aron and Kempf discussed in Stengers, *Histoire*, 107.

21. The gender aspect of masturbation ideas has been almost nonexistent in the literature. Exceptions include the important recent work of Isabel Hull, "'Sexualität'"; *Sexuality*, 258–63. See also Barker-Benfield, *Horrors*; "Spermatic," in *American Family* (1973); Cohen, "(R)evolutionary," *NCC* (1987).

22. HStAW, 211/394, 1–3. Digby, *Madness*, 210, and Dwyer, *Homes*, 102, note similiar diagnostic patterns at British and American asylums.

23. For examples, see Hufeland, *Kunst* (1798), 12–15; Schreger, "Onanie," *AEWK* (1832); Klein, "Selbstbefleckung," *EWmW* (1843).

24. The one exception is the case of a peasant girl whose doctor suspected her of onanism on the basis of (among other things) the fact that she lay in bed with her hands under the covers, was dreamy, and had rings around her eyes (no. 812). This case is so striking because it applies a paradigm of masturbatory illness which otherwise simply does not exist in the female cases. However, from time to time the asylum medical notes used terms of exhaustion in cases of female masturbators.

25. Despite the fact that satyriasis was a recognized illness in the literature, it can be found in only one male case (no. 235).

26. No. 673, 6 August, 1847.

27. No. 57, 28 October, 1816.

28. The word itself was never used, evoking as it did an earlier superstitious age shunned by enlightened physicians.

29. One finds it as far back as the ancient Greeks—in, for example, the poetry of Sappho. Ferrand, *Treatise*, 40.

30. No. 812, Basting report, 1842.

31. No. 1225, medical register, 9 March, 1844.

32. No. 95, medical register, 10 April, 1823.

33. "Sinnlosigkeit." The word sensuality ("Sinnlichkeit") is crossed out.

34. No. 830, August, 1846.

35. No. 338, 11 February, 1832.

36. No. 536, medical log, 11 September, 1841.

37. No. 113, medical register.

38. Nos. 242 and 590 are two exceptions.

39. No. 110, 25 August, 1832; 1 September, 1832.

40. No. 64, commitment and release reports, November, 1828; February, 1829.

41. No. 884, 21 June, 1846.

42. Of course, open masturbation in the asylum by male patients was considered an outrageous and "shameless" act. See, for example, the case of Adolph H. (no. 2594) discussed below.

43. On the antisocial aspects of masturbation, see Gilbert, "Masturbation," *Albion* (1980), 275–79; Laqueur, "Social" (1989).

44. No. 722, medical register, 1835.

45. No. 164, 9 June, 1835.

46. No. 2594, 26 May, 1847.

47. No. 264, 27 June, 1843.

48. No. 28, autopsy report, 1825.

49. No. 606, 27 February, 1845.

50. No. 495, 1839.

51. No. 722, 7 November, 1835.

52. Tsouyopoulos, "Influence," in *Brunonianism* (1988), 70–71.

53. "Brunonianism" in W.F. Bynum et al. (eds.), *Dictionary of the History of Science* (Princeton, 1981), 47.

54. Tsouyopoulos, "Doctors," in *Romanticism* (1990); idem, "Influence," 63–74.

55. Tsouyopoulos, "Doctors," 110.

56. Dörner, *Madmen*, 50; Schott, "Heilkonzepte" (1989).

57. Dörner, *Madmen*, 50.

58. A notable exception is the work of Isabel Hull.

59. The literature also recommended a speedy marriage, pregnancy, and in the most stubborn cases, the excision of the clitoris.

60. Tsouyopoulos, "Doctors," 110.

61. Shuttleworth, "Female," in *Body/Politics* (1990), also points out the contemporary focus in Britain on "excess" in female pathology as opposed to "loss" and "self-control" in both male masturbation and spermatorrhoea.

62. No. 2594, medical register, 30 May, 1847; 2 June, 1847.

63. Two influential studies are Hausen, "Polarisierung," in *Sozialgeschichte* (1976); Davidoff and Hall, *Family* (1987).

64. See the literature cited in note. 1.

65. Laqueur, "Orgasm," in *Making* (1987), 3; idem, *Making Sex* (1990).

66. *Nymphomanie*, 38–40.

67. Jessen, "Nymphomanie," 393–94.

68. Groneman, "Nymphomania," also makes this point quite forcefully.

69. No. 673, 3 August, 1847.

70. No. 358, 19 August, 1848.

71. No. 1075, 29 September, 1838.

72. No. 128, medical log, 16 January, 1830. On conceptions of femininity embedded in asylum practice, see also Showalter, *Female Malady* (1985), chapter. 3.

73. See, for example, Jessen, "Nymphomanie," 411. On the image in the eighteenth century, see "Geilheit," *ZUL* (1735), 642–43; Lipping, "Bürgerliche," in *Frauenkörper* (1986), 40. On gender metamorphosis before the eighteenth century, see Ferrand, *Treatise*, 230–31, 384–85.

74. Jessen, "Nymphomanie," 400.

75. The male fear of women is discussed at length in Delumeau, *Peur* (1978).

76. No. 541, 22 August, 1843.

77. No. 933, November, 1835.

78. No. 1231, 21 December, 1847. On the genital signs of male masturbation, see also Müller, *Entwurf* (1796), 138–39.

79. No. 606, 27 February, 1845.

80. Trepp, *Sanfte* (1995).

81. See, for example, Hausen, "Polarisierung,"; Davidoff and Hall, *Family*.

82. Hull, *Sexuality*, 248. See also Laqueur, "Orgasm"; Herzog, *Intimacy*.

83. Hull, *Sexuality*, 251–56.

Chapter 5

1. No. 187, medical log, 18 June, 1836; 13 August, 1836.

2. Medical log, 30 July, 1836.

3. Other material in the file reinforces this interpretation.

4. Nymphomania is no longer listed in the 1990 edition of the *Psychiatric Reference Guide to Diagnostic Criteria*. Consistent with the sexual revolution of the twentieth century, the focus is instead on illnesses of "inhibited" sexuality. One example of the nymphomania concept in contemporary popular culture is Marie Brenner, "Erotomania," *Vanity Fair* (September 1991): 189–265.

5. Busch, *Geschlechtsleben* (1839–45), 678.

6. Jessen, "Nymphomanie," 398. See also Louyer-Villermay, "Nymphomanie," *DSM* (1819), 563, 572–73; Esquirol, *Mental*, 342.

7. Jessen, "Nymphomanie," 363.

8. For British asylum patients, see Showalter, *Female*. One can assume these ideals were particularly important in nymphomania, given the way it was diagnosed primarily through external signs.

9. Nos. 311, 889, 95.

10. No. 151, 29 September, 1834.

11. Undated patient suicide note: "Meine Seele ist der Beschauung Gottes entzo-

gen . . ." Marianna had sought to kill herself by (allegedly) swallowing pins. She subsequently had a tearful reunion with her mother and was released one month later.

12. No. 66, 16 December, 1828.

13. 2 July, 1829.

14. No. 151, medical log, 18 October, 1834.

15. The "crisis" in contemporary medicine was the pinnacle of the disease, which begins the recovery process.

16. No. 151, letter to Lindpaintner, 28 April, 1835.

17. I do not mean to imply by this that middle-class patients were always more capable of controlling their feelings.

18. Frevert, *Krankheit* (1984), 116 ff; Lipp, "Innenseite," in *Arbeit* (1990). On Nassau, see Göbel, *Verarmung* (1846); Blum, *Staatliche* (1987).

19. This issue is dealt with further in the next chapter.

20. See, for example, Davis, *Society* (1975); Landes, *Women,* (1988).

21. Jessen, "Nymphomanie," 365 66.

22. No. 1085, 1844.

23. This is consistent with Foucault's thesis about the productive nature of power in modern institutions. Foucault, *Discipline*; idem, *Sexuality*, 92–95.

24. No. 124, 29 April, 1827. The "amorous" diagnosis is somewhat ambiguous: it could have meant either erotomania (obsession with a single love-object affecting only the mind) or an early stage of nymphomania (indiscriminate love of a carnal nature). But both referred to an uncontrollable state of desire, the former of the mind ("love"), the latter of the body ("sex").

25. Two examples: A single servant woman, living with her two brothers and "guardian," who was regularly "beaten at home," and began suffering from terrible nightmares and anxiety. After her commitment, it was said that she "preferred" it in Eberbach (no. 586); An extremely poor day laborer, who arrived at Eberbach in a "wretched [*elend*] condition." The patient said that he was "thankful and content" at Eberbach, and did not want to go home (no. 203).

26. No. 99, 14 February, 1824; medical log, 1824–31.

27. Medical log, November 1825; May 1826; October 1829.

28. Autopsy report, 1831.

29. The sociologist Erving Goffman discusses such a process in his seminal work on twentieth-century institutions of confinement, *Asylums* (1961).

30. No. 311, medical log, 30 January, 1836.

31. 13 February, 1836.

32. 11 September, 1836.

33. 14 February, 1835; 4 April, 1835; 1–8 August, 1840.

34. In German "sich entblössen" can mean either stripping or uncovering oneself.

35. Here "jealousy" (*Eifersucht*) meant that Elisabeth accused her husband of infidelity.

36. No. 231, Basting report, 1848.

37. No. 124, 3 July, 1826.

38. On the symbolism of removing the hat as a polite gesture of greeting in the nineteenth century, see Bausinger, "Bürgerlichkeit," in *Bürger* (1987), 125–27.

39. No. 124, 3 July, 1826.

40. Schulte, *Dorf*, 41-90.

41. See, for example, "Entblößung," *Handwörterbuch des Deutschen Aberglaubens* 2 (1929/30), 846–48; Christine de Pizan, *The Book of the City of Ladies*, 58.

42. Bergren, "Baubo," (1985).

43. See, for example, Gullickson, "Unruly," in *Gendered* (1992), 143.

44. No. 99, medical log, 8 August, 1829.

45. To be sure there were cases of patients undressing and ripping up their clothes before admission to the asylum. I do not examine these instances, but some of the following analysis is relevant to these cases as well.

46. No. 1993, medical log, 15 January, 7 June, 20 June, 1850.

47. No. 673, Basting report, 13 August, 1847; medical log 26 March, 1851.

48. No. 877, 25 January, 1847.

49. 23 September, 1848.

50. Lindpaintner to Nassau government, 1820, HStAW, 211/394 (1).

51. 1820 asylum house rules, quoted in Hötger, *Sozialstruktur*, 226. I have inferred the financial reasons for such a policy, though such reasons were not explicitly stated. The procedure outlined above is consistent with the general asylum approach to meeting expenses. The use of patient labor was another such cost-saving device.

52. Unlike the gesture of raising the skirt, acts of destroying the clothes were not exclusive to lower-class patients. However, the latter behavior did occur more frequently in such patients.

53. No. 877, 8 January, 1 April, 1848.

54. No. 95, medical log, 11–18 October, 1823.

55. Lindpaintner to Nassau government, 1820, HStAW, 211/394 (1).

56. Foucault, *Sexuality*. The English term was first used in the late nineteenth century. Davidson, "Sex," *Critical Inquiry* (1987), 23.

57. Jessen, "Nymphomanie," 28.

58. The time period of the events can only be estimated, since the passage is a summary written in August of 1846 of the patient's behavior since admission in mid-July of that year.

59. See the case of Christine F., chapter 6.

60. Female patients probably had some contact with other men, such as male attendants called in to assist with violent patients, workers in the asylum, or visiting relatives. They also may have been able to catch glimpses of male inmates from the correctional house and asylum when the latter worked outdoors. On the other hand, patients had frequent, regular, and direct contact with the male doctors and director, making these staff members, it seems to me, the likeliest candidates as the "men" who appear in the nymphomania files.

Chapter 6

1. No. 358, 27 December, 1848.

2. No. 934.

3. Grimm, *Deutsches Wörterbuch*, vol. 13, pp. 1524–26. This meaning appears in both the Catholic and Lutheran traditions.

4. No. 358, 21 August, 1848.

5. On sex as an economic transaction in peasant society, see, for example, Segalen, *Love* (1983), 24; Beck, "Illegitimität," in *Kultur* (1983), 135.

6. Benker, "Ehre," in *Frauenkörper* (1986), 18.

7. Schüler, "Sozialstruktur."

8. No. 889, medical reports of 16 August, 1827 and 5 May, 1832.

9. Hull, *Sexuality*, 29–52.

10. No. 8, 2 October 1814.

11. 1 February, 1814 and undated letter.

12. By contrast, the examining doctor had mentioned the rumor, and an Amt official wrote regarding Elisabeth's past that she was "inclined to promiscuity" (no. 358, 21 August, 1848).

13. No. 536, 5 September, 1841.

14. 16 August, 1841.

15. Schulte, *Dorf*, 171. On nineteenth-century, lower-class attitudes toward female sexuality, see also Lipp, "Ledige," in *Tübinger* (1986).

16. For example, Pinel, *Traité* (1801); Esquirol, *Mental*, 46.

17. "General Rescript" of July 7, 1818, reprinted in Hötger, "Sozialstruktur," 336–38; Lindpaintner to Nassau government, 1831, HStAW, 211/394 (2).

18. The fire event also implicated much or all of the community: the punishment meted out by the "farmers" and *Schultheiß* at the scene of the fire reflected a general suspicion and reproach cast upon Christine in the community. Her "preaching" to the "people" indicates the sense of community accusation; and, given the behavior described, by the time the doctor had been called in to examine her, she had certainly become a marginal and disturbing figure of whom the community wanted to rid itself.

19. No. 358.

20. No. 170, June 1830.

21. No. 967, 3 May, 1838; medical log, 8 March, 1845.

22. No. 128, 23 August, 1820.

23. No. 13, 26 June, 1819.

24. No. 99, 14 Febraury, 1824.

25. Lipp, "Ledige," 75.

26. Segalen, *Love*, 53, 43–46. On the power exercised by women through gossip, see Schulte, *Dorf*, 173–76.

27. No. 1428, October 1843.

28. No. 858, 4 October, 1846.

29. No. 13, 27 July, 1819.

30. Geertz, *Interpretation*, 9.

31. No. 889, medical reports of 16 August, 1827 and 5 May, 1832

32. For Nassau, see Hoffmann, *Rheinhessische*, 88.

33. The notion of symbolic capital is taken from Bourdieu, *Outline* (1977), 177–183.

34. No. 884, 1846.

35. 23 June, 1846.

36. Medical log, 1849-52.

37. Schulte, *Dorf*, 138; Benker, "Ehre," 12.

38. Schuebler, "Gesetze," *DVj* (1854), 63; Blum, *Staatliche*, 18.

39. Klein, "Hessen-Nassau," in *Grundriß* (1979), 120, gives the population figures by gender as 59,859 (adult) males and 65,790 (adult) females. This gender imbalance was probably the product of male emigration in response to the poor economic conditions in Nassau.

40. No. 95.

41. No. 66.
42. No. 1993.
43. Benker, "Ehre," 17.
44. No. 678.
45. No. 1368.
46. No. 673, medical report, 9 July, 1847.
47. At least five of the Jewish nymphomania cases were those of women who were both single and poor. Two other cases included a woman without means who had been abandoned by her husband, and a twenty-one-year-old girl whose economic situation could not be determined. See the more detailed discussion of *Schutz* and the discriminatory laws against Jews in chapter 8.
48. No. 153, 14 January, 1835.
49. Beck, "Illegitimität," 137; Benker, "Ehre," 14–17.
50. Lunbeck, "New Generation."
51. Lunbeck, "New Generation," 513.
52. No. 612.
53. No. 1993, 5 August, 1849.
54. 27 July, 1847.
55. This diagnosis he based on the character of her menstrual blood and the fact that it had stopped altogether right before the outbreak of the illness.
56. 1879 autopsy report.
57. Benker, "Ehre," 16.
58. 21 July, 1847.
59. 11 July, 1849. The presence of "deckhands" is explained by the fact that Anna's village, Niederlahnstein, was located on the Rhine.
60. 27 July, 1849.
61. Beck, "Illegitimität," 140–42.
62. Benker, "Ehre," 17.
63. In another context, that of working-class women in nineteenth-century Württemburg, Lipp, "Ledige," 85, comments on the internal conflict of single, lower-class women who had little stake in upholding the norms of sexual honor but, at the same time, remained internally bound by those norms.
64. No. 174, 2 April, 1825.
65. Schulte, *Dorf*, 69.
66. No. 720, 1830.
67. No. 1441, Eberbach admissions report, 1846; autopsy report, 1848.
68. No. 877, 16 November, 1846.
69. No. 95, Amt report, 29 January, 1823.
70. Medical report, 1 January, 1823; Amt interview of brother, 29 January, 1823.
71. Heerdt, "Madness," (1986).
72. Ibid., 361. Wild man also involved something not seen specifically in the Eberbach sources: dressing and acting like men.
73. Ibid., 361, 363.
74. Ibid., 363–66.

Chapter 7

1. Hare, "Masturbatory," 4.
2. Gilbert, "Masturbation," 269; idem, "Doctor," *JHMAS* (1975). Gilbert ex-

amined only cases of middle-class patients, which partly accounts for his conclusions.

3. No. 264, 7 September, 1842.

4. 12 October, 1842.

5. 18 October, 1842.

6. See, for example, Schulte, "Reinterpretations" (1984).

7. Report to Amt Höchst, 22 October, 1842.

8. 29 October, 1842.

9. 3 November, 1842.

10. 1 December, 1842.

11. Windt's release report gave as the only indication of masturbation "the observations of the doctor who treated him in Frankfurt."

12. 1 December, 1842.

13. As for "shyness" and "embarrassment," these reactions were common among the patients. In a case of suspected masturbation, however, they were read as one more confirmation of onanism.

14. No. 1241, 21 January, 1840.

15. No. 710, 3 April, 1846; 27 May, 1846.

16. No. 722, 7 November, 1835.

17. No. 164, 9 June, 1835.

18. Eberbach quarterly report to Nassau government, 1837, HStAW, 211/394 (3).

19. Symptoms that families and communities most often viewed as signs of mental derangement included dangerous and out-of-control behavior, as well as disobedience and not working.

20. No. 249, 13 December, 1841. The asylum considered the patient's opinion on this matter an "idée fixe," which, together with other faulty ideas, proved that the "faculties of thought and judgment are significantly disturbed."

21. Stengers and van Neck, *Grande*, 109–112, show that before the late seventeenth century, the medical literature never mentioned onanism as a cause of illness. Consistent with the Galenic (humoral) model of disease, it stressed instead the dangers of sperm *retention*. There was a glaring inconsistency in eighteenth- and nineteenth-century medicine, which, still often using a humoral model, advocated the necessity of ridding the body of the humor blood to preserve or restore health, while at the same time vehemently opposed the draining from the body of the seminal humor.

22. No. 249, 15 November, 1842.

23. No. 541, 22 August, 1843.

24. No. 230, February, 1841.

25. No. 26, 6 February, 1824.

26. No. 206, 1820 medical report.

27. *Accessists* were candidates for higher bureaucractic office.

28. No. 606, 17 February, 1845. One of the supposed effects of masturbation was that the "facial features have a peculiar character, something agitated, disrupted" (Schreger, "Onanie," 398).

29. The father's profession is unknown.

30. No. 820, "Lebenslauf" of the patient, 17 December, 1825. The author of this letter, together with a third brother (an *Oberleutnant*), later became a patient himself at Eberbach.

31. Foucault, *Sexuality*, 34–35.

32. No. 2594, medical report of Dr. Kiefel, 26 May, 1847.

33. 3 May, 1847. It can not be determined whether this letter preceded or antedated the communication between Herr B. and Dr. Kiefel.

34. 16 February, 1847.

35. 30 May, 1847. The connection between the insanity and onanism was explicitly made in a later report of 2 June, 1847.

Chapter 8:

1. Lessing, *Die Juden*, quoted in Gay (ed.), *Enlightenment* (1973), 750.

2. No. 107.

3. Goldstein, "Wandering," *JCH* (1985).

4. Gilman, "Jews," *JHBS* (1984); idem, *Difference* (1985); most recently, idem, *Case* (1993), 20–26.

5. "Jews," 150.

6. Ibid., 157.

7. Shorter, "Women," *Medical History* (1989).

8. HStAW, 211/394 (1).

9. Figures for the Jewish and gentile populations in Nassau are averages of the censuses of 1821, 1831, and 1843. HStAW, 210/11037(a); Vogel, *Beschreibung*, 428–29. Elsewhere in Germany, Jews likewise tended to be slightly overrepresented in asylums. See Fuchs, "Medicinische Statistik" (1833), 89; Ruer, *Irrenstatistik* (1837), 10.

10. Kober, "Juden," *NA* (1955), 224.

11. Goldstein, "Wandering," 532.

12. Poliakov, *History*, vol. 3 (1968), 52, discusses the nonviolent coping strategies of Jews as "peaceful means of resistance."

13. On the role of national characteristics in mental illness, see Esquirol, *Mental* (1965), 30–48; Heinroth, *Textbook*, vol. 2, 257–58; In his textbook *Allgemeine Diagnostik* (1832), 90–103, Friedreich discussed at length national characteristics, basing these largely on custom, habit, and even religious belief; still, no mention of Jews.

14. Proctor, *Racial* (1988).

15. Nipperdey and Rürup, "Antisemitismus," in *Geschichtliche* (1972); Sterling, *Judenß* (1969); Rürup, *Emanzipation* (1975).

16. See, for example, Heinroth, *Textbook*, 254–59.

17. See, especially, Lindpaintner to the Nassau government, 1820, HStAW, 211/394 (1).

18. No. 94.

19. Gilman, *Difference*, 12, 18.

20. Mosse, *Toward* (1978).

21. Richards, *Mental*, 269.

22. On the stereotypical "Jewish" appearance, dating back to the fifteenth century, see Mosse, *Germans* (1970), 63–64.

23. One exception is no. 476.

24. See, for example, Heinroth, *System* (1825), 336–47.

25. On the image of the Jew in eighteenth-century thought, see Katz, *From Prejudice* (1980). On medieval conceptions of Jews as allies of the devil intent on destroying Christianity, see Trachtenberg, *Devil* (1943).

26. Bering, *Stigma* (1992), 47–53.

27. For example, nos. 1225 and 216.

28. No. 107.

29. 2 May, 1832.

30. 2 December, 1829.

31. Medical log, 25 April, 1829.

32. Medical log, 25 July, 1829.

33. Schwenken, *Notizen* (1820), 43–44, 197. The "Torfdrucker" (or "Dorf-drucker") is described in Stuhlmüller, *Vollständige* (1823), xx, as a type of "market thief" whose "exclusive occupation consists in stealing money, watches, tobacco, pipes, and other such things out of the people's pockets at large cattle or other yearly markets and fairs." Abraham and his family are also listed in Stuhlmüller (pp. 42–43).

34. The village of Eckederoth was notorious as a safe haven for robber bands. Boehncke and Sarkowicz (eds.), *Räuberbanden* (1991), 18.

35. Schwenke, *Notizen*, 44.

36. Glanz, *Geschichte* (1968).

37. Glanz, *Geschichte*, 60–87, 118–20; Boehncke, *Räuberbanden*, 9–20.

38. Glanz, *Geschichte*, 87, 102.

39. Toury, (ed.), *Eintritt* (1972), 165–66.

40. Schwenke, *Notizen*, iv–v.

41. See also the description of the Jewish *Gauner* in an 1823 notice to the police authorities by the Bavarian government: Toury, *Eintritt*, 168–74.

42. Among the more amusing tactics these bands used to deflect suspicion from themselves onto the non-Jewish bands was the practice of leaving at the scene of the crime Christian objects, such as pork and the Host. Gentile bands picked up the tactic and left, in their turn, Jewish objects, such as the Ten Commandments. The police were onto all of this, and therefore knew how to simply reverse the relationship between sign and perpetrator. Glanz, *Geschichte*, 119–20.

43. See Goldstein, "Wandering," for an analysis of the trope of the Wandering Jew in late nineteenth-century psychiatry. The discourse on the itinerant *Gauner* Jew probably drew upon the Wandering Jew myth.

44. Since these manuals were expensive and published for internal police use. There is no communication about the Schwenken manual or any of the information it includes in Abraham's file.

45. Medical log, 15 August, 1830.

46. Medical log, 14–21 May, 1831.

47. Medical register, 19 September, 1829.

48. April 1832.

49. *Webster's New Collegiate Dictionary*, eighth ed. (Springfield: Merriam Co., 1981), 53.

50. Scholem, *Sabbatai Sevi* (1973).

51. Scholem, *Messianic* (1971), 61–62.

52. Ibid., 152.

53. Ibid., 160.

54. Seligenstadt (about seven miles to the south of Offenbach) and Friedberg, north of Offenbach, are two towns listed by Schwenken, *Notizen*, 44, where Abraham was under investigation.

55. Katz, *Out of the Ghetto* (1973), 27; idem., *Exclusiveness and Tolerance* (1961), 158–162.

56. The word "rabble" was used by an official in reference to the ambiguous and problematic residence status of Abraham and his family, who were presumed not to possess *Schutz* (30 March, 1829).

57. No. 73. There is no record of how he previously had made a living, but a prisoner from his wife's village said that the wife was a leaseholder.

58. Medical log, 5–12 September, 1829.

59. 19 October, 1828.

60. No. 1328.

61. No. 73, 29 December, 1828.

62. Eberbach quarterly report to Nassau government, 1826, HStAW, 211/395.

63. "On the 23rd, [MJ] was punished with eight hours of lock-up [*Krumm*] for being work-shy and dirty. Since then, he has spun one full spool, dirtied the bed four times instead of using the bedpan, urinated in his pants . . ." (20 January, 1829).

64. "Occurrence," 31 January, 1829.

65. Reports of 1 September, 1828; 27 November, 1828; 10 February, 1829.

66. 10 October, 1828.

67. Lunbeck, *Psychiatric*, 121–126. Her conclusion dovetails my own: "Psychiatrists were alert to racial variations in temperament, but they did not diagnose patients straightforwardly along racial or ethnic lines. More often than not, when they drew on racial psychology they did so to brand individuals not abnormal but *normal*, invoking race to account for and render inconsequential otherwise damaging behaviors."

Conclusion

1. Joan Acocella, "The Politics of Hysteria," *The New Yorker.* 6 April, 1998: 74. See also the interesting exchange about M.P.D. between Ian Hacking and Jean Comaroff. Hacking, "Two Souls," in *Questions* (1991), 433–77.

2. Ibid., 64–68.

3. Ibid., 68 and *passim*.

4. Ibid., 68.

5. Lunbeck, *Psychiatric*, 3.

6. Foucault, *Madness,* chap. 9.

7. For an incisive critique of Foucault's General Confinement thesis, see Midelfort, "Madness and Civilization," in *After the Reformation* (1980).

8. Foucault's *I Pierre* is an exception.

9. For a review of the issues and literature, see Kleinman, *Rethinking Psychiatry* (1988).

10. Ibid., 50–51.

11. Examples include Canning, *Languages* (1996); Coffin, *Politics* (1996); Scott, *Gender*; Herzog, *Intimacy.*

12. See chap. 3, pp. 76–77

13. Blasius, *Einfache*, 78.

14. Ibid. The first specialized psychiatric journal, *Allgemeine Zeitschrift für Psychiatrie,* was actually founded in 1844.

Works Cited

A. Unpublished Sources

Hessisches Hauptstaatsarchiv Wiesbaden (HStAW)

Section No.

430/1	Eberbach/Eichberg Asylum Patient Files
211/394 (1–3)	Eberbach Asylum Yearly Reports to Nassau Government, 1815–1844
211/395	Eberbach Asylum Quarterly Reports to Nassau Government, 1825–1828
210/3554 (2)	Nassau Organization of Medical Care, 1824–1839
210/3556 (a)	Nassau Examination of Medical and Pharmaceutical Candidates, 1845–1867
210/11037 (a)	Nassau Population Statistics, 1811–1854
210/6379	Appointment and Retirement of Medical Assistant Basting

Diözesanarchiv Limburg

B. Published Primary Sources

Anon. "Geilheit." *Großes vollständiges Universal-Lexikon,* edited by Zedler, vol. 10, 637–44. 1735. Reprint. Graz: Akademische Druck- u. Verlagsanstalt, 1961.

Basting, Andreas. "Wie können für Irrenanstalten menschenliebende Wärter und Aufseher gewonnen werden?" *Allgemeine Zeitschrift für Psychiatrie* 2 (1845): 421–474.

———. "Begünstigt das pennsylvanische Strafsystem der Entstehung des Wahnsinns?" *Allgemeine Zeitschrift für Psychiatrie* 4 (1847): 106–21.

————. "Bericht über die Oldenburgische Irrenanstalt." *Correspondenzblatt der deutschen Gesellschaft für Psychiatrie und gerichtliche Psychologie* (1866): 82.

Bienville, M.D.T. de. *Nymphomanie, worinnen von den Ursachen, Anfange und Fortgange dieses gefährlichen Übels gründlich gehandelt wird*. No. trans. Amsterdam: Johann Schreuder, 1772.

————. *Nymphomania, or, A dissertation concerning the furor uterinus*. Translated by E.S. Wilmot. London: J. Bew, 1775.

Biermann, "Aerztlich-psychologisches Gutachten über einen Zustand von Wahnsinn durch religiöse Schwärmerei . . ." *Archiv für medizinische Erfahrung* (January, February, 1831): 106–26.

Bird, Friederich, "Über die religiöse Melancholie." *Zeitschrift für die Anthropologie* 2 (1823): 229.

Blumröder, Gustav. "Über religiösen Trübsinn." *Blätter für Psychiatrie* 1 (1837): 14–26.

Brunn, Friedrich. *Mitteilungen aus meinem Leben*. Zwickau, 1893.

Bucknill, John Charles and Daniel H. Tuke, *Manual of Psychological Medicine* 1858. Reprint. New York: Hafner, 1968.

Burrows, George M. *Inquiry into Certain Errors Relative to Insanity*. London, 1820.

Burton, Robert. *Anatomy of Melancholy* (1621). New York: Tudor, 1938

Busch, Dietrich Wilhelm Heinrich. *Das Geschlechtsleben des Weibes in physiologischer, pathologischer, und therapeutischer Hinsicht*. Leipzig: Brockhaus, 1839–45.

Crichton, Alexander. *An Inquiry into the Nature and Origin of Mental Derangement*. 1798. Reprint. New York: AMS, 1976.

Emmermann, F.W. "Philipp Heinrich Lindpaintner." *Neuer Nekrolog der Deutschen* 26 (1850): 575–88.

Esquirol, Jean Etienne. *Mental Maladies. A Treatise on Insanity*. Translated by E.K. Hunt. 1845. Reprint. New York: Hafner, 1965.

Ferrand, Jacques. *A Treatise on Lovesickness*. 1623. Translated and edited by D. Beecher. Syracuse, N.Y.: Syracuse University Press, 1990.

Flemming, Carl Friedrich, "Nachtrag." *Allgemeine Zeitschrift für Psychiatrie* 6 (1849): 259–61.

Friedreich, Johannes Baptista. *Allgemeine Diagnostik der psychischen Krankheiten*. Würzburg: Strecker, 1832.

Fuchs, Dr. "Medicinische Statistik der Irrenhäuser und des Irrseyns." *Neues Magazin für philosophische, medizinische und gerichtliche Seelenkunde* 3 (1833): 45–133.

Göbel, F.H. *Über die Verarmung im Herzogtum Nassau: Ihre Entstehung und die dagegen anzuwendenden Mittel; nebst einer vorhergehenden allgemeinen Betrachtung über den Pauperismus*. Wiesbaden: L. Riedel, 1846.

Grohmann, Johann Christian. "Über religiösen Aberglauben und Mysticismus in der Geschichte der Menschheit." *Zeitschrift für die Anthropologie* 4 (1825): 193–307.

Heinroth, Johann Christian. *Geschichte und Kritik des Mysticismus aller bekannten Völker und Zeiten*. Leipzig: C.H.F. Hartmann, 1830.

————. *Textbook of Disturbances of Mental Life*. 2 vols. 1818. Translated by J. Schmorak. Baltimore: Johns Hopkins University Press, 1975.

————. *System der psychisch-gerichtlichen Medizin*. Leipzig, 1825.

Henke, Adolph. *Lehrbuch der gerichtlichen Medicin*. 10th ed. Berlin: Ferdinand Dümmler, 1841.

Hoffbauer, Johann Christoph. *Wie ärztlich-psychologische Gutachten organisirt und ausgefertigt sein müssen wenn sie den Zwecken des Richters entsprechen sollen.* Berlin: Albert Förstner, 1845.

———. *Untersuchungen über die Krankheiten der Seele und verwandten Zustände,* 3 vols. Halle: Johann Gottfried Trampen, 1802–1807.

Hudtwalcker, Martin. *Ueber den Einfluss des sogenannten Mysticismus und der religiösen Schwärmerei auf das Ueberhandnehmen der Geisteskrankheiten und des Selbstmordes, besonders in Hamburg.* Hamburg, 1827.

Hufeland, C.W. *Die Kunst das menschliche Leben zu Verlängern.* Jena, 1798.

Ideler, Carl Wilhelm, *Versuch einer Theorie des religiösen Wahnsinns.* Halle: Schwetschke und Sohn, 1848.

———. *Grundriß der Seelenheilkunde,* 2 vols. Berlin, 1835/38.

Jacobi, Maximilian. *Die Hauptformen der Seelenstörungen in ihren Beziehungen zur Heilkunde nach der Beobachtung geschildert.* Leipzig: Verlag der Weidmann'schen Buchhandlung, 1844.

———. "Irrenanstalten" *Encyclopädisches Wörterbuch der medicinischen Wissenschaften* 19 (1839): 62–197.

Jessen, Peter Willers. "Nymphomanie." *Encyclopädisches Wörterbuch der medicinischen Wissenschaften* 25 (1841): 357–415.

Lindpaintner, P.H. *Nachrichten über die Herzoglich Nassauische Irrenanstalt zu Eberbach im Rheingau von ihrer Begründung an bis zum Schlusse des Jahres 1842.* Wiesbaden: A. Scholz'schen Offizin, 1844.

———"Rechenschaft über die Verwaltung des Herzogl. Nassauishen Irrenhauses zu Eberbach im Rheingau im Jahre 1844," *Allgemeine Zeitschrift für Psychiatrie* 4 (1847): 70–73;

Klein Dr. "Selbstbefleckung." *Encylopädisches Wörterbuch der medicinischen Wissenschaften* 31 (1843): 513–25.

Louyer-Villermay. "Nymphomanie." *Dictionaire des Sciences Médicales* 36 (1819): 561–96.

Morel, Benedict-Augustin. "Pathologie Mentale en Belgique, en Allemagne, en Italie et en Suisse. Notice sur L'Hospice d'Eberbach." *Annales Médico-Psychologiques* 8 (1846): 18–41.

Müller, J.V. *Entwurf der gerichtlichen Arzneiwissenschaft,* vol. 1. Frankfurt: Andreáische Buchhandlung, 1796.

Pinel, Philippe. *Nosographie Philosophique, ou La Méthode de l'Analyse Appliquée a la Médecine.* 5th edition. Paris: J.A. Brosson, 1813.

———. *Traité Médico-philosophique sur l'Aliénation Mentale ou la Manie.* Paris: Richard, Caille et Ravier, 1801.

———. *A Treatise on Insanity.* Translated by D.D. Davis. 1806. Reprint. Washington, D.C.: University Publications of America, 1977.

Pizan, Christine de. *The Book of the City of Ladies.* Translated by Earl Jeffrey Richards. New York: Persea, 1982.

Reil, Johann Christian. *Rhapsodieen über die Anwendung der psychischen Curmethode auf Geisteszerrüttungen.* 1803. Reprint. Amsterdam : E.J. Bonset, 1968.

Roller, C.F.W.. *Die Irrenanstalt nach allen ihren Beziehungen.* Karlsruhe, 1831.

Rotteck, Karl von. "Aberglaube." *Das Staats-Lexikon* 1 (Altona, 1845): 85–90.

Ruer, Wilhelm. *Irrenstatistik der Provinz Westphalen.* Berlin: Enslin, 1837.

Schreger, Th. "Onanie." *Allgemeine Encyklopädie der Wissenschaften und Künste,* edited by Ersch and Gruber. Section 3, vol. 3 (1832): 398–401.

Schwenken, K. *Notizen über die berüchtigsten jüdischen Gauner und Spitzbuben*. Marburg: J.C. Krieger, 1820.

Soranus, *Gynecology*, translated by Owsei Temkin. Baltimore: Johns Hopkins, 1956.

Spengler, L. "Über die Predigerkrankheit in Schweden." *Allgemeine Zeitschrift Für Psychiatrie* 6 (1849): 253–59.

Stuhlmüller, Karl. *Vollständige Nachrichten über eine polizeyliche Untersuchung gegen jüdische . . . Gaunerbanden*. Plassenburg, 1823.

Tissot, S.-A.D. *Onanism, or, A Treatise upon the Disorders produced by Masturbation*. 4th ed. Translated by A. Hume. London: Richardson Urquhart, 1772.

Ulrich, August Leoppold. "Bemerkungen über die Wunderheilungen des Fürsten Hohenlohe und des Bauern Martin Michel, mit einem Rückblick auf die am Mittelrhein davon sichtbar gewordenen Wirkungen," *Zeitschrift für die Anthropologie* 2 (1823): 397–412.

Villaume, Peter. "Über die Unzuchtsünden in der Jugend." In *Allgemeinen Revision des gesammten Schul- und Erziehungswesens*, edited by J.H. Campe, vol. 7. Wolfenbüttel, 1787.

Vogel, C.D. *Beschreibung des Herzogthums Nassau*. 1843. Reprint. Niederwalluf: Dr. Martin Sändig, 1971.

Wachsmuth, Dr. "Bericht über die Irrenanstalt Eberbach aus dem Jahre 1828 an die K. französische Gesandtschaft." *Allgemeine Zeitschrift für Psychiatrie* 81 (1929): 242–55.

C. Secondary Works Cited

Acocella, Joan. "The Politics of Hysteria." *New Yorker* April 6, 1988: 64–79.

Adam, Alfred. "Die Nassauische Union von 1817." *Jahrbuch der Kirchengeschichtlichen Vereinigung in Hessen und Nassau* 1 (1949): 35–400.

Alexander, Franz G. and Sheldon T. Selesnick. *The History of Psychiatry: An Evaluation of Psychiatric Thought and Practice from Prehistoric Times to the Present*. New York: Harper & Row, 1966.

Anderson, Margaret Lavinia. "Piety and Politics: Recent Work on German Catholicism." *The Journal of Modern History* 63/1 (1991): 681–716.

Barker-Benfield, G.J. *The Horrors of the Half-Known Life: Male Attitudes toward Women and Sexuality in Nineteenth-Century America*. New York: Harper & Row, 1977.

———. "The Spermatic Economy: A Nineteenth-Century View of Sexuality." In *The American Family in Social-Historical Perspective*, edited by Michael Gordon, 336–72. New York: St. Martin's Press, 1973.

Bausinger, Hermann. "Bürgerlichkeit und Kultur." In *Bürger und Bürgerlichkeit im 19. Jahrhundert*, edited by Jürgen Kocka, 121–142. Göttingen: Vandenhoeck & Ruprecht, 1987.

Becker, Erich. "Die Gemeindeverfassung in Nassau seit dem Ausgang des 18. Jahrhunderts." *Rheinische Vierteljahresblatt* 1 (1932): 19–42.

Beck, Rainer. "Illegitimität und voreheliche Sexualität auf dem Land. Unterfinning, 1671–1770." In *Kultur der einfachen Leute: Bayerisches Volksleben vom 16. bis zum 19. Jahrhundert*, edited by Richard van Dülmen, 112–50. Munich: C.H. Beck, 1983.

Benker, Gitta. "'Ehre und Schande'—Voreheliche Sexualität auf dem Lande im ausgehenden 18. Jahrhundert." In *Frauenkörper, Medizin, Sexualität: Auf dem Wege zu einer neuen Sexualmoral*, edited by Johanna Geyer-Kordesch and Annette Kuhn, 10–27. Düsseldorf: Pädagogischer Verlag Schwann-Bagel, 1986.

Bergren, Ann. "Baubo: The Praise and Blame of the Female in Archaic Greece." Paper presented at the UCLA Faculty Seminar on Women, Culture and Theory, Los Angeles, May 1985.

Bering, Dietz. *The Stigma of Names: Antisemitism in German Daily Life, 1812–1933*, translated by Neville Plaice. Ann Arbor: University of Michigan Press, 1992.

Blackbourn, David. *Marpingen: Apparitions of the Virgin Mary in Bismarckean Germany*. New York: Knopf, 1993.

Blasius, Dirk. *Umgang mit Unheilbarem: Studien zur Sozialgeschichte der Psychiatrie*. Bonn: Psychiatrie-Verlag, 1986.

———. *'Einfache Seelenstörung': Geschichte der deutschen Psychiatrie 1800–1945*. Frankfurt/M: Fischer Taschenbuch Verlag, 1994.

———. *Der verwaltete Wahnsinn: Eine Sozialgeschichte des Irrenhauses*. Frankfurt: Fischer Taschenbuch Verlag, 1980.

———. *Kriminalität und Alltag. Zur Konfliktgeschichte des Alltagslebens im 19. Jahrhundert*. Göttingen: Vandenhoeck & Ruprecht, 1978.

Blessing, Werner K. *Staat und Kirche in der Gesellschaft*. Göttingen: Vandenhoeck & Ruprecht, 1982.

Blum, Peter. "Armut und Alkohol im Herzogtum Nassau." *Nassauische Annalen* 97 (1986): 65–81.

———. *Staatliche Armenfürsorge im Herzogtum Nassau, 1806–1866*. Wiesbaden: Selbstverlag der Historischen Kommission für Nassau, 1987.

Boehncke, Heiner and Hans Sarkowicz (eds), *Die deutschen Räuberbanden. Vol. I: Die Großen Räuber*. Frankfurt/M: Eichborn, 1991.

Bourdieu, Pierre. *Outline of a Theory of Practice*. Cambridge: Cambridge University Press, 1977.

Breit, Stefan. *"Leichtfertigkeit" und ländliche Gesellschaft. Voreheliche Sexualität in der frühen Neuzeit*. Munich: Oldenbourg Verlag, 1991.

Broman, Thomas. "Rethinking Professionalization: Theory, Practice, and Professional Ideology in Eighteenth-Century German Medicine." *Journal of Modern History* 67 (1995): 835–72.

Bynum, Caroline Walker. *Holy Feast and Holy Fast. The Religious Significance of Food to Medieval Women*. Berkeley: University of California Press, 1987.

Canning, Kathleen. "Feminist History after the Linguistic Turn: Historicizing Discourse and Experience." *Signs* 19 (1994): 368–404.

———. *Languages of Labor and Gender. Female Factory Work in Germany, 1850–1914*. Ithaca: Cornell University Press, 1996.

Carstairs, G.M. and R.L. Kapur, *The Great Universe of Kota: Stress, Change, and Mental Disorder in an Indian Village*. New York: Basic, 1969.

Castel, Robert. *The Regulation of Madness: The Origins of Incarceration in France*. Translated by W.D. Halls. Berkeley: University of California Press, 1988.

Chauncey, George. "From Sexual Inversion to Homosexuality: Medicine and the Changing Conceptualization of Female Deviance." *Salmagundi* nos. 58–59 (Fall 1982–Winter 1983): 114–46.

Cohen, Ed. "(R)evolutionary Scenes: The Body Politic and the Political Body in Henry Maudsley's Nosology of 'Masturbatory Insanity.'" *Nineteenth-Century Contexts* 11, no. 2 (1987): 179–191.

Coffin, Judith G. *The Politics of Women's Work: The Paris Garment Trades, 1750–1915*. Princeton: Princeton University Press, 1996.

Cominos, Peter T. "Late Victorian Sexual Respectability and the Social System." *International Review of Social History* 8 (1963): 18–48.

Cott, Nancy. "Passionlessness: An Interpetation of Victorian Sexual Ideology." In *A Heritage of Her Own*, edited by N. Cott and E. Pleck, 162–81. New York: Simon and Schuster, 1979.

Cunningham, Andrew and Nicholas Jardine (eds.), *Romanticism and the Sciences*. Cambridge: Cambridge University Press, 1990.

Davidoff, Leonore and Catherine Hall. *Family Fortunes. Men and Women of the English Middle Class, 1780–1850*. Chicago: University of Chicago Press, 1987.

Davidson, Arnold. "Sex and the Emergence of Sexuality." *Critical Inquiry* 14 (1987): 16–48.

Davis, Natalie Zemon. *Society and Culture in Early Modern France*. Stanford: Stanford University Press, 1975.

Delumeau, Jean. *La Peur en Occident, XIVe–XVIIIe Siècles: une Cité Assiégeé*. Paris: Fayard, 1978.

Demandt, Karl E. *Geschichte des Landes Hessen*. Kassel: Bárenreiter, 1980.

Devlin, Judith. *The Superstitious Mind: French Peasants and the Supernatural in the Nineteenth Century*. New Haven: Yale University Press, 1987.

Diethelm, Oskar. "La Surexcitation Sexuelle: Historique et Discussion Clinique." *L' Evolution Psychiatrique* 31 (1966): 233–45.

Digby, Anne. *Madness, Morality and Medicine: A Study of the York Retreat, 1796–1914*. Cambridge: Cambridge University Press, 1987.

Dörner, Klaus. *Madmen and the Bourgeoisie: A Social History of Insanity and Psychiatry*. Translated by J. Neugroschel and J. Steinberg. Oxford: Basil Blackwell, 1981.

Donnely, Michael. *Managing the Mind: A Study of Medical Psychology in Early Nineteenth-Century Britain*. London: Tavistock, 1983.

Douglas, Mary. *Purity and Danger: An Analysis of the Concepts of Pollution and Taboo*. London: Routledge, 1966.

Duden, Barbara. *Geschichte unter der Haut*. Stuttgart: Klett-Cotta, 1987.

Dwyer, Ellen. *Homes for the Mad: Life Inside Two 19th Century Asylums*. New Brunswick: Rutgers University Press, 1987.

Eisenbach, Ulrich. *Zuchthäuser, Armenanstalten und Waisenhäuser in Nassau*. Wiesbaden: Historische Kommission für Nassau, 1994.

Eley, Geoff. "Labor History, Social History, Alltagsgeschichte: Experience, Culture, and the Politics of the Everyday—a New Direction for German Social History," *Journal of Modern History* 61 (1989): 297–343.

Elias, Norbert. *The History of Manners. The Civilizing Process: Volume I*. New York: Pantheon, 1978.

Ester, Matthias M. "'Ruhe- Ordnung- Fleiß'. Disziplin, Arbeit und Verhaltenstherapie in der Irrenanstalt des frühen 19. Jahrhunderts." *Archiv für Kulturgeschichte* 71 (1989): 349–76.

Evans, Richard J. *Death in Hamburg: Society and Politics in the Cholera Years, 1830–1910*. Oxford: Clarendon, 1987.

———(ed.). *Rethinking German History: Nineteenth-Century Germany and the Origins of the Third Reich*. London: Unwin Hyman, 1987.

Feldmann, Detlef. "Die 'religiöse Melancholie' in der deutschsprachigen medi-

zinisch/theologischen Literatur des ausgehenden 18. und 19. Jahrhunderts,"
Medical Dissertation, Kiel, 1973.

Finkenrath, Kurt. *Sozialismus im Heilwesen: eine geschichtliche Betrachtung des Medizinalwesens im Herzogtum Nassau von 1800–66.* Veröffentlichungen aus dem Gebiete der Medizinalverwaltung, vol. 38, no. 6. Berlin: Richard Schoetz, 1930.

Firnhaber, Carl Georg. *Die Nassauische Simultanvolksschule*, 2 vols. Wiesbaden, 1881–83.

Fischer, Alfons. *Geschichte des deutschen Gesundheitswesens*, vol. 2. Hildesheim: G. Olms, 1965.

Foucault, Michel. *The History of Sexuality, vol. 1: An Introduction.* Translated by Robert Hurley. New York: Vintage, 1980.

———. *Madness and Civilization: A History of Insanity in the Age of Reason.* Translated by Richard Howard. New York: Vintage, 1973.

———. *Discipline and Punish. The Birth of the Prison.* Translated by Alan Sheridan. New York: Vintage, 1979.

Freidson, Eliot. *Profession of Medicine: A Study of the Sociology of Applied Knowledge.* New York: Dodd, Mead, 1970.

Freud, Sigmund. "Mourning and Melancholia." In *The Standard Edition of the Complete Psychological Works of Sigmund Freud.* Translated by James Strachey. London: Hogarth Press, 1957.

Frevert, Ute. *Krankheit als politisches Problem 1770–1880. Soziale Unterschichten in Preußen zwischen medizinischer Polizei und staatlicher Sozialversicherung.* Kritische Studien zur Geschichtswissenschaft, 62. Göttingen: Vandenhoeck & Ruprecht, 1984.

Fuchs, Konrad. "Zur Entwicklung der Sozialstruktur im Westerwald während des 19. Jahrhunderts." *Nassauische Annalen* 93 (1982): 61–74.

Gall, Lothar. *Bürgertum in Deutschland.* Berlin: Siedler, 1989.

Gay, Peter. *The Enlightenment. A Comprenensive Anthology.* New York: Simon and Schuster, 1973.

Geertz, Clifford. *The Interpretation of Cultures.* New York: Basic, 1973,

———. "'From the Native's Point of View': On the Nature of Anthropological Understanding." In idem, *Local Knowledge.* New York: Basic, 1983.

Giddens, Anthony. *Central Problems in Social Theory.* Berkeley and Los Angeles: University of California Press, 1979.

Giedke, Adelheid. *Liebeskrankheit in der Geschichte der Medicin.* Medical dissertation, Düsseldorf, 1983.

Gilbert, Arthur N. "Doctor, Patient, and Onanist Diseases in the Nineteenth Century." *Journal of the History of Medicine and Allied Sciences* 30, no. 3 (July 1975): 217–34.

———. "Masturbation and Insanity." *Albion* 12, no.3 (1980): 268–82.

Gilman, Sander. *Difference and Pathology: Stereotypes of Sexuality, Race, and Madness.* Ithaca: Cornell University Press, 1985.

———. "Jews and Mental Illness: Medical Metaphors, Anti-Semitism, and the Jewish Response." *Journal of the History of Behavioral Sciences* 20, no. 2 (April 1984): 150–59.

———. *The Case of Sigmund Freud. Medicine and Identity at the Fin de Siècle.* Baltimore: Johns Hopkins University Press, 1993.

Glanz, Rudolf. *Geschichte des niederen jüdischen Volkes in Deutschland.* New York: Leo Baeck Institute, 1968.

Goffman, Erving. *Asylums: Essays on the Social Situation of Mental Patients and Other Inmates.* New York: Anchor, 1961.

Goldstein, Jan. *Console and Classify: The French Psychiatric Profession in the Nineteenth Century.* Cambridge, Mass.: Cambridge University Press, 1987.

————. "The Wandering Jew and the Problem of Psychiatric Anti-Semitism in Fin-de-Siècle France." *Journal of Contemporary History* 20 (1985): 521–52.

Goulemot, Marie. "'Prêtons la Main à la Nature': Fureurs Utérines." *Dix-Huitième Siècle* 12 (1980): 97–112.

Groneman, Carol. "Nymphomania: The Historical Construction of Female Sexuality." *Signs* 19 (1994): 337–367.

Gullickson, Gay L. "The Unruly Woman of the Paris Commune." In *Gendered Domains. Rethinking Public and Private in Women's History,* edited by Dorothy O. Helly and Susan M. Reverby, 133–53. Ithaca: Cornell University Press, 1992.

Häbel, Hans-Joachim. "Land- und Forstwirtschaft." In *Herzogtum Nassau, 1806–1866: Politik, Wirtschaft, Kultur,* 173–85. Wiesbaden: Historische Kommission für Nassau, 1981.

Habermas, Jürgen. *The Structural Transformation of the Public Sphere.* Cambridge, Mass.: MIT Press, 1989.

Hacking, Ian. "Two Souls in One Body." In *Questions of Evidence: Proof, Practice, and Persuasion across the Disciplines,* edited by James Chandler, Arnold Davidson, and Harry Harootunian, 433–462. Chicago: University of Chicago Press, 1991.

Hare, E.H. "Masturbatory Insanity: The History of an Idea." *Journal of Mental Science* 108 (1962): 2–21.

Harris, Ruth. "Possession on the Borders: The 'Mal de Morzine' in Nineteenth-Century France." *The Journal of Modern History* 69/3 (1997): 451–78.

Hausen, Karin. "Die Polarisierung der 'Geschlechtscharaktere'—Eine Spieglung der Dissoziation von Erwerbs- und Familienleben." In *Sozialgeschichte der Familie in der Neuzeit Europas,* edited by W. Conze, 363–93. Stuttgart: Klett, 1976.

Hayd, Jürgen. "Die Hysterie und Nymphomanie dargestellt in Doktorarbeiten des 17. und 18. Jahrhunderts aus der Dr. Heinrich Laehr Sammlung." Medical dissertation, University of Munich, 1968.

Heerdt, Gilbert. "Madness and Sexuality in the New Guinea Highlands," *Social Research* 53 (1986): 349–67.

Herzog, Dagmar. *Intimacy and Exclusion: Religious Politics in Pre-Revolutionary Baden.* Princeton: Princeton University Press, 1996.

Hill, Teresa L. "Religion, Madness, and the Asylum: A Study of Medicine and Culture in New England, 1820–1840." Ph.D. dissertation, Brown University, 1991.

Hoffmann, Wilhelm. *Rheinhessische Volkskunde.* 1932. Reprint. Frankfurt/M: Wolfgang Weidlich, 1980.

Hölscher, Lucian. "Die Religion des Bürgers. Bürgerliche Frömmigkeit und Protestantische Kirche im 19. Jahrhundert." *Historische Zeitschrift* 250/3 (1990): 595–630.

Honegger, Claudia. *Die Ordnung der Geschlechter.* Frankfurt/M: Campus Verlag, 1991.

Hötger, Dirk. "Sozialstruktur des herzoglich-nassauischen Irrenhauses Kloster Eberbach, 1815–1849." Medical dissertation, University of Mainz, 1977.

Huerkamp, Claudia, *Der Aufstieg der Ärzte im 19. Jahrhundert: vom gelehrten Stand zum professionellen Experten. Das Beispiel Preussens.* Kritische Studien zur Geschichtswissenschaft, 68. Göttingen: Vandenhoeck & Ruprecht, 1985.

Hull, Isabel. *Sexuality, State, and Civil Society in Germany, 1700–1815*. Ithaca: Cornell University Press, 1996.

———. "'Sexualität' und bürgerliche Gesellschaft." In *Bürgerinnen und Bürger,* edited by Ute Frevert, 49–66. Göttingen: Vandenhoeck & Ruprecht, 1988.

Jäger, Wolfgang. "Der Strukturwandel des Staates und der Kirchen in Nassau zwischen Revolution und Restauration." In *Revolution und konservatives Beharren,* edited by Karl Otmar Freiherr von Aretin and Karl Härter, 175–95. Mainz: Philipp von Zabern, 1990.

Jetter, Dieter. *Zur Typologie des Irrenhauses in Frankreich und Deutschland (1780–1840)*. Wiesbaden: F. Steiner, 1971.

Katz, Jacob. *Exclusiveness and Tolerance; Studies in Jewish-Gentile Relations in Medieval and Modern Times*. London: Oxford University Press, 1961.

———. *From Prejudice to Destruction: Anti-Semitism, 1700–1933*. Cambridge: Harvard University Press, 1982.

———. *Out of the Ghetto; the Social Background of Jewish Emancipation, 1770–1870*. Cambridge, Mass.: Harvard University Press, 1973.

Kaufmann, Doris. *Aufklärung, bürgerliche Selbsterfahrung und die 'Erfindung' der Psychiatrie in Deutschland, 1770–1850*. Göttingen: Vandenhoeck & Ruprecht, 1995.

———. "'Hartnäckiger Eigensinn' oder 'temporeller Wahnsinn.' Der Fall der Witwe Anna K." *Journal Geschichte* 4 (August 1990): 46–59.

———. "'Irre und Wahnsinnige.' Zum Problem der sozialen Ausgrenzung von Geisteskranken in der ländlichen Gesellschaft des frühen 19. Jahrhunderts." In *Verbrechen, Strafen und soziale Kontrolle,* edited by Richard van Dülmen, 178–214. Frankfurt/M: Fischer Taschenbuch, 1990.

Kirchhoff, Theodor (ed.). *Deutsche Irrenärzte,* vol. 1. Berlin: J.Springer, 1921.

Kittsteiner, Heinz-Dieter. *Die Entstehung des modernen Gewissens*. Frankfurt/M: Insel, 1991.

———. "From Grace to Virtue: Concerning a Change in the Presentation of the Parable of the Prodigal Son in the 18th and Early 19th Centuries." *Social Science Information* 23/6 (1984): 955–975.

Klein, Thomas. "Hessen-Nassau." In *Grundriß zur deutschen Verwaltungsgeschichte 1815-1945,* edited by Walter Hubatsch, vol. 11, 117–40. Marburg: Johann-Gottfried-Herder-Institut, 1979.

Kleinman, Arthur. *Social Origins of Distress and Disease: Depression, Neurasthenia, and Pain in Modern China*. New Haven: Yale University, 1986.

——— *Rethinking Psychiatry, From Cultural Category to Personal Experience*. New York: The Free Press, 1988.

Knudsen, Jonathan. "On Enlightenment for the Common Man." In *"What Was Enlightenment?" Eighteenth-Century Answers and Twentieth-Century Questions,* edited by James Schmidt. Berkeley: University of California Press, 1994.

Kober, Adolf. "Die Juden in Nassau seit Ende des 18. Jahrhunderts." *Nassauische Annalen* 66 (1955): 220–50.

Kocka, Jürgen. "The European Pattern and the German Case." In *Bourgeois Society in Nineteenth-Century Europe,* edited by Jürgen Kocka and Allan Mitchell, 3–39. Oxford and Providence, R.I.: Berg, 1993.

Korff, Gottfried. "Zwischen Sinnlichkeit und Kirchlichkeit. Notizen zum Wandel populärer Frömmigkeit im 18. und 19. Jahrhundert." In *Kultur zwischen Bürgertum und Volk,* edited by Jutta Held, 136–48. Berlin: Argument-Verlag, 1983.

Kraepelin, Emil. *One Hundred Years of Psychiatry*. New York: Philosophical Library, 1962.

Kreuter, Alma (ed). *Deutschsprachige Neurologen und Psychiater. Ein biographisch-bibliographisches Lexikon von den Vorläufen bis zur Mitte des 20. Jahrhunderts*, vol. 2. Munich: K.G. Saur, 1996.

Kropat, Wolf-Arno. "Die Emanzipation der Juden in Kurhessen und in Nassau im 19. Jahrhundert." In *Neunhundert Jahre Geschichte der Juden in Hessen*, 325–49. Wiesbaden: Kommission für die Geschichte der Juden in Hessen, 1983.

———. "Herzogtum Nassau zwischen Reform und Reaktion, 1806–1866." In *Das Werden Hessens*, edited by Walter Heinemeyer, 517–44. Marburg: N.G. Elwert, 1986.

———. "Nassaus staatlicher Gesundheitsdienst." In *Herzogtum Nassau, 1806–1866: Politik, Wirtschaft, Kultur*, 247–51. Wiesbaden: Historische Kommission für Nassau, 1981.

Labouvie, Eva. *Verbotene Künste. Volksmagie und ländlicher Aberglaube in den Dorfgemeinden des Saarraumes 16.-19.Jahrhundert*. St. Ingbert: Röhrig Verlag, 1992.

Landes, Joan. *Women and the Public Sphere in the Age of the French Revolution*. Ithaca: Cornell University Press, 1988.

Laqueur, Thomas."Orgasm, Generation, and the Politics of Reproductive Biology." In *The Making of the Modern Body*, edited by C. Gallagher, T. Laqueur, 1–41. Berkeley: University of California, 1987.

———. *Making Sex: Body and Gender from the Greeks to Freud*. Cambridge, Mass.: Harvard University Press, 1990.

———. "The Social Evil, the Solitary Vice and Pouring Tea." In *Fragments for a History of the Human Body*, edited by Michel Feher, vol. 3, 335–42. New York: Zone, 1989.

Lerner, Franz. *Wirtschafts- u. Sozialgeschichte des Nassauer Raumes, 1816–1964*. Wiesbaden: Nassauischen Sparkasse, 1965.

Lipp, Carola. "'Fleißige Weibsleute' und 'liederliche Dirnen.' Arbeits- und Lebensperspektiven von Unterschichtsfrauen." In *Schimpfende Weiber und patriotische Jungfrauen: Frauen im Vormärz und in der Revolution 1848/49*, edited by Carola Lipp, 25–55. Moos and Baden-Baden: Elster, 1986.

———. "Ledige Mütter, 'Huren' und 'Lumpenhunde.' Sexualmoral und Ehrenhändel im Arbeitermilieu des 19. Jahrhunderts." In *Tübinger Beiträge zur Volkskultur*, edited by Utz Jeggle et al., 70–86. Tübingen: Tübinger Vereinigung für Volkskunde, 1986.

———. "Die Innenseite der Arbeiterkultur. Sexualität im Arbeitermilieu des 19. und frühen 20. Jahrhunderts." In *Arbeit, Frömmigkeit und Eigensinn*, edited by Richard van Dülmen, 214–259. Frankfurt/M: Fischer Taschenbuch Verlag, 1990.

Lipping, Margita. "Bürgerliche Konzepte zur weiblichen Sexualität in der zweiten Hälfte des 18. Jahrhunderts: Rekonstruktionsversuche am Material medizinischer und pädagogischer Texte." In *Frauenkörper, Medizin, Sexualität: Auf dem Wege zu einer neuen Sexualmoral*, edited by Johanna Geyer-Kordesch and Annette Kuhn, 28–42. Düsseldorf: Pädagogischer Verlag Schwann-Bagel, 1986.

Loetz, Francisca. *Vom Kranken zum Patienten: 'Medikalisierung' und medizinische Vergesellschaftung am Beispiel Badens, 1750–1850*. Stuttgart: Franz Steiner, 1993.

Lüdtke, Alf (ed.). *The History of Everyday Life. Reconstructing Historical Experiences and Ways of Life*. Translated by William Templer. Princeton: Princeton University Press, 1995.

Lunbeck, Elizabeth. *The Psychiatric Persuasion. Knowledge, Gender, and Power in Modern America*. Princeton: Princeton University Press, 1994.

———. "A New Generation of Women: Progressive Psychiatrists and the Hypersexual Female." *Feminist Studies* 13, no. 3 (Fall, 1987): 513–43.

MacCormack, Sabine. *Religion in the Andes. Vision and Imagination in Early Colonial Peru*. Princeton: Princeton University Press, 1991.

MacDonald, Michael. *Mystical Bedlam: Madness, Anxiety and Healing in Seventeenth-Century England*. Cambridge: Cambridge University Press, 1981.

———. "Anthropological Perspectives on the History of Science and Medicine." In *Information Sources in the History of Science and Medicine*, edited by Pietro Corsi and Paul Weindling. London: Butterworth, 1983.

———. "Religion, Social Change, and Psychological Healing in England, 1600–1800." In *The Church and Healing*, edited by W. Sheils, 101–25. Oxford: Basil Blackwell 1982.

MacDonald, Robert. "The Frightful Consequences of Onanism." *Journal of the History of Ideas* 3 (1967): 423–31.

Marcus, Steven. *The Other Victorians; A Study of Sexuality and Pornography in Mid-Nineteenth-Century England*. New York: Basic, 1964.

Maaskant-Kleibrink, Marianne. "Nymphomania." In *Sexual Asymmetry. Studies in Ancient Society*, edited by Josine Blok and Peter Mason, 275–96. Amsterdam: J.C. Gieben, 1987.

Matz, Klaus-Jürgen. *Pauperismus und Bevölkerung: Die gesetzlichen Ehebeschränkungen in den süddeutschen Staaten während des 19. Jahrhunderts*. Stuttgart: Klett-Cotta, 1980.

McCandless, Peter. *Moonlight, Magnolias, and Madness: Insanity in South Carolina from the Colonial Period to the Progressive Era*. Chapel Hill: University of North Carolina Press, 1996.

Micale, Mark. *Approaching Hysteria. Disease and its Interpretations*. Princeton: Princeton University Press, 1995.

Midelfort, Erik. "Sin, Melancholy, Obsession: Insanity and Culture in 16th-Century Germany." In *Understanding Popular Culture: Europe from the Middle Ages to the Nineteenth Century*, edited by Steven L. Kaplan, 113–45. Berlin: Mouton, 1984.

——— "Madness and Civilization in Early Modern Europe: A Reappraisal of Michel Foucault." In *After the Reformation*, edited by B.C. Malament, 247–65. Philadelphia: University of Pennsylvania Press, 1980.

Mooser, Josef, Regine Krull, Bernd Hey, and Roland Greßelmann (eds.). *Frommes Volk und Patrioten: Erweckungsbewegung und soziale Frage im östlichen Westfalen, 1800 bis 1900*. Bielefeld: Verlag für Regionalgeschichte, 1989.

Mosse, George. *Germans and Jews; The Right, the Left, and the Search for a "Third Force" in Pre-Nazi Germany*. New York: H. Fertig, 1970.

———. *Toward the Final Solution: A History of European Racism*. New York: H. Fertig, 1978.

Neuman, R.P. "Masturbation, Madness and the Modern Concepts of Childhood and Adolescence." *Journal of Social History* (spring, 1975): 1–27.

Niedergassel, Hermann. "Die Behandlung der Gesisteskranken in der Irrenanstalt Eberbach im Rheingau in der Zeit von 1815–1849 anhand alter Krankengeschichten." Medical dissertation, University of Mainz, 1977.

Nipperdey, Thomas. "Verein als soziale Struktur in Deutschland im späten 18. und frühen 19. Jahrhundert." In *Gesellschaft, Kultur, Theorie. Gesammelte Aufsätze zur neueren Geschichte*, edited by idem, 174–205. Göttingen: Vandenhoeck & Ruprecht, 1976.

———. *Germany from Napoleon to Bismarck, 1800–1866*. Translated by Daniel Nolan. Princeton: Princeton University Press, 1996.

——— and Reinhard Rürup. "Antisemitismus." In *Geschichtliche Grundbegriffe*, vol. 1, edited by Werner Conze, Reinhart Koselleck, and Otto Brunner, 129–53. Stuttgart: Ernst Klett, 1972.

Obeyesekere, Gananath. *Medusa's Hair. An Essay on Personal Symbols and Religious Experience*. Chicago: University of Chicago Press, 1981.

Paletschek, Sylvia. *Frauen und Dissens: Frauen in Deutschkatholizismus und in den freien Gemeinden, 1841–1852*. Göttingen: Vandenhoeck & Ruprecht, 1990.

Phayer, Fintan Michael. *Religion und das Gewöhnliche Volk in Bayern in der Zeit von 1750–1850*. Munich: Stadtarchiv, 1970.

Poliakov, Léon. *The History of Anti-Semitism*, vol. 3. New York: Vanguard, 1968.

Poovey, Mary. *Uneven Developments. The Ideological Work of Gender in Mid-Victorian England*. Chicago: University of Chicago Press, 1988.

Proctor, Robert. *Racial Hygiene: Medicine under the Nazis*. Cambridge, Mass.: Harvard University Press, 1988.

Reill, Peter Hanns. "Anti-Mechanism, Vitalism and their Political Implications in Late Enlightened Scientific Thought." *Francia* 16/2 (1989): 195–212.

———. "Science and the Construction of the Cultural Sciences in Late Enlightenment Germany: The Case of Wilhelm von Humboldt," *History and Theory* 33 (1994): 345–66.

Richards, Graham. *Mental Machinery. The Origins and Consequences of Psychological Ideas, 1600–1850*. Baltimore: Johns Hopkins University Press, 1992.

Riley, Denise. *"Am I That Name?" Feminism and the Category of "Women" in History*. Minneapolis: University of Minnesota Press, 1988.

Ripa, Yannick, *Women and Madness: The Incarceration of Women in Nineteenth-Century France*. Translated by C. du Peloux Menagé. Minneapolis: University of Minnesota Press, 1990.

Risse, Guenter B. "Hysteria at the Edinburgh Infirmary: The Construction and Treatment of a Disease, 1770–1800." *Medical History* 32 (1988): 1–22.

Rosenberg, Hans. *Politische Denkströmungen im deutschen Vormärz*. Göttingen: Vandenhoeck & Ruprecht, 1972.

Rothman, David. *The Discovery of the Asylum*. Boston: Little Brown, 1971.

Rousseau, G.S. "Nymphomania, Bienville and the Rise of Erotic Sensibility." In *Sexuality in Eighteenth-Century Britain*, edited by Paul-Gabriel Boucé. Manchester: Manchester University Press, 1982.

Rürup, Reinhard. *Emanzipation und Antisemitismus*. Göttingen: Vandenhoeck & Ruprecht, 1975.

Russett, Cynthia Eagle. *Sexual Science: The Victorian Construction of Womanhood*. Cambridge, Mass.: Harvard University Press, 1989.

Sabean, David. *Power and the Blood. Popular Culture and Village Discourse in Early Modern Germany*. Cambridge: Cambridge University Press, 1984.

———. "Production of the Self during the Age of Confessionalism," *Central European History* 29/1 (1996): 1–18.

Saurer, Edith. "Religiöse Praxis und Sinnesverwirrung. Kommentare zur religiösen Melancholiediskussion." In *Dynamik der Tradition*, edited by Richard van Dülmen, 213–305. Frankfurt/M: Fischer Taschenbuch, 1992.

Schär, Markus. *Seelennöte der Untertanen. Selbstmord, Melancholie und Religion im Alten Zürich, 1500–1800.* Zürich: Chronos, 1985.

Scharfe, Martin. "Subversive Frömmigkeit. Über die Distanz unterer Volksklassen zur offiziellen Religion. Beispiele aus dem württembergischen Protestantismus des 18. Jahrhunderts." In *Kultur zwischen Bürgertum und Volk*, edited by Jutta Held, 117–35. Berlin: Argument-Verlag, 1983.

Schatz, Klaus. *Geschichte des Bistums Limburg.* Mainz: Gesellschaft für mittelrheinische Kirchengeschichte, 1983.

Schieder, Wolfgang. "Kirche und Revolution: Sozialgeschichtliche Aspekte der Trier Wallfahrt von 1844." *Archiv für Sozialgeschichte* 14 (1974): 419–54.

Schings, H.J. *Melancholie und Aufklärung.* Stuttgart: Metzler, 1977.

Schmid, Pia. "Hausfrau, Gattin, Mutter: Zur bürgerlichen Definition von Weiblichkeit um 1800 im Spiegel einiger deutschsprachiger Zeitschriften." In *Die ungeschriebene Geschichte: Historische Frauenforschung* 5. Historikerinnentreffens. Vienna: Wiener Frauenverlag, 1984.

Scholder, Klaus. "Grundzüge der theologischen Aufklärung in Deutschland." In *Aufklärung, Absolutismus, und Bürgertum in Deutschland*, edited by Franklin Kopitzsch, 294–318. Munich: Nymphenburger Verlagshandlung, 1976.

Scholem, Gershom. *The Messianic Idea in Judaism.* New York: Schocken Books, 1971.

———. *Sabbatai Sevi: The Mystical Messiah, 1626–76.* Princeton: Princeton University Press, 1973.

Scholz, C. "Herzogthum Nassau." In *Das Armenwesen und die Armengesetzgebung in europäischen Staaten*, edited by A. Emminghaus, 141–57. Berlin: F.A. Herbig, 1870.

Schrenk, Martin. *Über den Umgang mit Geisteskranken.* Berlin: Springer-Verlag, 1973.

Schuebler, E. "Die Gesetze über Niederlassung und Verehelichung in den verschiedenen deutschen Staaten." *Deutsche Vierteljahresschrift* 17 (1854): 55–138.

Schüler, Winfried. "Die Revolution von 1848/49." In *Herzogtum Nassau, 1806–1866: Politik, Wirtschaft, Kultur*, 19–35. Wiesbaden: Historische Kommission für Nassau, 1981.

———. "Sozialstruktur und Lebensstandard." Ibid., 105–22.

———. "Wirtschaft und Gesellschaft im Herzogtum Nassau." *Nassauische Annalen* 91 (1980): 131–44.

———. "Die katholische Partei im Herzogtum Nassau während der Revolution von 1848." *Archiv für mittelrheinische Kirchengeschichte* 34 (1982): 121–42.

Schulte, Regina, *Das Dorf im Verhör: Brandstifter, Kindsmörderinnen und Wilderer vor den Schranken des bürgerlichen Gerichts, Oberbayern 1848–1910.* Reinbek, Germany: Rowohlt, 1989.

———. "Reinterpretations of Peasant Life: A Nineteenth-Century Scientific Approach." *German Historical Institute* London, 1984.

Schwedt, Herman H. "Die katholische Kirche nach der Säkularisation." In *Herzogtum Nassau, 1806–1866: Politik, Wirtschaft, Kultur*. 275–82. Wiesbaden: Historische Kommission für Nassau, 1981.

Scott, Joan. *Gender and the Politics of History.* New York: Columbia University Press, 1988.

Scribner, Robert W. "Elements of Popular Belief." In *Handbook of European History, 1400–1600*, vol. 1, edited by Thomas A. Brady Jr., Heiko A. Oberman, and James D. Tracy, 231–62. Leiden: J. Brill, 1994.

Scull, Andrew. *Museums of Madness: The Social Organization of Insanity in Nineteenth-Century England.* New York: St. Martin's, 1979.

————. *The Most Solitary of Afflictions: Madness and Society in Britain, 1700–1900*. New Haven: Yale University Press, 1993.

Segalen, Martine. *Love and Power in the Peasant Family; Rural France in the Nineteenth Century*. Translated by Sarah Matthews. Oxford: Basil Blackwell, 1983.

Sheehan, James. *German Liberalism in the Nineteenth Century*. Chicago: University of Chicago Press, 1978.

Shorter, Edward. "Women and Jews in a Private Nervous Clinic in Late Nineteenth-Century Vienna." *Medical History* 33, no. 2 (April, 1989): 149–83.

Showalter, Elaine. *The Female Malady: Women, Madness and English Culture, 1830–1980*. New York: Pantheon, 1985.

Shuttleworth, Sally. "Female Circulation: Medical Discourse and Popular Advertising in the Mid-Victorian Era." In *Body/Politics*, edited by Mary Jacobus, Evelyn Fox Keller, and Sally Shuttelworth, 47–68. New York and London: Routledge, 1990.

Smith-Rosenberg, Carroll. "The Hysterical Woman: Sex Roles and Role Conflict in Nineteenth-Century America," *Social Research* 39 (1972): 652–78.

————. "Puberty to Menopause: The Cycle of Femininity in Nineteenth-Century America." In *Clio's Consciousness Raised*, edited by M. Hartman and L. Banner, 23–37. New York: Harper & Row, 1974.

Sperber, Jonathan. *Popular Catholicism in Nineteenth-Century Germany*. Princeton: Princeton University Press, 1984.

————. "Bürger, Bürgertum, Bürgerlichkeit, Bürgerliche Gesellschaft: Studies of the German (Upper) Middle Class and its Sociocultural World." *Journal of Modern History* 69/2 (1997): 271–97.

Spierenburg, Pieter. "The Sociogenesis of Confinement and Its Development in Early Modern Europe." In *The Emergence of Carceral Institutions: Prisons, Galleys, and Lunatic Asylums, 1550–1900*, edited by Pieter Spierenburg, 9–77. Rotterdam: Erasmus Universiteit, 1984.

Spitz, R.A. "Authority and Masturbation." *Yearbook of Psychoanalysis* 9 (1953): 113–45.

Stengers, Jean, and Anne van Neck. *Histoire d'une Grande Peur: La Masturbation*. Brussels: University of Brussels, 1984.

Steitz, Heinrich. *Geschichte der Evangelischen Kirche in Hessen und Nassau*. Marburg: Trautvetter und Fischer, 1977.

Sterling, Elenore. *Judenhaß. Die Anfänge des politischen Antisemitismus in Deutschland (1815–1850)*. Frankfurt/M: Europäische Verlagsanstalt, 1969.

Taylor, Charles. *Sources of the Self: The Making of the Modern Identity*. Cambridge, Mass.: Harvard University Press, 1989.

Tomes, Nancy J. *A Generous Confidence. Thomas Story Kirkbride and the Art of Asylum-Keeping, 1840–1883*. Cambridge: Cambridge University Press, 1984.

Toury, Jacob, ed. *Der Eintritt der Juden ins deutsche Bürgertum: Eine Dokumentation*. Tel Aviv: Diaspora Research Institute, 1972.

Trachtenberg, Joshua. *The Devil and the Jews*. New Haven: Yale University Press, 1943.

Treichel, Eckhardt. *Der Primat der Bürokratie: burokratischen Staat und bürokratische Elite in Herzogtum Nassau, 1806–1866*. Stuttgart: Franz Steiner, 1991.

Trenckmann, Ulrich. *Mit Leib und Seele. Ein Wegweiser durch die Konzepte der Psychiatrie*. Bonn: Psychiatrie-Verlag, 1988.

Trepp, Anne-Charlott. *'Sanfte Männlichkeit' und 'selbstständige Weiblichkeit'—Frauen und Männer im Hamburger Bürgertum zwischen 1770 und 1840*. Göttingen: Vandenhoeck & Ruprecht, 1995.

Tsouyopoulos, Nelly. "The Influence of John Brown's Ideas in Germany." In *Brunonianism in Britain and Europe*, edited by W.F. Bynum and Roy Porter, 63–74. London: Wellcome Institute for the History of Medicine, 1988.

———. "Doctors Contra Clysters and Feudalism: The Consequences of a Romantic Revolution." In *Romanticism and the Sciences*, edited by Andrew Cunningham and Nicholas Jardine, 101–18. Cambridge: Cambridge University Press, 1990.

Veith, Ilza, *Hysteria: The History of a Disease*. Chicago: University of Chicago Press, 1965.

Verwey, Gerlof. *Psychiatry in an Anthropological and Biomedical Context*. Dordrecht: Reidel, 1985.

Wachsmuth. "Aus alten Akten und Krankengeschichten der Herzoglich nassauischen Irrenanstalt Eberbach." *Psychiatrisch-Neurologischen Wochenschrift* 27 (1925), 29 (1927).

Walton, John. "Lunacy in the Industrial Revolution: A Study of Asylum Admissions in Lancashire, 1848–50," *Journal of Social History* 13 (1979): 1–22.

Wettengel, Michael. *Die Revolution von 1848/49 im Rhein-Main-Raum*. Wiesbaden: Selbstverlag der Historischen Kommission für Nassau, 1989.

Wiesing, Urban. *Kunst oder Wissenschaft? Konzeptionen der Medizin in der deutschen Romantik*. Stuttgart: Frommann-Holzboog, 1995.

Zilboorg, Gregory. *A History of Medical Psychology*. New York: W.W. Norton, 1941.

Index

Adam, Alfred, 82
Alltagsgeschichte, 5, 7, 186
Awakening, 36, 42, 47

Basting, Andreas, 21–22, 66, 82, 112, 155, 179, 181, 202 n. 45
Beck, Rainer, 142
Benker, Gitta, 122
Bienville, M.D.T. de, 87
Biermann, Johann Karl, 46
Bird, Friederich, 37, 44–45
Blasius, Dirk, 74
Blumröder, Gustav, 44, 46
body, 60–61, 95–96, 106–7
bourgeoisie, 10–11, 185
    and class formation, 40–41
    definition of, 193 n. 9
    patient experiences of madness, 30–31, 56–58, 104–6, 159 f., 184
    and the public sphere, 28–29
    and religious belief, 39–41
    and the self, 41, 44, 81
    and sexuality, 79, 86, 95 f., 103, 122, 126–27, 159 f.
Brown, John, 93

Bürgerrecht, 134–35
Burrows, George M., 44
Busch, Dietrich, 103
Bynum, Caroline Walker, 8–9

Charcot, Jean-Martin, 85, 163
conscience. *See also* patients; penal institutions
    in Christianity, 72
    in the Enlightenment, 72, 78
    historiographical models of, 71–72
    in rural society, 72–73, 78–80
    and social relations, 79–81

direct psychic method, 25–26
dissimulation, 13–14, 152–53, 170, 172 f., 178 f.
Dörner, Klaus, 25, 27
Duden, Barbara, 60

Eberbach asylum
    administration, 20–24
    admissions rate, 17
    and authority, 25–29, 66–67
    clothing policy, 114–16
    in comparative perspective, 20

233